COMPARATIVE PHYSICAL EDUCATION AND SPORT VOLUME 4

COMPARATIVE PHYSICAL EDUCATION AND SPORT VOLUME 4

Edited by

Herbert Haag, PhD

University of Kiel
Federal Republic of Germany

GV
205
.I623
1984
West

Dietrich Kayser

Federal Institute of Sport Science
Federal Republic of Germany

Bruce L. Bennett, PhD

Ohio State University
United States of America

Human Kinetics Publishers, Inc.
Champaign, Illinois

ASU WEST LIBRARY

Library of Congress Cataloging-in-Publication Data

International Seminar on Comparative Physical
    Education and Sport (4th: 1984 : Malente,
    Germany and Kiel, Germany)
    Comparative physical education and sport, volume 4.

    "Proceedings of the Fourth International Seminar on
Comparative Physical Education and Sport held April 29-
May 5, 1984, at Malente/Kiel, West Germany"—T.p. verso.
    Includes bibliographies.
    1. Physical education and training—Congresses.
2. Sports—Congresses. I. Haag, Herbert, 1937–
II. Kayser, Dietrich. III. Bennett, Bruce Lanyon,
1917–   . IV. Title.
GV205.I623 1984   613.7   86-15287
ISBN: 0-87322-077-3

Proceedings on the Fourth International Seminar on Comparative Physical Education and Sport held April 29-May 5, 1984, at the University of Kiel, Malente/Kiel,
Federal Republic of Germany.

Developmental Editor: Patricia Sammann
Production Director: Ernie Noa
Assistant Production Director: Lezli Harris
Copy Editor: Kristen Gallup
Typesetter: Theresa Bear
Text Layout: Leah Freedman
Cover Design and Layout: Julie Szamocki

ISBN: 0-87322-077-3

Copyright © 1987 by Human Kinetics Publishers, Inc.

All rights reserved. Except for use in a review, the reproduction or utilization
of this work in any form or by any electronic, mechanical, or other means, now
known or hereafter invented, including xerography, photocopying, and recording,
and in any information storage and retrieval system, is forbidden without the
written permission of the publisher.

Printed in the United States of America

10 9 8 7 6 5 4 3 2 1

Human Kinetics Publishers, Inc.
Box 5076 Champaign, IL 61820

Contents

Contributors

Bruce L. Bennett
501 Loveman Avenue
Worthington, Ohio 43085, USA
(Tel. (614) 885-7038)

Erich Beyer
Friedrich-Naumann-Str. 47
7500 Karlsruhe 21, FRG
(Tel. 0721/75 44 27)

Eric F. Broom
The University of British Columbia
6081 University Boulevard
Vancouver, British Columbia V6T 1W5, Canada
(Tel. (604) 228-4764)

Clemens Czwalina
Institut für Sportwissenschaft
Universität Hamburg
Rothenbaum Chaussee 80
2000 Hamburg 13, FRG
(Tel. 04102-59290)

Nanda Fischer
Technische Universität München
Connollystrasse, ZHS
8000 München 40, FRG
(Tel. 089-35491326 or 089-607524)

Margo Gee
School of Recreation, Physical and Health Education
Dalhousie University
Halifax, Nova Scotia B3H 3J5, Canada
(Tel. (902) 423-7796)

Ommo Grupe
Institut für Sportwissenschaft
Universität Tübingen
Wilhelmstr. 124
7400 Tübingen, FRG
(Tel. 07071-29 26 28)

Herbert Haag
Institut für Sport und Sportwissenschaften der Christian-Albrechts-

Universität Kiel
Abt. Sportpädagogik
Olshausenstrasse 40
2300 Kiel, FRG
(Tel. 0431-880-3770)

Zygmunt Jaworski
Akademia Wychowania Fizycznego
ul. Marymoncka 34
01-813 Warszawa, Poland
(Tel. 34-60-81)

Dietrich Kayser
Bundesinstitut für Sportwissenschaft
Carl-Diem-Weg
5000 Köln 47 Müngersdorf
Postfach 400 109/110
5000 Köln 40, FRG

Wolfgang Kneyer
Institut für Sport und Sportwissenschaften der Christian-Albrechts-
Universität Kiel
Abt. Sportpädagogik
Olshausenstrasse 40
2300 Kiel, FRG
(Tel. 0431-880-3767)

March L. Krotee
Division of Physical Education
University of Minnesota
218 Cooke Hall
Minneapolis, Minnesota 55455, USA

Annette Krüger
Institut für Sport und Sportwissenschaften der Christian-Albrechts-
Universität Kiel
Abt. Sportpädagogik
Olshausenstrasse 40
2300 Kiel, FRG

Arnd Krüger
Institut für Sportwissenschaften
Georg-August-Universität Göttingen
Spranger Weg 2
3400 Göttingen, FRG

Pawel Kudlorz
Akademia Wychowania Fizycznego
ulica Wiejska 1
PL-80-336 Gdansk, Poland

Darío Menanteau-Horta
Dept. Rural Sociology

University of Minnesota
St. Paul, Minnesota 55108, USA

Brian Pendleton
Department of Physical Education and Political Science
Vancouver Community College
Langara Campus
100 West 49th Avenue
Vancouver, British Columbia V5Y 2Z6, Canada

João Piccoli
Federal University of Pelotas
Dept. of Physical Education
Rio Grande del Sur
Brazil

John C. Pooley
School of Recreation, Physical and Health Education
Dalhousie University
Halifax, Nova Scotia B3H 3J5, Canada

T. Neville Postlethwaite
Dept. of Comparative Education
Universität Hamburg
Sedanstr. 19
2000 Hamburg 13, FRG
(Tel. (040) 41 23 3717)

Erhard Rehbein
Institut für Sport und Sportwissenschaften der Christian-Albrechts-
Universität Kiel
Olshausenstrasse 40
2300 Kiel, FRG

John E. Saunders
University of Queensland
Brisbane, Australia 4067
(Tel. (07) 377 11 11)

Rainer Schams
Silberbreite 9
3400 Göttingen, FRG
(Tel. 0551-65352)

Joy Standeven
Brighton Polytechnic
Chelsea School of Human Movement
Trevin Towers, Gaudick Road, Eastbourne
East Sussex, BN20 7SP, England, Great Britain
(Tel. Eastbourne 21400)

D. Margaret Toohey
California State University
1250 Bellflower Blvd.

Long Beach, California 90840, USA
(Tel. (213) 498-4086)

Aniko T. Varpalotai
1-41 Clergy St. W.
Kingston, Ontario K7L 2H8, Canada
(Tel. (613) 544-2586)

Ralph C. Wilcox
Hofstra University
Hempstead, New York 11550, USA
(Tel. (516) 650-5815)

Klaus Willimczik
Fakultät für Psychologie und Sportwissenschaften
Universität Bielefeld, Abt. Sportwissenschaft
Universitätsstrasse, Postfach 8640
4800 Bielefeld 1, FRG
(Tel. 0521-106-5127)

Earle F. Zeigler
Faculty of Physical Education
The University of Western Ontario
London, Ontario N6A 3K7, Canada

Zofia Żukowska
Akademia Wychowania Fizycznego
W. Warszawie
Zakland Pedagogiki AWF
ul. Marymoncka 34, 01-813 Warszawa, Poland
(Tel. 34-04-31)

Preface

The proceedings are grouped by the four major topics of the symposium. The papers included are main papers and additional short papers. All the presentations have been edited by the Committee, especially for composition and correct English usage. This editorial work is not easy when dealing with an international group of authors. At this point, I would like to thank Prof. Dr. Bruce L. Bennett, formerly of Ohio State University, Columbus, OH, U.S.A, and Wiss. Director Dietrich Kayser, Federal Institute of Sport Science, Cologne, F.R.G., for their educational help.

Since the intent of this symposium was to analyze, discuss, and clarify the understanding and nature of comparative physical education and sport, these proceedings are a basic handbook for this field. The topics discussed in each part are as follows:

Part I

Content and research methodology of comparative physical education and sport

Part II

Comparative research on physical activity within schools

Part III

Comparative research on physical activity outside of schools

Part IV

Teaching of courses in comparative physical education and sport in higher education

Thus the proceedings start with metatheoretical reflections, which are especially important for a young scientific field. Then concrete examples are given of research work in comparative physical education and sport. They conclude with teaching in higher education which is important, since knowledge and research results have to be transferred to practice, otherwise science loses its justification.

Human Kinetics Publishers has agreed to publish the proceedings from ISCPES symposia, starting with Volume 3. Thus the work of the ISCPES will be made available every 2 years, giving it visibility and encouraging the continuous growth of the field of comparative physical education and sport.

Prof. Dr. Herbert Haag, M.S.
Abt. Sportpädagogik
Institut für Sport und Sportwissenschaften der
Christian-Albrechts-Universität Kiel

Welcome Speeches

It is my privilege and pleasure to welcome you very cordially as the participants of the Fourth International Seminar on Comparative Physical Education and Sport on behalf of the Christian-Albrechts-University at Kiel. Kiel University, founded in 1665, is proud to have you with us for this important symposium, taking place for the first time in a European country.

As the head of Kiel University, I would like to welcome in particular Dr. Peter Bendixen, Minister of Cultural Affairs of the federal state of Schleswig—Holstein; Mr. Sauerbaum, the president of the city council of the city of Kiel; Mr. Hans Hansen, president of the Sport Federation of Schleswig-Holstein; and Professor Dr. Kirsch, head of the Federal Institute of Sport Science in Cologne and president of the International Council of Sport Science and Physical Education.

Christian-Albrechts-University sees in the fact that your society has asked the Institute of Sport and Sport Sciences (ISS) to take over the local organization and preparation in Kiel as well as in Malente a vivid acknowledgment of the scientific and practical effort made by the ISS during the last decade. I want to thank you very warmly for your decision.

I also would like to wish you a successful meeting, with the exchange of new experiences in fruitful discussions that may lead to gaining new friends and meeting old ones. Furthermore, I wish you enough leisure time at Malente and Kiel for you to see much of our beautiful country of Schleswig-Holstein, the land between the North Sea and the Baltic, in the fine weather we are accustomed to having.

Prof. Dr. G. Griesser,
President of the Christian-Albrechts-University Kiel

During the last decades more and more young people in our countries have traveled abroad. I appreciate this very much. A stay in a foreign country offers opportunities to gain impressions about history and culture, economy and education, different ways of thinking and living, and the beauty of nature and landscape. But besides the personal advantages for everyone who travels abroad, foreign youth-exchange contributes much to international peace and understanding. I believe that the process of unifying Europe, (which sometimes seems too slow), and the development of the Atlantic partnership are partially due to the large number of personal bonds across our national borders.

What pertains to young people also applies especially to those who are responsible for the future of the younger generation and for the educational system of a country, including politicians, teachers, and of course, scientists dealing with the teaching and training of the young. So I am very glad, indeed, that Professor Haag and the staff of his department have made "Comparative Physical Education and Sport" one of the main themes of their scientific work. In close cooperation with universities in Germany and other countries, especially in Scandinavia, Poland, Canada, and the United States of America, they have received stimuli and encouragement for further studies, and the results of their scientific work have found expression in the development of our curricula. New physical education programs have been developed during the last 5 or 6 years, and a special interest has been taken in health education. Undoubtedly, "Physical Activity Within Schools," one of the themes of this symposium, is a most important and effective means of health and recreation education. I think that our curricula have been quite up-to-date, as they have been developed in close cooperation with the Institute of Sport and Sport Sciences of Kiel University.

After the International Seminars in Israel, Canada, and the United States, the Fourth International Seminar on Comparative Physical Education and Sport is now being held with us in the north of the Federal Republic of Germany. I consider this a vote of confidence in Kiel University and in Professor Haag and his organizing committee. I hope that after these 6 days you will not be disappointed, neither by the interesting themes of the symposium and the scientific outcome nor by the additional happenings and experiences of these days. I think this symposium will again result in better understanding of concepts in other countries; in clearer judgment concerning our own situation in physical education and sport; and in learning from others and thus receiving valuable knowledge and stimuli for improving our own educational systems.

I have no doubt that this symposium will contribute to further development in this special and important field of education.

You have come to Schleswig-Holstein to discuss the themes of this symposium. In spite of the importance of the themes and in spite of the fact that discussions on educational problems sometimes take more time than available in a well-planned program, I do hope you will have a chance to enjoy the additional items of the program as well so that you may experience Kiel, the capital of Schleswig-Holstein, and a very beautiful part of Schleswig-Holstein, which is—as not a few foreigners say—one of the most charming areas in North Germany, with pretty little towns like Malente.

When you leave on May 5, I hope you all may agree that the Fourth International Seminar on Comparative Physical Education and Sport has been a very successful one and that you have spent a very nice and interesting time in our country with old and new friends from all over the world.

Dr. P. Bendixen
Minister of Cultural Affairs of the State of
Schleswig-Holstein

I welcome all participants of the Fourth International Seminar on Comparative Physical Education and Sport on behalf of the municipal council of Kiel, the capital of Schleswig-Holstein.

I am very proud that this symposium, which takes place every other year, is being held in the Federal Republic of Germany for the first time, after Wingate in Israel, Halifax in Canada, and Minneapolis—St. Paul in the United States.

The professional level, the new goal-point, different methods and changed organization, the more intensive application of techniques, and the intensification of scientific work do change the research, doctrinal teaching, and practice of sports in a very elementary way. These changes are still going on. Knowledge is growing old in sports also, and the learning process must continue. Maintaining sound physical, mental, and spiritual fitness is more necessary today then ever before.

The necessary improvements are possible for everyone, by studying the literature and by participating in meetings, congresses, conferences, and classes. These meetings have three main aspects:

- To mediate new experiences in an appealing way
- To discuss questions and problems, because discourse today is essential
- To encourage and make human contacts possible

In my opinion the third aspect is the most important one. I am very glad that, because of a very good program including receptions and community arrangements, we will find a big platform for these human contacts.

As my last words, I want to thank everyone for the good organization of this symposium, especially the Institute of Sport and Sport Sciences of the Christian-Albrechts-University in Kiel and its Department of Sport Pedagogy.

Ladies and gentlemen, I hope you'll have a pleasant stay here in our northwest federal state.

E. Sauerbaum
President of the City Council of the City of Kiel

In the name of the Landessportverband Schleswig-Holstein (LSV), I extend greetings to the participants of the Fourth International Seminar on Comparative Physical Education and Sport.

We represent the actively engaged sports people of Schleswig-Holstein in different sport disciplines organized in the typical German form of sport clubs. In the whole Federal Republic of Germany, approximately 18 million people belong to sport clubs. In Schleswig-Holstein we have 760,000 members in more than 2,200 clubs.

The LSV is cooperating very closely with the Institute of Sport and Sport Sciences (ISS) of the University of Kiel in different dimensions. We know that the ISS has many international relations. These include Pennsylvania State University in the United States; Carnegie Institute in Leeds, Great Britain; the University of Jordan, in Amman, Jordan; and the Academy of Physical Culture in Gdansk, Poland. Furthermore, a great deal of work exists in so-called developing countries like Peru, Indonesia, Jordan, and Zambia.

The ISS has an open-mindedness toward international work, and therefore we feel that it was a very good decision to choose Kiel and Malente as the setting for the Fourth International Seminar on Comparative Physical Education and Sport. We are very happy that the symposium is taking place in our "Sport und Bildungszentrum Malente," situated in the "Holsteinische Schweiz," one of the nicest parts of Germany.

We know that the world today needs international understanding and cooperation. Comparative research as discussed during this symposium helps to facilitate international work. In this sense we hope that the symposium is successful, and we wish the best for all participants.

Hans Hansen
President of the Landessportverband
Schleswig-Holstein

First, I welcome you on behalf of the International Council of Sport Science and Physical Education (ICSSPE/CIEPSS). Our colleague Herbert Haag, in his paper for this symposium, has called the ICSSPE "the parent-organization of physical education and sport as well as for sport science on a world-wide basis." Nominations like these may cause us difficulties because, in the biological sense, parents are older than children. Our eldest "child," the Fédération Internationale d'Education Physique (FIEP), was born in 1923, the "parent" ICSPE not earlier than 1958. These circumstances may be one reason why we like to call ourselves an umbrella organization of sport science and physical education.

I do not want to discuss the details of our organization. Copies illustrating its organic structure are available. In Article 17 of our new statutes dating back to January 1st, 1983, the committees and areas of work are described. Thereafter, the Council shall conduct its work in three areas concerned with:

• the development of individual scientific branches of sport science and their cooperation and integration;
• the practical application and use of sport-scientific results in various fields of physical education and sport; and
• the promotion of information, documentation, and propaganda in the field of sport, physical education, and sport science.

I would like to stress that ICSSPE is the only nongovernmental organization in the field of sport and sport science, maintaining consultative and associate relations with UNESCO in Category A since 1971. In November 1983, ICSSPE received the official status of a "recognized organization" by the International Olympic Committee (IOC). The agreement, which will take the form of annual protocols, is to include informative and consultative services in areas of mutual interest, mutual participation in important events of both organizations, and research activities carried out by the ICSSPE on behalf of the IOC. In this way, ICSSPE cooperates with both top-level organizations of sport, one in the field of nongovernmental organizations and the other on the governmental side.

In the organic structure mentioned earlier, you will find a committee called "Sport Pedagogy." I would like to ask you to discuss during this symposium in what way your organization can cooperate within and with this new committee.

Second, I would like to welcome you in my capacity as Director of the Federal Institute of Sport Science (BISp) in Cologne. This institution is the basis of ICSSPE's work in this period of election. The Secretary General of ICSSPE, Werner Sonnenschein, is a staff member of the BISp. The Institute is part of the Ministry of the Interior in Bonn, and I would also like to extend a wish of welcome from our Minister, Dr. Friedrich Zimmermann, to all of you.

The BISp again is very lucky to cooperate with the Institut für Sport und Sport-wissenschaften at the Christian-Albrechts-Universität Kiel. We already have worked together several times before, especially at the time of the 1977 congress of the ICHPER. Our colleague, Herbert Haag, guarantees not only effective cooperation, but also full success.

Prof. Dr. A. Kirsch
Director of the Federal Institute of Sport Science
President of ICSSPE

PART I

Content and Research Methodology of Comparative Physical Education and Sport

CHAPTER 1

A Theoretical Framework for Comparative Physical Education and Sport

Ommo Grupe

The following is not a real concept or, as Herbert Haag puts it, a "theoretical framework" at all. Instead, it is a statement of some outlines and conceptions concerning the status and standard of present research in this area.

First, the German Sport Federation (DSB) is the umbrella organization of the approximate 20 million athletes in sport associations in the Federal Republic of Germany and all physical education teachers, coaches, sport physicians, sport psychologists, sport historians, and sport pedagogues. The DSB also includes the few people that already occupy themselves with questions concerning comparative physical education and sport science. The DSB is delighted not only because this Congress takes place in our country, but also because we find the theme and problem of the Congress extraordinarily important. This brings me to my second point.

It seems to us that the scientific treatment of such comparative topics not only can directly improve the relationships among the participants but also, and above all, can help sport and sport organizations to make the most of their potential to improve and consolidate international relationships. We must, especially in these times of political tension and nuclear threat, do everything to recognize this potential so that we can evaluate properly and adapt consequently. In this respect, we have not only a scientific task but also an important political task to fulfill in a practical sense as well as in a theoretical scientific respect. The latter includes gathering, sorting, and systemizing critically (i.e., in a scientifically proven way), and catching up on and presenting knowledge of differing and similar developments, traditions, goals, conditions, and requirements for sport and physical education in different nations, cultures, social systems, and continents. In his book, *Sport Pedagogy: Content and Methodology,* Haag presents an impressive diagram (1978, p. 244).

This knowledge is not just of physical education in its strict sense, but also of various areas of sport and the questions and problems that arise

3

in these areas—education of teachers, sport physicians, and coaches; competitive sports; top-level sports; professionalizing and commercialization of sport; extracurricular sports; participation of women; sport for the "handicapped"; spread of sports; collegiate sports; sport for everyone; building sport facilities—and in various scientific perspectives—historical, social scientific, cultural-anthropological, and economical. The conclusions of such studies and their results can, in this way, give science a practical meaning and sense.

Nixon and Jewett convincingly described this relationship with respect to comparative physical education in their book *An Introduction to Physical Education* in the chapter "Physical Education Around the World": "Comparative education is one of the subdivisions of the theory of education. This special field of education concentrates on the investigation and interpretation of educational policies and practices in various cultures and countries throughout the world" (Nixon & Jewett, 1980, p. 94).

They quote Bereday, who wrote:

> Comparative education seeks to make sense out of the similarities and differences among educational systems. It catalogs educational methods across national frontiers; and in this catalog each country appears as one variant of the total score of mankind's educational experience. If well set off, the like and the contrasting colors of the world perspective will make each country a potential beneficiary of the lessons thus received (Bereday, 1964, p. 43).

Nixon continues:

> The result of these investigations and analyses is a set of general principles that provides guidance to policy-makers, administrators, and other active participants in the conduct and direction of educational systems.

> At the theoretical level, comparative education is considered to be a general social science that employs theories, hypotheses, models, and laws to clarify the fundamental processes of education. Important relevant data collected by the formal research methods can be categorized and their functional interrelationships can be examined. The hypotheses of the theoretical comparative educational scientist can be tested in the crucible of experience. This field is coming to be recognized as a discipline in its own right (Nixon & Jewett, 1980, p. 94).

In summarizing the values of comparative studies and research, Nixon refers to Lauwerys: "Through contrast and comparison, we are led to a better and deeper understanding of what we ourselves do. And sometimes we learn that practices and arrangements which we thought were based upon reason and experience are, in fact, based only on prejudice or on an unreasoning reverence for tradition" (Lauwerys, 1973, p. viii).

What Nixon writes is valid for both sport and sport science. Robert Decker from Luxembourg showed just a few weeks ago in the journal *Sportunterricht* (1984, pp. 51-58) how useful such careful comparative descriptions can be when he described the completely different development of physical education in the Federal Republic of Germany and France in detail. The development differs not only in its educational concepts and foundings but also in its many methods and processes.

From comparisons like these, not only can we get to know each other better, but also prejudices can be eliminated, mutual understanding can be promoted, and cooperation can be improved. This brings us to the third point.

The science of sport and physical education is still a very new science in all countries of the world; in comparison with the classic sciences, the science of sport and physical education has just begun. Thus it is not surprising that this new science's methods, questioning, self-assessment, and quality standards are still quite uncertain. The fact that this science is often, too often, brought into the public limelight—in tow of sport—does not serve to eliminate this uncertainty or contribute to a cautious assessment of the science's own achievements. Adding to this problem, we have, on the one hand, the scientific unsettledness of the sport phenomenon; on the other hand, we have the immense dynamics and vivacity of sport's worldwide development. These, combined with the scientific problems that ensue and the need for distance and objectivity that must distinguish science in the problem areas of sport (e.g., drug abuse, doping, technical and other manipulations, and children in top-level sports).

The following can be said about this scientific unsettledness of sport. Without a doubt, sport, as it is presently known, belongs to that class of phenomena that has not yet been investigated with regard to its consequences and structures and on which no general information is available. First impressions of sport are that it is not complicated, is without problems, has a clear structure, is understandable in its obvious relationships, and needs no science and no comparative research. Such seeming transparency is perhaps responsible for its intensity and attractiveness.

However, it should not be overlooked that there is not much information available on the real position of sport with respect to the individual, social life, sport's social relevancy, and education. This may explain why sport has not been free of misunderstanding, wrong interpretation, and ideology. The systematic interest of serious research has barely reached the field of sport. Medicine can provide some information on the healthful aspects of sport (i.e., its prophylactic, rehabilitative, and therapeutic dimensions), but not much information is available on the many relationships between social relevancy and sport or on its real possibilities in education. The available scientific results are not at all in agreement with the obvious public importance and the usage and misusage of sport.

This was, at least, the situation until a few years ago, which was certainly no favorable starting point for the beginning and development of comparative research in physical education and sport. Several things have changed since then. Not only has research improved, but the impact of science on sport also has shown a marked increase. This is not only true of top-class sport which, without the knowledge supplied by various scientific disciplines (i.e., sports medicine, sports psychology, biomechanics, or scientifically based training) and without its rigorous application in practice, could scarcely have attained the levels of performance achieved today. It is also true of other fields of sport. For instance, sport instruction increasingly is being influenced in its planning, organization, and content by theoretical and empirical scientific considerations. Thus much of what we have learned about the educative effects of sport and exercise has emerged not simply as a result of random experience, but also as a result of scientific research. Thus prophylactic measures concerning health and rehabilitation based on the therapeutic effects of sport and exercise have become subject to guidelines provided as a result of scientific research. Hence, mass sport receives as much assistance from scientific research into motivation and the stimulation of interest as it does from research into its significance for the health of the sportsperson. Sports for the elderly would be indefensible were it not for the relevant research that has been conducted in the fields of gerontology, medicine, and sports medicine. Anthropological, pedagogical, sociological, historical, and cultural research deepen our knowledge of sport and make both direct and indirect contributions to improving the way in which we assess, plan, and organize this social phenomenon above and beyond the pure increase in knowledge that the research brings. At least we hope this is the case.

Better conditions for qualified scientific comparisons were created with this development; the work of this organization can, on the one hand, profit from this development and, on the other hand, promote it.

Nevertheless, problems of establishing a comparative sport-science theory remain because exactly at that point of its development where sport science has not yet mastered itself and its own constitution and standards completely, it arises as a new scientific branch. This branch will not easily prove itself before the unity of sport science is established, considering the inconclusive clarification of the status of sport science in most countries—its methods and procedures, its research areas and relationship to sport, its associations and cooperation with other sciences, and its already beginning decay into separate disciplines such as sport psychology, sport pedagogy, sport sociology, sport history, sport philosophy, and so forth.

Of course all leading scientists have always agreed that science cannot be limited to national frontiers, that the scientific community is a worldwide community, and that internationalism, tolerance, and pluralism, along with scientific seriousness and quality, must be among their principles of action. But the consequent investigation of questions that all nations are concerned with—systematic comparison and qualified insight into mutuality, individuality, and differences—are all things that sciences had not recognized and had not accepted as important tasks until very late. It is therefore more important that scientists ponder their self-understanding and their principles thoroughly and communicate with each other—above all, in international circles—to find a common direction.

Another difficulty should be mentioned. Of course, as we know, questions concerning the scientific foundations of the fields of sport-science theory—especially in physical education—have been discussed for several years. These discussions have been held on different levels of competency and have ended with different results. However, important questions have not been answered. For example, where does sport science belong? It cannot be categorized with only one science; it is an interdisciplinary, integrated science that arises from its content. How can sport science be developed with regard to methods and questions? Concerning comparative research, it is necessary to discuss such general elements of sport science, but it is also important to discuss the specific ones. At least three elements should be mentioned: interdisciplinarity, internationalism, and pluralism.

With the assertion of sport science as an interdisciplinary science, only a common object, not a community of methods and theory development, is required. However, the common basis in terms of research objectives is not quite clear. Sport is an area that is many-sided and can be divided into several subareas that are judged quite differently.

With the claim of being an integrated science—a science that involves somewhat different questions and divergent results—the interdisciplinary nature of the research concept is provided. This is a format that is discussed within methodological questions for sport science to a great extent. *Interdisciplinary* means that problems of the science evolve not only from the specific methods and techniques that immediately lead to problems related to a single science, but also from sport. This stress on integration for the development of sport science and that on the necessity of interdisciplinary research thus have a close relationship.

Interdisciplinary views within sport science, however, still have to be developed because appropriate methods, techniques, and questions are still lacking. These cannot be derived from sport science itself. Corresponding behavior patterns of the researchers that generally can be described by terms, teamwork, or ability for cooperative work are necessary. We have to discuss and perhaps solve this problem in comparative research.

In this respect, internationalism as a second element does not only demand participation from a wide range of countries, but it also requires an international orientation. However, nobody can forcibly create such an orientation. We can only try to provide the opportunity for all people to work together and cooperate in the interest of scientific progress, regardless of differences in viewpoints and philosophies and to freely exchange opinions on the various problems without discrimination by conducting a fair debate whenever controversial points tend to give rise to conflict. Understanding, fairness, and readiness to engage in open discussion, as well as friendliness and tolerance, make up the substantial elements of such internationalism.

Another element still to be mentioned is pluralism. The concept of "scientific pluralism" gains color and topicality together with internationalism. Only realization of pluralistic concepts and attitudes, and respect for national peculiarities and interests can lead to international communication and cooperation, which are so essential, and provide the impulse toward further developments in the science of sport. Here, of course, certain obstacles can be discerned, such as the language barrier and the various national traditions and established views, that are often difficult to explain.

Nevertheless, these difficulties and problems need not be obstacles; instead, they can serve as challenges, and if this is true, then this meeting will bring sport science further on its international way.

References

Bereday, G.Z.F. (1964). *Comparative methods in education*. New York: Holt, Rinehart and Winston.

Decker, R. (1984). Die "Psychomotorik". Entwicklungstendenzen und Zielrichtung der teutschen und französischen Bewegungsforschungsrichtung "Psychomotorik" [Developmental and orientation trends in German and French motoric research]. *Sportunterricht, 33*, 51–58.

Haag, H. (1978). *Sport pedagogy: Content and methodology*. Baltimore: University Park Press.

Lauwerys, J.A. (1973). *Education at home and abroad*. London: Rutledge and Kegan Paul.

Nixon, J.E., & Jewett, A.E. (1980). *An introduction to physical education* (9th ed.). Philadelphia: Saunders College.

CHAPTER 2

Comparative Education in General: Aims, Content, and Research Methodology

T.N. Postlethwaite

To begin, it is proper that I define the way I am using the term *comparative education*, for there is no universal agreement among educators about what it should mean. I define *education* as the planning, conduct, and results of formal and nonformal schooling. *Compare* means examining two or more educational entities by putting them side by side and looking for similarities or differences between or among them. This can apply to comparisons within or between systems of education. Comparisons "within," for example, could be a comparison of the aims of sport education in several schools of education within a country, and comparisons "between" could be a comparison of national programs of physical education. This meaning of comparative will be used as the main focus of this paper but is somewhat restrictive. The Comparative and *International* Education Society introduced the word *International* because many people did not compare, but rather described, analyzed, or proposed particular aspects of education in other countries.

Content includes the major themes typically dealt with in comparative education publications. Some writers simply describe features of education. Some interpret such descriptions. Some point out similarities and differences. Others measure achievement in different school subjects and compare such achievement in different school systems. Some go further and analyze the relationships between in- and out-of-school factors thought to affect achievement. This could be achievement between students, between classes, between schools, between regions within a country, between countries, or between classes or students from a number of countries pooled together. Authors then compare and interpret the differential effects of such determinants in different school systems.

The content can include the historical evolution of educational systems, the goals of education and how and why they change over time, structures and enrollments and how and why they change over time, studies of how systems of education are financed, educational administration, curriculum development, teacher preparation and supply, student achievement, and so on. Later in this paper, I categorize content according to major fields of education, simply to show that there are various ways of categorizing such content.

Methodology is normally defined as the systematic study of methods. However, in this context I take it to mean a review of the various types of approaches used in inquiry as pursued in comparative education. *Research* I define as the diligent, systematic investigation of educational phenomena.

I propose to speak a little about the aims of comparative education before proceeding to content and methods. At the very end I shall give some examples of ongoing international research in which I am participating. (I hope that by the end of the presentation there will be more clarity about content and methods and that we all will not still be confused.)

Aim

When well done, comparative education can deepen our understanding of our own education and society. Comparative education can be of assistance to policymakers and administrators and can be a valuable component of teacher education programs. Or, as Noah has said, "comparative education can help us understand better our own past; locate ourselves more exactly in the present; and discern a little more clearly what our education future may be". These contributions can be made via work that is primarily descriptive; through work that seeks to be analytic or explanatory; through work that is limited to just one or a few nations; and through work that relies on nonquantitative, as well as quantitative, data and methods.

I would postulate four major aims.

To identify what is happening elsewhere that might help improve our own system of education. What are the principles involved in, say, an innovation such as "Mastery Learning," which had such a success in South Korea, and what are the procedures necessary to implement the principles?

Similarities and differences exist between systems of education—in goals, in structures, in financing mechanisms, in the scholastic achievement of age groups, and so on. Indeed, differences and similarities also exist between subparts of a system. Only recently I saw a paper on differences in mathematics achievement between the bottom halves of the distribution of students in England and of students in the Federal Republic of Germany. Basically, the comparison showed that the bottom half of the German distribution was higher than the English, although at the top end of the distribution the English were higher. Thus here is an example not of comparing means but of comparing distributions. Another book I recently saw presented changes in mathematics curricula between 1960 and 1980 in a series of countries and looked for similarities and differences in not only the curricula profiles but also in the reasons given for such changes.

The English/German comparison was undertaken because the English believed that Real and Hauptschul education was better in Germany than its equivalent was in England; the researcher wanted to find out if this was true or not. If indeed it was better, then a second question is about the concomitants of such achievement in Germany. The curriculum book allowed any one nation to compare its curriculum with that of other nations. In terms of curriculum, England would also learn, from comparisons with Germany, whether or not its bottom half achievement was lower.

To describe similarities and differences in educational phenomena between systems of education and to interpret why these exist.   Not only are inputs to and processes within systems described, but the philosophies of systems (viz., such catchwords as *equality, democratization, arabization,* etc.) and outcomes (achievement in many subjects) also are described. One major question, not only of academic but also of practical use, concerns why the philosophies and outcomes are what they are. Phrased differently, what are the determinants of such philosophies or outcomes?

To estimate the relative effects of variables (thought to be determinants) on outcomes; these effects can be estimated both within and between systems of education.   Within education there is a great deal of speculation about what affects what. How much evidence, for example, do the people who teach methods at teacher training establishments have about the effectiveness of the methods they promulgate? What about home versus school effects on outcomes? Under what conditions for what sorts of outcomes are they different? If we can agree on a definition of, say, equality of education (do we mean, for example, access to education, promotion through the system, treatment, achievement, or all of these?), then what are the major societal, political, economic, and educational determinants of achieving such equality? I often quote the example of having once asked 10 eminent professors of education what, to them, was the most important school factor to determine between-school differences in a country; I received eight different answers. It is only through systematic, analytic study that one can finally assert that factors A and B have a major impact, that factors C and D have a moderate impact, and that factors E, F, and G have no impact. Remember that during the 1960s there were many proponents of language laboratories for improving the acquisition of a foreign language. And yet, in a study conducted in 1971 on the learning of French as a foreign language in eight countries, the carefully amassed and analyzed data showed that there was no difference in achievement in French between those students who were exposed to language labs and those students who were not exposed. Thus it was a myth that language labs as used in 1971 had an effect on the learning of any of the four language skills.

To identify general principles concerning educational effects.   Let us take a hypothetical example (as in Table 1). Assume that a model has been postulated whereby certain variables are held constant before examining the relationship between other variables (in this case Variables 1, 2, and 3) with the outcomes. The resultant relationship is often estimated by a regression coefficient. In Table 1, A-G represent different systems of education. Variable 1 is significant in all systems, Variable 2 is not significant in any system, and Variable 3 is sometimes significant and sometimes

Table 1 Hypothetical Set of Significant Relationships with Outcomes

| Variables | System of education | | | | | | |
	A	B	C	D	E	F	G
1	✓	✓	✓	✓	✓	✓	✓
2	–	–	–	–	–	–	–
3	✓	–	–	✓	–	–	✓

not significant. In the first case the variable is a determining factor, in the second case it never is, and in the third case it is in some systems and not in others. Thus for the systems A-G we seem to have general (*universal* is too grand a term) principles for Variables 1 and 2 but not for Variable 3. A question of interest to comparative education is, of course, why Variable 3 is sometimes important and other times not.

I feel sure that this is probably an incomplete list and that not all will agree with it, but it does contain a lot of what is done in the area of comparative education.

Content

In the February 1983 issue of *Comparative Education Review*, a bibliography was compiled from 18 different journals (but not including the "CER") of all articles (about 200) published by these journals in the first half of 1982. Over 100 articles were country-specific, and a further 25 specified themes in Europe, a few were on Latin America, and 8 were on developing countries. Topics such as "Recent Trends in Norwegian Higher Education," "Italian Universities: Prospects Offered by New Legislation," "Inefficiency in the French System of Higher Education," "The Soviet Schools' New Frontiers," "The United Kingdom: Becoming and Staying Literate," "International Education: A United States Perspective," "Educational Regionalization in Colombia," "The Re-emergence of Private Education in China," "Universal Primary Education and Rural Development in Nigeria," "Vocational Education in Algeria," "Education and Endogenous Development in Africa," "Theses on Basic Education and Village Development in Black Africa," and "The Development and Training of Teachers for Remote Rural Schools in Less-Developed Countries" all give some flavor of the type of content covered.

Of the remaining 50-odd articles, 10 were on ideological or social science approaches in comparative education, 6 were on teaching and classroom practices, 6 were on economics of education and planning, 4 were on literacy, 4 were on educational administration, and fewer than 4 were on such topics as goals of education; women in education; historical analyses of educational reform, curriculum, minorities, political psychology, student protest; and so on. All of this shows great diversity, both in terms of countries and themes.

My friend and colleague, Murray Thomas, who is the head of the International Education Program at the University of California at Santa Barbara, recently produced a framework for comparing writings about educational systems. In an attempt to convince readers of the desirability or undesirability of an educational plan, policy, or practice, he classified writings in terms of the following models: descriptive, explanatory, assessment, or evaluation, planning, and propagandistic. When reviewing articles in recent issues of *Comparative Education Review* from the viewpoint of such models, he suggested that authors who employ the descriptive model exclusively have very little chance of having their articles published. But those who employ explanatory/assessment or assessment/propagandistic models have good chances of having their articles published given that the geographical educational scopes of the articles are attractive to the editors and that the authors' arguments are lucid. It is for people such as you to decide whether or not Thomas is right and to what extent modes or biases come and go with different review panels in different years.

Let me try to give a brief overview of some of the major themes being covered by comparative educators at the beginning of the 1980s.

Country Studies

What the Germans call "Auslandspädagogik" is still a major theme. Either a total educational system is described—as Murray Thomas and I do in our regional series: South East Asia (1980), East Asia (1983), Pacific (1984) in which we have chapters describing each national system and a final chapter making certain comparisons among the systems in the region—or a subpart of an educational system is taken (e.g., vocational education in a particular country).

A recent trend is to make a country study and examine the political, economic, social, and educational development all at once—what has been called "the development of education in a total societal context" (Nestvogel, 1985).

Themes Within and Between Countries

The major trend, however, has been to move away from country system descriptions and to examine themes either in a national or an international context. Some major themes which I have identified follow.

Economics of education. Subthemes within this area include education financing, cost-benefit in education employment, earnings and education, economic development and education, educational expenditures, educational dropouts and wastage, female labor force participation and education, economic performance and education of immigrants, income distribution and education, labor market theories and education, labor quality and education, on-the-job training, rates of return, sex earnings differentials, skill excess and shortage, economics of teacher supply, and youth unemployment and education.

Educational planning and policy. Here the major subthemes are decentralization, demography in planning, dependency, equality, ideology in educational policy, policies for the education of immigrant children, multilateral and bilateral aid to education in third world countries, school language policies, legitimacy in educational policy, literacy and numeracy, modernization and education, nonformal education, educational planning and social change, planning teacher supply, planning vocational education, history of education planning, educational reform policies, regional disparities, school mapping, and training abroad, as well as some of the subthemes mentioned under the economics of education.

Preschool education. Basically, work here has been descriptive only, but some rudimentary attempts have been made to estimate the effects of different types of preschooling.

Teaching and teacher education. Many studies describe teacher education in one or more systems. Some studies of teaching have been forthcoming (e.g., Dunkin & Biddle, 1974). But very often the meta-analyses attempted are based only on U.S. data (cf. Walberg & Hartel, 1980). Two new international studies are underway: (a) the effect of teacher instructional and management variables on growth in mathematics achievement in 5th grade students and (b) the effect of various methods of teaching particular mathematics topics to 7th and 8th grade students (International Association for the Evaluation of Educational Achievement, in press).

Very often, however, the themes treated by examining data within single countries are architecture of instructional spaces, class size, school size, classroom climate, classroom management, competition in the classroom, content coverage (or opportunity to learn), modes of evaluating teaching, compulsory versus optional inservice training of teachers, the intent and operationalization of various teaching methods (e.g., direct instruction, discussion, group work, mastery learning, and so on), homework, the role of laboratory schools, microteaching, the use of paraprofessionals, paradigms for research on teaching, reading readiness, questioning techniques, the teaching of minority groups, teacher centers, and so on.

Human development. The only direct comparative education book in human development that I know of is *Comparing Theories of Child Development* (Thomas, 1979), in which 23 theories of child development are described and compared. Otherwise, I know only of country studies (e.g., *Multilingualism in the Soviet Union*, Lewis, 1972) or attempts to examine themes by pulling together experiences from various countries. Such themes include attitude development, attitude differences, creativity, delinquency, concept formation (usually à la Piaget), adolescence, language acquisition, moral development, self-concept, sex characteristics and roles, and effects of television on children.

Curriculum. Here the major studies involve what is in the curriculum (as general or specific educational objectives) in specific subject areas and examine similarities and differences (e.g., Steiner, 1980; Travers, 1984). Given evidence from a series of studies about opportunity to learn influencing differences not only between countries but also within countries, several publications have dealt with this aspect of the curriculum. Several studies in developing countries have shown the importance of adequate textbook supply, and this has produced writings on the production, distribution, and availability in the classroom of curricula textbooks and other materials. The differential effect of different curricula are often reported (cf. *Studies in Educational Evaluation*). The work of various national centers of curriculum development is also reported (see, for example, the publications of the African Curriculum Organization or the Asian Programme for Innovation and Educational Development from the UNESCO Regional Office in Asia).

Educational statistics. The work of UNESCO, OECD, and the World Bank is most notable in this area. One of the major problems facing comparative educators is collecting valid and reliable data. UNESCO undertakes the task of attempting to collect comparable, reliable data and then standardizing them. (A selection of some publications is given in the bibliography.) Trend data are particularly useful.

Higher education. Subthemes here focus on the historical development of higher education, the transfer of academic models, curriculum, student unrest, student loans, enrollment expansion, and, more recently, the identity crisis of schools of education.

Nonformal education. The major emphasis here has been on assessing successful, innovative, and transferable programs. Coombs's and his associates' publications (Coombs & Ahmed, 1974; Coombs, Prosser, & Ahmed, 1973), as well as the first major study on 74 programs in Africa (Sheffield & Diejomaoh, 1972) come to mind. Distance education (McAnany, Oliveira, Orivel, & Stone, 1982) is also often under the heading of nonformal education.

Adult education. Subthemes in adult education deal partly with nonformal education in developing countries mentioned above but also deal with the concepts and practices of lifelong and recurrent education, literacy and numeracy studies (including mass campaigns), education for minority groups (handicapped, imprisoned), legislation, the genesis of policies, the translation of policies into programs, participation and motivations for participation (especially among women), roles of various religious and voluntary bodies in adult education, community education, education in the military, lifespan education, the role of museums and libraries, education for leisure, paid educational leave, and peoples' high schools and peoples' universities.

The themes listed are by no means exhaustive (e.g., vocational, industrial, and business education as well as sport education have been omitted). You could no doubt add to the list. What is obvious to me is that there seems hardly to be a domain of education where comparative educators have not dared to tread. Very often the authors undertaking national descriptions or comparisons do not consider themselves comparative educators. They see themselves as economists, historians, or human development specialists and so on.

Methods

Noah has said that "research workers in comparative education have for the most part relied upon concepts and models drawn from history, philosophy, psychology, and the several social sciences" (1985, p. 869). This is a safe statement, but I find, when discussing methods with students, that there is a lot of confusion because several dimensions are mixed up. Terms such as *sociohistorical, ethnographic, anthropological, empirical, hypothetico-deductive, hermeneutic, critical approach,* and the like are used. Terms such as *qualitative* or *quantitative* are often attached. Further terms such as *positivist, Marxist,* and *relativist* are added on. And finally, comments are made about the researcher having or not having a vested interest in the research. So that "positivist, quantitative, empirical with the researchers producing 'objective' results to policymakers" might be a typical cliché used about a method. I propose to examine these dimensions and then suggest a way of proceeding practically, which might rid us of the rhetoric in the debate.

The word *method* is difficult. Some people refer to the "empirical method." Those working in the empirical field might refer to a host of methods of data collection or statistical analyses. Hence, in English, it would be better to refer to *approaches* when referring to hermeneutics, empirical research and the like. As has been seen, several approaches exist. No one researcher will be familiar with all approaches. Hence, teamwork is needed for some problems. Not only should different disciplines be involved (e.g., economics, sociology, education), but often different approaches should be involved. The nature of the problem should determine the one or several approaches to be used.

Kazamias (1961) used the word *approach* in a different way. He distinguished between "old" and "new" approaches. Old approaches, for him, were descriptive and prescriptive—what is and what should be. New approaches were philosophical, functional, and problem-oriented. These were, he maintained, microcosmic, more analytic, and more scientific.

Then there is a problem of quantitative versus qualitative. The debate has been particularly violent during the 1970s and continues. Personally, I can not see what all the fuss is about. In nearly every research project concerning systems of education, both are needed. Mind you, I cannot help observing that I sometimes suspect that some of the more vociferous proponents of qualitative research, and those who totally exclude the utility of quantitative research, are innumerate.

Epstein (1983) has written about the neo-positivist, neo-Marxist, and neo-relativist ideologies embedded in research methodology. Not only are procedures (methods) important, but the ideology that precedes and colors a methodology is also important. Ideology produces bias, and each ideology produces its own type of bias. But surely none of the practitioners of schools of thought believe or have ever believed that they were value-(ideology) free. Their implicit and explicit values are involved in the problems they select to study, in their conceptualization of their theories and models, in the ways (methods) they use to tackle the problem, in the criteria for proof that they use, and in their interpretations of their data. We are all victims of our own experiences. Put in another way, the interpretation of data depends on the memory, introspection, and testimony of the interpreter. Our task is to make our perspectives clear in the write-up of our studies so that a reader of a different persuasion knows that it is *that* author with *that* perspective or *those* perspectives who tackled *that* problem in *that* way with *those* results. This is easier said than done.

A further dimension added to method, quantitative/qualitative, and ideology is the different meanings around the word *research*. Let me distinguish two differences. A first difference is the perceived role of the researcher. One group of researchers believes that research is undertaken to have an impact on society (i.e., they have a vested interest). Many of the adherents of the 'critical approach' school believe this. A second group of researchers believes that the results of a research project are to be given to policymakers to increase the knowledge base for decision-making, but they believe that their work is finished once they have made the results available. Other researchers believe that their results have added to the stock of human knowledge, and that is that. A second dimension asks the question, What research approach is good for what problem? My own belief is that approaches such as hermeneutical or critical are primarily hypothesis or theory or model generating. The ethnographic/anthropological approaches are good both for theory generation and for theory testing. The same is true of the empirical approach.

Let me say that I do not think the above is true only of comparative education; it applies to all educational and social science research. And the problem is that very often various mixes of the above dimensions are given; often the people discussing the issues are not clear about which aspect they are discussing.

The result is often total confusion—at least in my head. Of course, more thought needs to be given to such issues, and we must always be sensitive to the possible biases in the methods we use.

However, to conduct research in comparative education I believe that the following are reasonable procedures (methods) in tackling any subject:

1. Clearly define the problem(s) to be investigated.
2. Decide on and define the universe of study.
3. Select theories[1] or formulate models to be tested (where appropriate) or describe data to be used for analysis to generate theory.
4. Clearly describe the methods to be used and the reasons for using them (here the ideologies can be made clear).
5. Specify the indicators in 3.
6. Where necessary, collect data, documents, and so forth.
7. Analyze.
8. Interpret (but again show possible biases).
9. Conclude.

What is important in any study is that the methods are clear and that the researcher has taken all possible steps to avoid alternative explanations (i.e., someone reviewing the research and saying, "Ah yes, but if you had considered variable x, which you have not, then the explanation would have been very different"). Furthermore, any research should show that the researcher has been systematic and analytic in the work undertaken. Where interpretation is a major feature of the work, then the interpreter's sociopolitical views should be made clear.

Within the type of research that I indulge (i.e., using empirical methods), certain obvious precautions must be taken. These include, for example, ensuring that the following takes place:

- The variable is carefully defined, and the indicators used to collect the information are appropriate in each system of education. The question may be the same or may have to be different.
- The defined target populations are comparable for the purpose of the study. Further, ensure that probability samples with very similar standard errors of sampling are drawn.
- The measures are comparable for all different types of variables: input, process, outcome, and context.
- General and country-specific models are tested.

Each particular approach has its own technical problems, but what is common to all approaches is the problem of comparing like with like and producing a valid measure in each system for a particular variable.

Examples of Empirical Research

Finally, let me turn to one type of comparative education study on which I feel most competent and most comfortable to speak, namely the type conducted by the IEA, of which I have been chairman since January 1978 and have served since 1962.

In the mid 1950s, certain educators were interested in differences and similarities in inputs, processes, and outcomes of school systems. They were not particularly interested in the varying percentages of an age group going through to the terminal grade of secondary school or in how many years of education there were up to the terminal grade, but rather they were interested in what had been learned by these students and in how learning was affected by such manipulable factors as the percentage in school and the number of years of education. This is only one example of the types of interest. There were many more, but all could be subsumed under the four aims of comparative education stated earlier in this paper. What was clear, however, was that outcomes would have to be measured such that they could be brought onto a common scale. The educators banded together to undertake such work. Few among them would have called themselves comparative educators. To begin with, there was a preponderance of measurement people—psychometricians, statistical analysts, and general educators. As time has passed, other forms of expertise have been added; by 1984 there were these categories of people plus economists, sociologists, curriculum and methods experts, and a sprinkling of people who call themselves comparative educators. However, most of them are staff members of educational research institutes. There is a strong empirical component in the work, but some curriculum analysis of a quantitative and qualitative nature is also undertaken.

From 1959 to 1961, a feasibility study was undertaken. From 1962 to 1967, the first major study was undertaken in mathematics achievement in 12 countries. This was followed in the period 1967-1975 by studies in six other subject areas, namely science, reading comprehension, literature, English as a foreign language, French as a foreign language, and civic education in up to 21 countries. Apart from volumes that reported *all* results (i.e., international publications), each national educational research institute typically published a result of the national analyses. There were, of course, many secondary analyses published in academic journals. An annotated bibliography of most of these publications exists (Postlethwaite & Lewy, 1979).

What I would like to do is to describe briefly the major projects being undertaken in the 1980s. There are seven projects.

Second mathematics study. This is being conducted in 26 countries and has two major parts. The first part measures mathematics achievement of 13-year-olds and terminal secondary students and attempts to identify the main determinants of differences in achievement between students in each country. The second part examines the growth in achievement between the beginning and the end of the year in the modal grade of 13-year-olds and attempts to identify the determinants (in terms of what happens in classrooms) of differential growth. As a by-product, it will also be possible in those countries participating in the first and second mathematics studies to assess differences in achievement between 1964 and 1981. A second by-product is an analysis of the changes in the mathematics curriculum between these dates, a summary of reasons for such changes, and an analysis of similarities and differences of changes over countries.

Second science study. This is being conducted in 38 countries. Its aims are similar to the second math study except there is no component examining growth in science achievement over the period of a year.

Classroom environment study. This is being conducted in 14 countries. It is a very detailed study of achievement growth over a period of 1 year (typically Grade 5 mathematics), and it examines the effect of just over 100 different teacher behavior and teacher management variables on such growth.

Written composition study. This is being conducted in 15 countries and examines achievement in different kinds of written composition and the effect of in- and out-of-school factors on such achievement.

Transition from school to work. This study is about to begin, and the number of countries participating is still not definite but likely will be between 20 and 30. The intention is to follow young people from school to work to identify in-school factors (including career guidance) and out-of-school factors affecting such matters as earnings, job satisfaction, realization of job expectations and aspirations, search time for employment, levels of job mismatch, patterns of transition, and so on. This study is clearly a longitudinal study and will last about 8 years.

Preprimary study. This is another study that is about to start. About 20 countries will participate. Again it is a longitudinal study in which 4-year-olds will be followed until the end of their first grade in primary school. Some countries may follow the children through school for a much longer time. The aim of the study is to examine the effect of different settings in which 4-year-olds find themselves (at home, in kindergarten, in nurseries, etc.) on cognitive, affective, and socialization outcomes.

Item banking. This project is the development of a prototype of an international item bank linked to national item banks. The international bank will contain items in mathematics, science, and English as a foreign language. Each item will be classified by objective and school level; each item will also have psychometric properties, such as a scaled value, attached to it. National item banks will be able to use items from the international bank. Item writing is a highly skilled task, but with many examples available it should make life easier for the many item writers throughout the world. One by-product will be that, with the use of such items, it will be possible to place any individual from one country on a scale for another country. Thus Johann taking Abitur can be compared with Jean taking the Baccalaureat or John taking G.C.E. 'A' levels.

Further to these ongoing projects, IEA is considering projects on "Learning the Language of Instruction When it Is Different from That of the Mother Tongue," "The Learning of Values in School," "Practical Skills," and "The Use of Microcomputers in Schools."

Basically, for a project to be undertaken by IEA it must satisfy various criteria:

- It must add to knowledge *and* have high potential for improving the education of children;
- Sufficient countries must wish to participate; and
- IEA must be the appropriate organization to undertake it.

These are examples of some studies underway in a number of countries. They are, as I have said, strongly empirical in their approach and, as such, are criticized by some whose preference is for other approaches. But, again as I have said before, the argument should not be about method. The most appropriate methods should be selected. The problem is to have high quality thinking and measurement in whichever combination of methods is selected.

I hope that what I have said gives you a flavor of the type of work going on in the areas of comparative education that I know about. I know nothing of comparative sport education but look forward to learning about it.

Note

1. The best criteria for judging theory that I have seen are in *Comparing Theories of Child Development* by R.M. Thomas, 1979: "A theory is better if it accurately reflects the facts of the real world of children; A theory is better if it is stated in a way that makes it clearly understandable to anyone who is reasonably competent; A theory is better if it not only explains why past events occurred but also accurately predicts future events; A theory is better if it offers practical guidance in solving daily problems; A theory is better if it is internally consistent; A theory is better if it is economical in the sense that it is founded on as few unproven assumptions as possible and requires simple mechanisms to explain all the phenomena it encompasses; A theory is better if it is falsifiable or disconfirmable; A theory is better if it stimulates the creation of new research techniques and the discovery of new knowledge; and A good theory is self-satisfying. It explains development in a way that we feel makes good sense" (p. 18-23).

References

Coombs, P.H., & Ahmed, M. (1974). *Attacking rural poverty: How nonformal education can help*. Baltimore: Johns Hopkins.

Coombs, P.H., Prosser, R.C., & Ahmed, M. (1973). *New path to learning: For rural children and youth*. Essex, CT: International Council for Educational Development.

Dunkin, M.J., & Biddle, B.J. (1974). *The study of teaching*. New York: Holt, Rinehart & Winston.

Epstein, E.H. (1983, February). Currents left and right: Ideology in comparative education. *Comparative Education Review*, **17**(1).

Gezi, I. (Ed.). (1971). *Education in comparative and international perspectives*. New York: Holt, Rinehart and Winston.

International Association for the Evaluation of Educational Achievement. (In press). *IEA: Activities, institutions and people*. Oxford: Pergamon Press.

Kazamias, A.M. (1961, October). Some old and new approaches to methodology in comparative education. *Comparative Education Review*, **5**, 90-96.

Lewis, E.G. (1972). *Multilingualism in the Soviet Union*. The Hague: Mounton and Co., N.C.

McAnany, E.G., Oliveira, J.B., Orivel, F., & Stone, J. (1982). Distance education: Evaluating new approaches in education for developing countries. *Evaluation in Education: International Progress*, **6**(3), pp. 289-380. Oxford: Pergamon Press.

Nestvogel, R. (1985). *Bildung und Gesellschaft in Algerien: Anspruch und Wirklichkeit*. Hamburg: Institut für Afrika Kunde.

Noah, H.J. (1985). Comparative education: Methods. In Husén, Tosten, & Postlethwaite (Eds.), *International encyclopedia of education: Research and studies*. Oxford: Pergamon Press.

Noah, H.J. (1985). Comparative education: Methods. In Husén, Tosten, & Postlethwaite (Eds.), *International encyclopedia of education: Research and studies*. Oxford: Pergamon Press.

OECD. (1967). *Methods of statistical needs for educational planning*. Paris: OECD.

Postlethwaite, T.N., & Lewy, A. (1979). *Annotated bibliography of IEA publications* (1962-1978). Stockholm: University of Stockholm, IEA.

Postlethwaite, T.N., & Thomas, R.M. (1980). *Schooling in the ASEAN region*. Oxford: Pergamon Press.

Sheffield, J.R., & Diejomaoh, V.P. (1972). *Non-formal education in African development*. New York: African-American Institute.

Steiner, H.G. (Ed.). (1980). Comparative studies of mathematics curricula. *Materialien und Studien*, **19**.

Thomas, R.M. (1979). *Comparing theories of child development*. Belmont, CA: Wadsworth.

Thomas, R.M., & Postlethwaite, T.N. (1983). *Schooling in East Africa*. Oxford: Pergamon Press.

Thomas, R.M., & Postlethwaite, T.N. (1984). *Schooling in the Pacific Islands*. Oxford: Pergamon Press.

Travers, K.J., & Westbury. (In press). *The international mathematics curriculum*. Oxford: Pergamon Press.

Walberg, A.J., & Hartel, E.H. (1980). Research integration: The state of the art. *Evaluation in Education: International Progress*, **4**(1), 1-106. Oxford: Pergamon Press.

Bibliography

Altback, G., Arnove, F., & Kelly, P. (Eds.). (1982). *Comparative education*. New York: Macmillan.

Carroll, J.B. (1975). The teaching of French as a foreign language in eight countries. In *International studies in evaluation* (Vol. V). New York: John Wiley & Sons.

Cowen, R., & Stokes, P. (Eds.). (1982). *Methodological issues in comparative education*. London: The London Association of Comparative Educationists.

Gezi, I. (Ed.). (1971). *Education in comparative and international perspectives*. New York: Holt, Rinehart and Winston.

Holmes, B. (1981). *Comparative education: Some considerations of method*. London: George Allen & Unwin.

Noah, H.J., & Eckstein, M.A. (1969). *Toward a science of comparative education*. London: Macmillan.

Thomas, R.M. (Ed.). (1983). *Politics and education: Cases from eleven nations.* Oxford: Pergamon Press.

United Nations. (1982). *Directory of international statistics* (Vol. 1). New York: Dept. of Internal Economics and Social Affairs, Statistical Office.

UNESCO. (1981). *World school-age population until year 2000: Some implications for the education sector.* Paris: UNESCO.

UNESCO International Bureau of Education. (1977). *Educational statistics: National and international sources and services.* Paris: UNESCO, Education Documentation and Information. (No. 202)

CHAPTER 3

Comparative Physical Education and Sport Needs Bifocal Eyeglasses

Earle F. Zeigler

An opportunity to offer some thoughts about Theme A, or the "content and research methodology session" of our field of interest, at this Fourth Symposium of the International Society for Comparative Physical Education and Sport represents one of my most interesting and challenging assignments in recent memory.

My interest in the international and comparative aspects of our field dates back to the late 1940s when I and my family first "bravely" emigrated from the United States to Canada—that frozen land somewhere to the north where Eskimos, somewhat bilingual people with fur coats, Indians, skis, hockey pucks, beavers, and mounted police with Boy Scout hats live. The fact that we left Canada in 1956 to work at universities like Michigan and Illinois but then returned to Western Ontario in 1971 has provided many experiences that we treasure on both sides of the border. However, it was not until 1968 when I first got a taste of what might really be called "international relations" at the Wingate Institute in Israel under the tutelage of the "peripatetic Israeli," more formally known as Dr. Uriel Simri.

From 1949 to 1968, therefore, it was a privilege to both observe and work closely on the North American continent in what was then called the area of international relations. The late Dorothy Ainsworth and others stimulated us and were most encouraging to those of us who in the 1950s were true neophytes. So-called comparative physical education and sport was truly embryonic at that stage, barely beginning to receive impetus from the disciplinary thrust that impacted upon our field and many others in the mid 1960s. The 1970s took us a bit farther along, but who among us would argue that we have yet achieved a state of "early maturity" in the early 1980s? (This point is immediately apparent as we observe what comparativists in the field of professional education were able to accomplish between 1960 and 1980.)

The task is not to trace the history of the comparative and international aspects of our field's endeavor. In some ways we are too close to this period to gain true historical perspective. It will be attempted, however, to carry out an analysis proceeding from the underlying argument or thesis that the field of comparative physical education and sport should approach its task by using bifocal eyeglasses, so to speak.

Such an analogy may be made because there is a need to view our specialized endeavor in ever-greater detail through the employment of highly refined research methodology. At the same time, there is a concurrent need to place the field and its research and scholarly endeavors in a broader perspective within the individual cultures that are increasingly resembling what might be called an embryonic world culture. Thus, to continue with the eyeglasses analogy, the need is "to see both near and far with our bifocals" as the world moves into the 21st century.

Finally, from the standpoint of introductory comments the presentation is divided into six main sections as follows: (1) social considerations viewed broadly; (2) recent trends in the area of comparative education; (3) a proposal for a consensual definition of the field; (4) two basic questions to resolve—Question 1: What shall we compare? and Question 2: How shall we make such a comparison? (5) a call for "data, knowledge, and wisdom"; and (6) concluding statement.

Social Considerations Viewed Broadly

In previous papers, findings from the investigations of certain social science and humanities scholars were presented and have turned out to be truly prophetic in nature. Consider, for example, the 1970 declaration of Isaac Asimov, who argued that, along with civilization's increasing tempo, a "fourth revolution," a different sort of a revolution than the type to which we had been accustomed, had indeed descended upon us (Asimov, October 24, 1970). He was referring to a fourth revolution in the area of communications that will move the world toward the idea of a "global village."

Moving from the invention of speech to the invention of writing, to the mechanical reproduction of the printed word, and now to relay stations in space, all people on earth are being confronted with a blanketing communications network that is making possible interpersonal relationships hitherto undreamed of by man. This is the highly urgent reason why comparative analysis of sport and physical education is no longer merely a pleasant diversion, a broadening experience, and an opportunity to promote international relations and goodwill. As important as these aspects are to life enrichment, in the area of communications the world is now confronted with a race for survival—a race "between the coming of the true fourth revolution and the death of civilization that will inevitably occur through growth past the limits of the third revolution" (p. 18). In other words, technological advancement in the area of communications has brought us to the point where we are being well-informed about the world's tragic happenings before we have created a situation in which cooperation and sharing have become the operative mode of existence. Thus the "signs of breakdown are everywhere, and the problems introduced by our contemporary level of technology seem insuperable" (Asimov, October 24, 1970, p. 19).

The conclusion to be reached here is that in all fields of endeavor we must truly learn to communicate in a greatly improved manner with people everywhere. Such cooperation, despite the apparent diversity of cultural values and norms that is often only superficial, is absolutely essential if the world as we have known it is to continue (Zeigler, 1975, pp. 466-471). Further support for this contention that the hopes and ideals of the people are not dissimilar comes from the findings of Kaplan, who observed at first hand certain recurring elements in the various world philosophies. Despite the suspicions engendered daily through the various media, he theorized that there are indeed four recurring themes of rationality, activism, humanism, and preoccupation with values present in the leading world philosophies (Kaplan, 1961, pp. 7-10).

Thus, admittedly in our small way, organizations such as the International Society for Comparative Physical Education and Sport (ISCPES) offer hope to sport and physical education professionals from a significant variety of countries as they plan for the future. We can help our cultures move forward to what Glasser has described as a "civilized identity society" in which the concerns of humans will again focus on such concepts as self-identity, self-expression, and cooperation—this time within a world culture that places much greater emphasis on sharing as opposed to "selfish survival" by the exploitation of other people and their natural resources (Glasser, 1972).

Recent Trends in the Area of Comparative Education

Wisdom suggests that we look very briefly at what seems to have transpired in the area of comparative education during the past few decades. Fortunately, we can call on comparative education's special issue on "The State of the Art" that appeared in the late 1970s (*Comparative Education Review*, 1977). Most helpful here is a paper entitled "Intellectual and Ideological Perspectives in Comparative Education: An Interpretation" by Kazamias and Schwartz (1970). Specifically, these scholars reviewed the past 20 years in regard to the definitional orientation and the research methodology and techniques employed in analysis during that period. Kazamias and Schwartz inquired as to whether comparative education was an art, a science, or a combination of both. They asked whether it was a discipline or an area of study on which several disciplines are brought to bear, whether it was a theoretical or an applied activity, and whether its techniques of analysis should be "empirico-statistical, historical, or philosophical." Finally, in regard to the determination of appropriate subject-matter for study, they pondered over the focus for investigation—that is, should they emphasize school-centered problems or school-society relationships (Kazamias & Schwartz, 1970, p. 153). Obviously, those of us in physical education and sport who have been around since the late 1950s are hearing questions that have a most familiar ring.

Time and space do not permit us the luxury of reviewing this historical analysis in detail, but we can report to you that significant change in subject matter focus and research methodology began to occur within comparative education in the late 1950s. The new lines of thought placed emphasis on (1) structural-functionalism from the field of sociology, (2) development education because of renewed concern for the so-called Third World, and (3) empirico-statistical research techniques that were in the ascendancy in the sociocultural and behavioral sciences generally (Kazamias & Schwartz, 1977, p. 157). Also interesting to us in physical education and sport is the observation by Kazamias and Schwartz that when this heavy disciplinary orientation became the vogue in comparative education, it seemed that the results of the investigations being carried out became increasingly useless to teachers as they sought to carry out their professional assignments. Bennett, Howell, and Simri sense this deficiency when they state that "comparative educators need to be careful not to study just those issues and cases that lend themselves to scientific inquiry"(Bennett, Howell, & Simri, 1983, p. 16). They also lament a further deficiency—the fact that "unfortunately, writers of comparative education have had little interest in physical education and sport," and that "references to our subject-matter are virtually nonexistent" (Bennett et al., 1983, p. 18).

To conclude this brief discussion of recent trends in scholarly investigation within comparative education, the thrust in the 1960s was toward development education and modernization based on instrumental means of bringing about such desired change. Possible strategies for change were viewed from the standpoints of economics, political science, sociology, and psychology (Kazamias & Schwartz, 1977, pp. 169-173). Finally, in the 1970s, there was continuing use of methodological empiricism as it applied to problems that had been emerging steadily and increasingly since the late 1950s. There has been continued concern, nevertheless, about the social order and consensus and theories of development and modernization, but such concern has been based almost exclusively on the employment of value-free investigation to develop findings and subsequent generalizations. More constructive dialogue among those concerned, less "cannibalistic poaching" on other disciplines in favor of greater identity for comparative education, and an improved relationship with work of the practicing professional—the teacher—was recommended (Kazamias & Schwartz, 1977, pp. 175-176). To these sentiments it only can be said "Amen!"

Proposal for a Consensual Definition of the Field

If we in this field need "to see both near and far with our bifocal eyeglasses" as we move toward an uncertain future, we should adopt a consensual definition to the effect that our domain includes "developmental physical activity in sport, dance, play, and exercise." As part of an effort to close the developing gap, or perhaps to reverse the direction of present movement within the field, Dr. Laura J. Huelster, Professor-Emerita, University of Illinois, and the author have developed a taxonomical table to explain the proposed areas of scholarly study and research using our nomenclature—sport and physical education terms only—along with the accompanying disciplinary and professional aspects (see Table 1) (Zeigler, 1983, p. 58).

Table 1   Developmental Physical Activity in Sport, Dance, Play, and Exercise

Area of scholarly study and research	Subdisciplinary aspects	Subprofessional aspects
Background, meaning, and significance	History Philosophy Comparative analysis	International Professional ethics
Functional effects of physical activity	Exercise physiology Anthropometry and body composition	Fitness appraisal Exercise therapy
Sociocultural and behavioral aspects	Sociology Psychology Anthropology Political science Geography Economics	Application of theory to practice
Motor development and control	Psycho-motor learning Physical growth and development	Application of theory to practice
Mechanical and muscular analysis of motor skills	Biomechanics Neuro-skeletal musculature	Application of theory to practice
Management/administration	Theory about the management function (derived largely from the behavioral sciences)	Application of theory to practice
Program development	Theory about program development, including general education; professional preparation; intramural sports and physical recreation; and special physical education and sport (including instructional methodology)	Application of theory to practice
Measurement and evaluation	Theory about the functions of measurement and evaluation to the subject of developmental physical activity in sport, dance, play, and exercise	Application of theory to practice

Admittedly, you may regard this recommendation as controversial. This does not worry us at all because we do not regard this material as being etched in stone. As a matter of fact, we have made a number of minor alterations in the table during the past several years, including several that have been added in the version that you see here. We are anxious to receive sound, constructive criticism from a variety of sources. The point to be made is that together we will all be developing a consensual definition that may well stand the test of time.

You will see in Table 1 that we have tentatively agreed upon eight areas of scholarly study and research that are correlated with their respective subdisciplinary and subprofessional aspects. These eight areas are (a) background, meaning, and significance; (b) functional effects of physical activity; (c) sociocultural and behavioral aspects; (d) motor development and control; (e) mechanical and muscular analysis of motor skills; (f) management/administration; (g) program development; and (h) measurement and evaluation.

You will notice immediately that there is a balanced approach between what we have identified as the subdisciplinary aspects of our field (a through e) and what we have called the subprofessional or concurrent professional components (f through h). By this we mean that what many have called—often in a semiderogatory tone—professional writing (e.g., curriculum studies or investigations into the teaching/learning process) is to be regarded as scholarly if and only if the best available research methodology and accompanying techniques have been employed. Furthermore, it is also professional writing in the sense that it should ultimately serve the best interests of the profession. Similarly, what many have regarded as more scholarly, scientific endeavor (e.g., exercise science investigation) is to be regarded as such only if it too is well-done.

Most importantly, note that the names selected for the eight areas do not include terms that are currently part of the names or the actual names of other recognized disciplines and that are therefore usually associated by the public—and also by our colleagues on campus—with these other related disciplines. Our position is simply that we must promote our own discipline of developmental physical activity in sport, dance, play, and exercise, and at the same time work cooperatively to the extent that our scholarly interests overlap. If scholars with degrees in our field who are employed for the greater percentage of their time continue to claim that, for example, they are *sociologists* of sport or *physiologists* of exercise, it will just be a matter of time before these other disciplines awake to the importance of what we believe to be our professional task. The end result, if this were to occur, would be semitrade status for our profession.

The Two Basic Questions to Resolve

Granting that we may be able to achieve a modicum or "irreducible minimum" of agreement as to a definition for our profession/discipline, there are two basic questions that should be answered to the best of our ability: (a) *What* shall be compared, and (b) *How* shall it be done? In regard to the first question (the *what*), ongoing scholarly endeavor should provide us with accurate descriptions of (a) what is actually occurring in the eight areas of scholarly study and research, (b) what social forces are influencing the development of the field, and (c) what recurring professional concerns and problems are confronting the profession.

Moving from the *what*, or the content aspect of our endeavor, we are confronted with the *how*, or the research methodologies and techniques to be employed. Here it seems logical that comparative sport and physical education scholars should not be limited solely to Bereday's recommended approach (1964). Also, I hasten to assert that his recommended technique is just that—a very fine and useful *technique*. It is *one* technique of a broad, descriptive method of research—but this will be addressed a bit further on.

Question 1: What Shall We Compare?

The first question to be answered on an ongoing basis under this heading was indicated above as ''What is occurring?'' Here I want to emphasize that, in my opinion, professionals in our field should elevate their sights far beyond what happens under our aegis within some level of the educational system. By this I mean that we should be extending our considerations so that they include an age range with a ''womb-to-tomb'' orientation. This is why Dr. Huelster and I have broadened the name to be applied to our area to ''developmental physical activity'' or ''human motor performance'' in sport, dance, play, and exercise. We are recommending that our field should have concern for the so-called normal individual, the accelerated person, and also the individual who, for some reason or other, may need special physical education (or a specific program of developmental physical activity) temporarily or permanently as part of his or her lifestyle.

Broadening our scope in this manner means that we should assume both disciplinary concern and professional concern for the type of developmental physical activity provided for the preschool child, and then we should follow through all the way on to what type of physical activity is desirable for older citizens. Obviously, there is a need for attention to all age groups; if we in this profession do not get fully involved, some other less-qualified group will take over. In fact, by our sins of omission, this has already taken place to a degree. Assuming this responsibility means that all of the eight areas of scholarly study and research should be included in this way (e.g., functional effects of physical activity or management/administration).

A second consideration under ''What shall be compared?'' should be the ongoing analysis of the various social forces and influences that impact the type of developmental physical activity provided to—or perhaps even urged upon—citizens of all ages. Under this heading I have postulated that we should be considering (a) the influence of societal values and norms, (b) the type of political state, (c) the level of nationalism present in a country, (d) the approach to economic theory and practice, (e) the impact of religion, (f) the concern for ecology, (g) the level of science and technology present, and (h) the concept of *progress*. All of these forces or influences exert a greater or lesser amount of impact upon the type and level of developmental physical activity present within a country or culture.

Thirdly, under the category of content for comparison, I have identified a number of professional concerns or perennial problems with which our profession has been faced—and which give every indication of being with us for the foreseeable future. These have been reported in the literature for many years (see, for example, Zeigler, 1975, 1977, 1979) and are now time-tested concerns for the profession in the sense that a substantive body of literature has accrued relative to each of these perennial problems. They are as follows: (a) program development (or what shall be included or taught); (b) instructional methodology (or how it should be presented in the teaching/learning process); (c) the overall approach to professional preparation or training; (d) the concept of the 'healthy body' (or what constitutes sound health); (e) the role of women, handicapped people, and ethnic minorities in sport and physical education; (f) the role of dance and music in developmental physical activity; (g) the use of leisure for the purpose of developmental physical activity; (h) the delineation of amateurism, semiprofessionalism, and professionalism in sport; (i) the approach to management/administration in sport and physical education; and finally (j) the concept of progress (or what constitutes professional progress). (Note that the concept of progress is viewed both as a social influence and a professional concern.)

Despite this three-pronged approach to "What shall be compared?" that has just been recommended for your consideration, I hasten further to call to your attention—if you have not already examined it thoroughly—what I consider to be perhaps the best job on conceptualizing our task in this area that has been offered for our consideration to date. I am referring to Donald Morrison's "Towards a Conceptual Framework for Comparative Physical Education" as presented in *Methodology in Comparative Physical Education and Sport*, by Howell, Howell, Toohey, and Toohey (1979, pp. 89-119). In this conceptual framework—an approach that I commend for your reconsideration at this time—the broad headings recommended for the analysis of a system of physical education are as follows: (a) ecological setting, (b) sociocultural system, (c) development and change of systems of physical education, (d) the system of physical education itself from sociocultural, economic, political, school system, and coordinating organizations' standpoints, and (e) structures and functions of physical education organizations. Here, indeed, we have a fine taxonomy from which to proceed as to "What shall we compare?" and I believe that what I have presented above offers excellent supplementation (and vice versa).

Question 2: How Shall We Make Such a Comparison?

Now it is time to take a look at the question of research methodologies and techniques that might be applicable to this area of scholarly study and research in sport and physical education (or, as I am recommending for consideration, developmental physical activity in sport, dance, play, and exercise). As we approach this question in our field, please keep in mind what was being urged upon comparative education in the 2 decades between 1950 and 1970. It went something as follows: (a) more systematic and less impressionistic investigations, (b) more empirical and analytical and less speculative and descriptive analyses, (c) a more microcosmic than macrocosmic approach to problems, and (d) a more scientific as opposed to philosophical or historical type of research—the presumption being, of course, that much more reliable data would be forthcoming if these criteria were applied to all investigations (Kazamias & Schwartz, 1977, p. 163). I suggest that these criteria have more than a familiar ring to us in this field and that probably others present at this symposium will be urging similar criteria for us in the 1980s.

Whatever criticisms the comparative education scholars or we ourselves may have for the methodological approaches to research and scholarly endeavor that have been followed in their field or ours, I do not propose here to assume a negative or critical role about how good or bad we may have been or may be now. That is water over the dam. Now there is every reason for us to be positive and prospective in this regard as we look forward to the possibility of the "global village" concept gradually becoming a reality because of technological advancement in the area of communications.

Having opted for a prospective mode above, I believe it to be logical at this time that so-called comparative scholars in sport and physical education should employ all of the research methods and techniques available to men and women who have an interest in developmental physical activity in sport, dance, play, and exercise that extends beyond the borders of their respective countries. In my opinion this should perhaps be the only criterion that should be employed when we invite scholars to attend our meetings and take part in our affairs.

The implications to be drawn from this recommendation are that we should be encouraging all types of scholars within our field who have scholarly interests that extend beyond the borders of their respective countries to consider getting involved with us in the future development of comparative sport and physical education at the international level. Until now it has been those people in our field with scholarly *historical* interests who have joined us, not to mention a relatively few who have what might be called a social-science approach. This has been fine, and we have indeed made some headway, but it is not enough for now and for the future—that is, the progress has been too slow keeping the rate of change in the world in mind.

What this recommendation adds up to is simply that there is an urgent need for comparative studies of all types that could, and should, involve scholars who employ historical, experimental group, and descriptive methods of research and philosophical analysis, respectively, as they seek answers to the problems and concerns of developmental physical activity in sport, dance, play, and exercise all over the world. Immediately, we must recognize, of course, that there are a number of different approaches to each of the research methods available. For example, a number of different historical interpretations are being employed in the latter half of the 20th century (e.g., that objectivity is an unattainable ideal), not to mention the many new techniques developed to aid the historian in his or her work (e.g., use of computers for analysis and development of demography). Such new techniques contribute, of course, to the micro-cosmic nature of present-day historical investigation.

Most of the studies that are carried out in the name of comparative physical education and sport fall in the category typically known as descriptive research method—that is, the investigator uses one or more techniques of what used to be called *survey research* (a term that has largely been abandoned because it was too narrow and limited in most people's opinions). Any and all techniques of descriptive (method) research are employed to discover one or more facts that are presumably related to the problem(s) under investigation. A good way to understand just when and where historical research ends and descriptive research begins is for the researcher, perhaps with the advice of associates, to ask himself or herself when historical data become blurred; it is impossible to evaluate the findings truly and clearly within an appropriate perspective. However, I do not believe that this matter can be determined arbitrarily and categorically.

At any rate, the "research waters" often become muddied by careless use of terminology and by an inability on the part of some investigators to understand that there are at least 12-15 different techniques employed by social science researchers that fall under the category of the descriptive method of research. Bereday's so-called comparative method is nothing other than one of the useful techniques of the descriptive method. Thus I believe it is very confusing when we hear or read such terms as *anthropological research, behavioral research, educational research, psychological research, methodological research, scientific research, social-scientific research, and sociological research,* to name some of the leading terms. Assuredly what is meant in almost every instance is that research in a specific subject matter or grouping of subject matters is being discussed. The point to be made is simply that there are three broad methods of research— historical, experimental group, and descriptive methods (using a control mechanism)—that contain within them a vast array of techniques often involving some type of statistical analysis. It should be obvious to all of us that the descriptive method of research must be a strong ally of scholars interested in comparative sport and physical education.

The third broad method of extant research has often been called experimental research, but I think it is much wiser to designate it as the experimental group method of research. I see such careful definition as being most important, because we might use an experimental technique with descriptive research to determine the status of some state or condition (e.g., we can test a group to see how many sit-ups each member can do in a period of 60 s) and, using the word in two different ways, tend to make the concept 'experimental' carry too much weight. Control is actually the most important factor for the researcher to keep in mind here, because he or she has the opportunity to manipulate factors and variables before the study or experiment is carried out. There can be randomization, and there can be a control group. The researcher can strive to control all of the variables except one. In such a case, the control of the situation is obviously greater, and therefore the probability that such-and-such may be truly related to this-and-that is greater as well.

Obviously, the problem that the researcher faces when consideration is given to the use of the experimental group method of research in some aspect of comparative sport and physical education is obtaining acceptance for the type of study undertaken. Leaders and members of organizations simply are not ready socially or psychologically to permit their organizational groups to be used as guinea pigs either experimentally or in a control group. There is typically great concern about the time necessary to carry out such a study and the possible effect of negative findings that may result from the study. This negative feeling is doubled or tripled when the researcher is dealing with a profit-making organization in North American culture.

Notwithstanding the difficulty of using this method when you enter the area of behavioral research—that is, using those research methods and techniques applicable to investigations in which people are involved in social, interpersonal situations—at this point we have not yet been able to describe accurately even those investigations that have been carried out. Thus we have not yet developed an acceptable, embryonic, taxonomic classification to describe comparative sport and physical education. Accordingly, it has not been possible to employ an integrative technique that would result in a synthesis of published findings and some reasonably tenable theory from which testable assumptions would undoubtedly emanate. Thus what occurs typically is that a scholarly person who wishes to undertake investigation almost of necessity executes some sort of an ad hoc, descriptive study—a study that is only rarely elevated to the point where something akin to Bereday's comparative technique may be applied. (Here I hasten to state that there have been some fine studies employing one or more techniques of descriptive method, but rarely have there been investigations where appropriate sampling and statistical techniques were used to provide an acceptable means of testing a theoretical proposition.)

If indeed we are not able to employ the experimental group method of research based on a research paradigm because of a variety of difficulties with which we are confronted at this point (i.e., random sampling of subjects and the random assignment of subjects to groups and treatment to groups, including even the assignment of people and/or groups as control groups), what can we do to improve the situation? Of course we cannot blithely proceed with erroneous, cause-and-effect assumptions based on the application of the historical and elementary descriptive methods only, followed by a conclusion that "after this, therefore caused by this" (the famous post hoc, ergo propter hoc fallacy). Thus if we decide that we must employ what has been called *ex post facto research techniques* of what is really the descriptive method, then we have to be most careful not to gloss over the fact that we have not been able to control the independent variables; therefore our investigation has an inherent weakness.

Before concluding this all-too-brief discussion of research methodologies and techniques, I must say some good words about ex post facto research despite its inherent limitations (i.e., the inability to manipulate independent variables, randomize subjects, and interpret directly). This approach to research can at least cope, to a degree, with investigations that do not readily lend themselves to the institution of these desirable characteristics. In fact, some important variables are not capable of being manipulated (e.g., personality factors), and therefore this approach is probably the only way that any type of semicontrolled inquiry is possible. In conclusion, we need well-executed studies of both types, and we will have to be satisified with what is available to us at this time and do the best that we can with it (Kerlinger, 1973, pp. 378-382, 390-392).

Finally, in response to the question as to how comparison may be carried out, I must say a few words about what has often mistakenly been designated as philosophic research. Let me say right away that I am now completely convinced that there is no such thing as philosophic research in the sense that new facts or knowledge can be uncovered. It was not always so, of course, because early philosophers believed that philosophy should serve a function not unlike that which we attribute to contemporary science today. But present-day science and its exacting methods and techniques have forced the large majority of British and North American philosophers at least to challenge the fundamental basis of philosophic activity.

By this admission I do not mean to imply that I personally do not see an important place for both speculative and normative philosophizing about our work. Nevertheless, I do recognize that what has been called *philosophic analysis*—the analytic tradition, if you will—dominates the discipline at present. It means that philosophy tends to be somewhat of a handmaiden to science through the use of techniques designated as conceptual and language analyses, not to mention a variety of other approaches all involved with some form of critical analysis. As a matter of fact, I believe that most approaches to philosophizing can be helpful to those of us who are interested in comparative sport and physical education if the approaches are well-executed. This is why I have been arguing strongly that a more well-balanced approach to philosophizing would be most helpful at present. By this I mean that philosophic endeavor can and should be both macroscopic and microscopic in its outlook. This is not to say that a given sport and physical education philosopher would necessarily be obligated to follow both approaches, only that professionals in the field and the general public both need advice at a time when the societal values and norms are being challenged so mightily on all fronts in a truly troubled world.

The Need for "Data, Knowledge, and Wisdom"

Early on in this paper I called for a consensual definition of our entire field or discipline by suggesting that we might call it "Developmental Physical Activity in Sport, Dance, Play, and Exercise." Whatever we eventually decide to call it, and however we may classify it taxonomically, I say to you that professionals in our field are drowning in data, starving for knowledge, and typically lacking in wisdom. Lest you think I am being too harsh in speaking about our field, let me say quickly that all professions are facing a similar problem to a greater or lesser degree. That is their problem, of course, but I have been attempting to devise a plan that might work for us.

The terms that I just used are *data, knowledge,* and *wisdom.* The term *data* refers to factual information—the type of material available through scholarly investigation with which we are being overwhelmed daily. We know that this information is out there somewhere, but I challenge you to find the results of the specific study that you need at the very time that you want to put it to use. The term *knowledge* refers to facts that are inventoried in the form of ordered generalizations that represent tenable theory. Such theory can be employed by professional practitioners, and it also contains testable assumptions upon which further research can be based. Tell me, if you can, where to find such inventoried facts and data.

By use of the concept of *wisdom,* I refer to that attribute or competency that mature professionals should employ when making decisions as to what should or should not be done—wise decisions such as are based on tenable theory in keeping with societal values and norms. Here too I challenge you to show where our professionals in the field have the ever-present opportunity to relate to outstanding people in the various areas of our field for advice and guidance. If these statements are accurate, and I believe that they are, that is why I feel constrained to assert that most people in our field are "drowning in data, starving for knowledge, and typically lacking in wisdom." Obviously, our responsibility in comparative sport and physical education is very great indeed. Our task is broader than the provision of data, knowledge, and wisdom within one country. Ours is a worldwide task and responsibility as we strive to bring the benefits of our scholarly and professional endeavor to all people in the approximately 156 countries that are currently constituted in the world.

Concluding Statement

Finally, I offer for your consideration several suggestions, recommendations, and what I feel are reasonable conclusions as follows:

- We should all be grateful that the International Society for Comparative Physical Education and Sport was established. It provides us with an international forum for the dissemination of both subdisciplinary and subprofessional data.
- In carrying out our professional and scholarly endeavors, we should strive to interest outstanding people from all areas of our field in the work of the Society.
- We need people who will identify primarily with the comparative technique of descriptive method to develop the necessary data and knowledge about sport and physical education on a global level.
- We should work for increased recognition of comparative sport and physical education within our profession in our own countries. For example, among the thousands of names included in a recent major

directory of physical educators in higher education in the United States, not one person identified himself or herself with the area of comparative sport and physical education. Obviously this seems to bespeak a surprising narrowness and insularity of outlook that must be overcome through the efforts of our members. How could this happen, you might ask? It was simple; there was no opportunity given to make such an identification. . . . That very fact tells us something, doesn't it?

- The challenge is there for us to meet if we can. We should ensure that our task and our responsibility are defined both broadly from the standpoint of breadth of outlook and narrowly from the standpoint of specialization of research interests. The approaches of the members of this society and those whom we enlist should be both macroscopic and microscopic. We need professional leaders with vision in the area of international relations—people who can comprehend the long-range goals and lead us down the correct paths to world peace and international cooperation. We also need scholars who will carry out both broadly based and narrowly defined investigations that will provide us with sound knowledge and theory upon which to base our professional work.

Now it is up to us to see what can be accomplished before we have another opportunity to meet again 2 years from now. Where are your bifocal eyeglasses?

References

Asimov, I. (1970, October 24). The fourth revolution. *Saturday Review*, 17-20.

Bennett, B.L., Howell, M.L., & Simri, U. (1983). *Comparative physical education and sport* (2nd ed.). Philadelphia: Lea & Febiger.

Bereday, G.Z.F. (1964). *Comparative method in education* (pp. 11-27). New York: Holt, Rinehart and Winston.

Glasser, W. (1972). *The identity society*. New York: Harper & Row.

Kaplan, A. (1961). *The new world of philosophy*. Boston: Houghton Mifflin.

Kazamias, A.M., & Schwartz, K. (1977). Intellectual and ideological perspectives in comparative education: An interpretation. *Comparative Education Review*, **21**(2/3), 153-176.

Kerlinger, F. (1973). *Foundations of behavioral research* (2nd ed.). New York: Holt, Rinehart & Winston.

Morrison, D. (1979). Towards a conceptual framework for comparative physical education. In M.L. Howell, R. Howell, D. Toohey, & D.M. Toohey (Eds.), *Methodology in comparative physical education and sport* (pp. 89-119). Champaign, IL: Stipes.

Zeigler, E.F. (1975). *Personalizing physical education and sport philosophy.* Champaign, IL: Stipes.

Zeigler, E.F. (1977). *Physical education and sport philosophy.* Englewood Cliffs, NJ: Prentice-Hall.

Zeigler, E.F. (1979). *A history of physical education and sport.* Englewood Cliffs, NJ: Prentice-Hall.

Zeigler, E.F. (1983). Relating a proposed taxonomy of sport and developmental physical activity to a planned inventory of scientific findings. *Quest,* **35**(1), 54-65.

CHAPTER 4

Interdisciplinary Methodology as the Basis for an Interdisciplinary Sport Science?

Klaus Willimczik

If one established an empirical distribution of the publications on the philosophy of sport science and marked the number of publications on the vertical axis and the year of publication on the horizontal axis, the graphic representation would show a sharply declining curve, because the number of philosophical-theoretical treatises on sport science has strongly decreased. If one furthermore analyzed the fewer number of publications as to what new vistas they contain, the tendency pointed out would even increase.

Even though it is simplifying and thus provocative, one could say, nonetheless, that the philosophical-theoretical discussion in sport science is marking time or that there is nothing new in the philosophical-theoretical discussion in sport science.

The causes for this surely deplorable situation are to be seen on three different levels. First, the extreme decrease in interest in the philosophical foundations of sport science which is to be noted since the mid 1970s coincides with the institutional recognition of sport science. In the Federal Republic of Germany alone, more than 100 chairs in sport science were created as a result of the enthusiasm reigning at that time in educational policy. The coincidence of the institutional and financial acknowledgement of sport science, on the one hand, and the diminishing interest in a philosophical foundation of sport science, on the other hand, is by no means accidental. There is reason to suppose or even suspect that the interest in the philosophy of science was not intrinsic (i.e., that interest was not primarily on material grounds in a philosophical-theoretical foundation). Rather, it was a matter of the recognition of sport science as an academic discipline and of the acknowledgement of one's own work.

Apart from the acknowledgement of sport science as an academic discipline, a second cause for the diminishing interest in a philosophical-theoretical foundation is to be seen in the work of general philosophy of science. Discussions in this area have reached such a degree of sophistication and such a level of abstraction that working sport scientists, as well as scientists in general, find themselves unable to participate. The practicing scientist no longer recognizes his or her own problems in the problems dealt with by the philosophers of science. And what is even worse yet, the problems appear to the scientist as pseudoproblems because they are void of any consequence for his or her work. It is quite irrelevant to sport scientists interested in the motivational structure of pupils, in motor learning processes, or in the impact of training programs on endurance whether they proceed from theories characterized as 'statement view' or as 'nonstatement view.' It is of little consequence for the scientists' work whether they have a critical-rational or a neo-Marxist conception of science.

I would not have dared to blame an entire scientific discipline if this reproach had not already been raised more than 2 decades ago by a distinguished empiricist and theoretician of science. I refer to Lazarsfeld and the statement he made in 1962: ''Either we must become our own methodologists, or we must muddle on without the blessings of the methodological clergy'' (p. 470).

With the third cause for the stagnation in philosophical-theoretical discussion, sport scientists, both those working empirically and those working theoretically, are addressed. As will be substantiated in the first main section of this paper, a universally acknowledged catalog of requisite criteria and structural models for sport science exists. But where are the scientists who bridge philosophy of science, on the one hand, and science itself, on the other (i.e., meta-theory and theory)? Or, to put it more concretely, today sport science undisputedly passes for an interdisciplinary science. The status of interdisciplinarity is generally delimited from an additive or a multidisciplinary status. Is it possible to show that this differentiation is also present in practical scientific work, or is it also a pseudoproblem—one of the blessings of the methodological clergy?

The aim of this paper is to explore a footpath for bridging the gap between philosophical foundation, on the one hand, and empirical work, on the other. That is to say the purpose is to find out whether the philosophical-theoretical criteria that sport science is required to meet can be fulfilled by the latter in everyday scientific work, and if so, to what extent.

Let us begin with a recapitulation of the criteria that are universally acknowledged as fundamental for sport science. Doing so, some brief remarks will be made on the importance that each single criterion has for practical work in sport science.

In a second step, a detailed examination will be made to determine whether there is an interdisciplinary research methodology on which an interdisciplinary sport science might be founded. As it has been resolved to avoid a high level of abstraction and rather to descend into the 'low grounds' of empiricism, one can proceed only exemplarily in this part of the paper.

Finally, the ideas presented will be applied to the specific problems of sport pedagogics. It will be shown to what extent the problems pointed out for sport science are also problems of sport pedagogics, and where the problems of sport pedagogics go beyond the problems of sport science.

The Current State
of Philosophical-Theoretical Discussion

In my article published in 1980 (English version published in 1983) the philosophies of sport science available in Eastern and Western Europe as well as in America were submitted to a comparative analysis. There is considerable universal agreement on the philosophical-theoretical foundation of sport science. This applies as well to the so-called 'philosophical basis' of the discipline, which according to the Eastern European view is characterized as 'politics of science,' as to the emergence of sport science as an academic field of inquiry, the structure of sport science, and the requisite criteria for sport science.

Perhaps it was the lack of differing opinions or of opposite views that made us believe that the philosophical-theoretical problems of sport science could be solved. And it is readily admitted that the significance of the unanimity in the philosophical-theoretical discussion on the meta-theory of sport science was overestimated. Now the following question seems to be of crucial importance: How great, actually, is the correspondence between philosophical-theoretical superstructure and practical work in sport science? To be in a position to answer this question, a brief overview of the philosophical-theoretical criteria that are universally recognized will be given. They will be examined under two aspects: Are the respective criteria for sport science still required at all? and In which way can they be fulfilled by practical sport science?

Relevant problems. The relevance of the problems that a discipline deals with is generally substantiated along two lines: Either the interest is in the refinement of theories (then the problems treated are discipline-oriented), or the interest of the scientist is in the problems of everyday life that, in general, are very complex. Disciplines concerned with the complex problems of everyday life are referred to as *interdisciplinary sciences*.

The problems of sport science arise from everyday life, and their relevance is recognized by society and its institutions—the ministries and the political parties. This equally holds true for the domain of public schools and for leisure, for aspects of both the individual and society, and for educational objectives such as health and communication. It likewise applies to both the private and the public spheres.

Specific field of inquiry. Notwithstanding the fact that this criterion continues to be unanimously required for sport science and has been claimed since Kant, it can be considered outdated today. Against this criterion it can be argued that, in practice, the real world is not divided up into special domains that the different scientific disciplines deal with as their specific subject matter. Rather, the subject matter of a discipline is constituted by research methodology and thereby is given its special character. Kant expressed himself along these lines when he spoke of the constitution of a subject matter through methodology. What is meant by this perhaps becomes clear if one bears in mind that when human beings—and also human beings engaged in sport—are the object of inquiry of a discipline, they are viewed quite differently depending on whether they are analyzed using individual characteristics according to the atomistic theory of the behaviorists or whether they are interpreted as holistic beings, as in gestalt psychology. In a similar way, human beings engaged in sport are seen from different perspectives depending on whether they are the subject matter of biomechanics, sport psychology, or sport philosophy.

Specific concepts. Undoubtedly, there are specific concepts that serve as approaches for scientific work. Unlike philosophical-theoretical literature, these are not specific to individual disciplines; they are claimed to have supradisciplinarity. This equally holds for the behavioristic approach, cybernetics, the systems theory, or for the approaches of action theory that just recently came into fashion. Not only are they claimed to be valid for psychology or pedagogics or sociology or sport science, but they also are to be used for explaining phenomena irrespective of the fact that these pertain to the physical or the social sciences. Thus concepts seem not to be suited for establishing individual disciplines.

Systematic organization of the body of knowledge. Still today, this criterion is considered to be of crucial importance for research. The systematic organization of the body of knowledge in terms of theories is both the starting point and the final objective of any research activity.

Likewise, it is not easy for the single disciplines to fulfill this criterion. It is relatively easy to fulfill it by the disciplines dealing with narrowly limited problems which are, as they are termed, discipline-oriented. Extremely problematic and controversially discussed, however, is the question of whether interdisciplinary theory-building is possible. Whether one assumes a positive or negative attitude to the possibility of interdisciplinary theories primarily depends on the concept of theory that one takes as a basis. If one advocates formal theories, then this problem field overlaps with that of concept formation. For example, cybernetics, which also is a conceptual approach, has been labeled as an interdisciplinary theory.

But if one demands interdisciplinary theories for sport science, these ought to be substantive theories. Whether these theories may be possible at all is still very controversial in the philosophy of science. In my opinion, there cannot be such theories. Revealing corresponding structures that exist between the theories of different fields of inquiry and correlating theories of different domains depending on the problems treated are all that we can expect to achieve. Thus a sport scientist who teaches the impact of endurance training as it is performed in schools has to consider the theories on adaptation and motivation and emotions without a "theory of endurance training in schools" being the result.

With that, the problem of interdisciplinary theory-building has surely not been given full treatment. Undoubtedly, interdisciplinary theory formation is of crucial importance for the establishment of an interdisciplinary sport science. Here ends the discussion of this criterion because the main subject of the paper is to look into the possibility of an interdisciplinary methodology for research.

Specific terminology.   The demand for a specific terminology may be considered secondary. It is subordinate in the sense that scientific terminologies cannot be viewed as isolated, they can only be viewed as being embedded in specific theories. A scientific terminology without a corresponding theoretical background is not possible.

But if scientific terminology is not possible without theory, and if several theories are (or must be) admitted for sport science, then there can be no coherent terminology in sport science. In practical research work it is not required, though. For the practicing scientist it is a matter of course that force in physics and strength in sport physiology are not defined in the same way. Rather, also with a view to terminology, an attempt must be made to reveal corresponding structures in the parallel existing terminologies.

Meaningful history.   This criterion directly depends on the theory-criterion because it cannot be meant that a discipline already exists for a long time. Rather, it is required that, as Nixon expressed it, "an impressive body of time-tested works" exists (1967, p. 47). The demand for a meaningful history hence says that theories that have been tested often and proven sound must be available.

Institutionalization of a discipline.   The fulfillment of this criterion has to be considered separately according to the different countries. For the Federal Republic of Germany it can be regarded as entirely fulfilled. There are chairs in sport science in almost all universities; in many universities sport science even has its own departments. A Federal Institute for Sport Science exists, and there are various national and international associations that coordinate sport science. However, one must be aware of the fact that this criterion is only of secondary importance. Institutionalization is a sign for the social recognition of the problems that sport science deals with, but it furnishes no details on the scientific character of work in sport science.

Specific methods of inquiry.   Also for this criterion it must be stated that the specificity of research procedures and techniques is no longer required. What is required with a certain emphasis is an acknowledged research methodology as prerequisite for the scientific quality of work. Or let it be put more clearly: The importance recently lost by the hitherto treated criteria has been gained by research methodology. In other words, the recognition of a field of inquiry as an academic discipline today largely, if not exclusively, depends on whether its work can be called 'scientific' and whether the research methodology used is in accordance with general scientific principles. This is why this criterion will be considered in more detail. The central aim is to find out whether the research methods acknowledged in the individual disciplines exist in a state of mutual isolation from one another in an interdisciplinary sport science or whether there may be something such as a problem-oriented research methodology that would justify speaking of an interdisciplinary research methodology and subsequently of an interdisciplinary sport science. If this proved to be impossible, one would have to be more moderate in one's demands on an interdisciplinary sport science.

An Approach Toward a Problem-Oriented Research Methodology

Research methodology is divided into a number of special fields that are in varying dependent relationships with each other. These include data gathering, data processing, experimental designing, sampling techniques, and constructing models for explaining the phenomena investigated. Because of necessary limitations, only data collection will be considered in the following.

The essential item of this part of research methodology is the theory of errors. It is used to prove that findings are not only knowledge, but that they are scientific knowledge. In this connection it must be borne in mind that the concept of error as it is used in science has another meaning in everyday life. Whereas in colloquial speech *error* and *false* are used as synonyms, the scientist employs the term *error* to designate the portion of a proposition that is attributable to influencing factors beyond his or her control.

Such errors may occur in manifold ways in sport science. To assess the respective margin of errors and take this margin into account to interpret research findings, manifold procedures and techniques have been developed for the individual disciplines of sport science.

It can be assumed that the theories of error in the individual disciplines are in keeping with their respective subject matters. Furthermore, in philosophical-theoretical discussion it is claimed that interdisciplinary sciences such as sport science should be based on the parent sciences relating to the individual disciplines. Therefore the discussion on research methodology of sport science can neither aim at principally questioning the theories of error of the individual disciplines nor at developing new theories of error for the individual disciplines separate from the parent disciplines. The aim of sport science—and of this paper—can only be the following:

- To reveal the sources that are considered as causes of errors in the individual disciplines.
- To look for corresponding structures in the calculus of error as it is performed in the individual disciplines to determine to what extent identical or different causes for potential errors exist.
- To analyze which disciplines are possibly dealing with the same errors and those errors' causes but are only starting from different approaches.
- To assess whether—and, if so, to what extent—an interdisciplinary research methodology for sport science is possible at all.

Because of both their underlying subject matter and the history of science, principal differences concerning the treatment of errors exist with respect to the following two areas of scientific inquiry: (1) the physical sciences and (2) the social sciences.

The subject matter of the physical sciences is inanimate nature, which is supposed to be subject to deterministic laws. This means that scientists can proceed from the fact that events occur with absolute certainty and not stochastically. For free fall $g/2\, t^2$ always holds—and not only with a high probability!

If exceptions to this rule are observed, they are because of the fact that, for example, air resistance was not sufficiently taken into consideration; they are not because the formula for the velocity of fall is incorrect or because the falling object behaves in a different way.

Thus variations in measurement occurring in practical research cannot and need not be traced back to a fluctuation in the object of measurement. They can be attributed exclusively to the process of measurement (i.e., measuring instruments or experimenters). It is only consequent and legitimate to limit the calculus of error to this source of error.

Do such conditions also apply to sport science or some of its subdisciplines? What was described as being the subject matter of the physical sciences could most likely apply to biomechanics and sport medicine, the parent sciences of which see themselves as physical sciences (though not consistently with respect to sport medicine).

Biomechanics is defined as the science of the mechanical description, explanation of the phenomena, and causes of movement, when taking the conditions of the organism as a basis. From this in principle, a generally acknowledged definition follows that the subject matter of biomechanics principally differs from that of mechanics. Whereas the latter focuses on inanimate nature, the subject matter of biomechanics is the organism (only) considered from its mechanical aspect. With that, however, it is no longer justifiable to confine oneself to errors of the process of measurement. Rather, the object of measurement—a human being—has to be taken into consideration as a source of possible variations occurring in the values measured: this is a matter of course, for example, in motor research. (Only those researchers whose object of investigation is limited to sport equipment may confine themselves to a purely natural/scientific calculus of error).

Thus in the motor ability test of backward balancing, it is assumed that the individual variations in the number of backward steps in the first place is because of the fact that the test person—the object of investigation—behaves otherwise than inanimate nature (i.e., not deterministically, but variably). He or she is not in a position to reproduce the result of the test without errors. In the social-scientific theory of errors, the source of errors is designated as trait fluctuation or lacking trait stability, respectively. It is determined via the test criterion of reliability.

Still another source of errors has to be considered when a human being is the object of investigation. A researcher who wants to make propositions on takeoff power by means of a jump-and-reach test or who strives for insight into endurance by means of the Cooper test does not claim to measure the respective motor ability with these tests. The result of measurement—the height in inches or the distance in minutes—is only an externally visible and measurable indicator for a not directly observable and measurable ability. Thus the height is measured in inches and the distance in yards, and the underlying takeoff power or the underlying endurance capacity is inferred from these indicators. Doing so, the researcher is aware of the fact that any propositions on a latent ability are flawed primarily for two reasons. The first is because of the fact that motor abilities in principle cannot be isolated completely; they are more-or-less complex. Thus endurance (especially in the anaerobic sphere) always also involves strength, speed, and coordination components. And speed (at least speed of locomotion in sport) always is determined also by a strength element.

A second reason is that the execution of a working load in a motor test is necessarily linked to motor skills. For endurance capacity these usually include bicycling on the bicycle or running on the treadmill. The great importance this has for the measurement of endurance becomes obvious if one considers the fact that, within the domain of high-performance sport, one proceeds more and more to developing endurance tests that are specific to the different types of sport, such as putting the rower on a rowing ergometer. It must be emphasized, however, that endurance is not in the least measured in a more "pure" form this way. Rather, the specific skills required by the different types of sport (i.e., the technical level of an athlete) enters as a decisive factor into the process of measurement. It can be assumed that the more the endurance of an athlete is overestimated, the better developed are his specific skills (i.e., the higher his technical level). In this sense, running and bicycling constitute rather complex skills that greatly influence the measurement process.

The fact that any ability is necessarily linked to a skill concerning the working load in the process of measurement raises the objection to motor ability tests—that they are not precise enough and thus that they do not meet scientific standards. This likewise also applies to the measurement of motor abilities in biomechanics and sport physiology because the working load as a source of errors is the same for each of the three research areas. Varying levels of error can only be caused by the validity of indicators and the measurement of indicators. Thus the rather simple measuring methods (yardstick and stopwatch) used in sport motor tests (which, strictly speaking, constitute mechanical measuring methods) are generally contrasted with the rather complicated measuring instruments used in biomechanics (high-frequency cameras, platforms for dynamic tests, electromyography) and in sport medicine (instruments for analyzing lactate, etc.). As for the indicators, the motor performances (running distance, jumping distance, and throwing range, and scores for successful or unsuccessful attempts) are paralleled in biomechanics in mechanical parameters such as maximum power, impulse, and so forth and in sport medicine, for example, in maximum oxygen uptake capacity or lactate concentration.

Including psychological factors into the reflections on a comparative theory of errors yields no principally new points of view. Supposing that psychic characteristics are not directly observable—and this is normally assumed in psychology—the same sources of error have to be taken into consideration as in motor tests that also fall in the range of psychology. If the construction of scales for measuring attitudes, self-concept, anxiety, motivation, and so forth is often more difficult than the design of motor tests, then this is because of the definition and measurement of indicators. Propositions on latent (i.e., invisible) psychic characteristics are mainly based on the responses of test people to (provocative) stimuli or test items. These stimuli or test items correspond to the working load in biomechanical, sport-physiological, or motor tests, respectively. The responses given (yes/no answers or more differentiated answer possibilities) constitute the indicators directly measured. The attitude, self-concept, or anxiety value is formed by summing up scores attained for the responses given to a number of test items that are believed to be a satisfying operationalization of the respective theoretical construct, such as 'social consequences anxiety' or 'hope for success.' Thus from a set of individual indicators, conclusions may be drawn about a not directly observable personality trait.

The summation of individual responses is also paralleled in motor tests in which the prolongation of the test serves to increase reliability.

Observation and sociometry are other widely used methods of data-gathering in psychology.

As to errors occurring in the use of observation, it must be stated that they have to be viewed and likewise differentiated as cinematography within biomechanics. If one confines oneself to observing only manifest characteristics and making propositions only on these (e.g., ball course; frequency of getting the ball), then the calculus of error can be limited to objectivity and reliability viewpoints because validity is largely obvious, or trivial, respectively. A biomechanical analysis and a (psychological) observation then primarily differ with respect to the characteristics that are of interest in the respective case and with respect to the scope and exactness of data collection.

If observation, however, is used to disclose latent dimensions (e.g., social-psychological relationships between individuals), then the characteristics observed rank equally with sport performances as indicators of motor abilities and with responses given to test items as indicators of the underlying attitudes.

Indicative of the present state of an interdisciplinary theory of errors is the discussion on the quality of sociometry, for though sociometry itself constitutes a complex method of data collection, this is hardly taken into consideration in the corresponding calculi of error. The complexity of the sociometric method consists in the fact that it is a data-processing technique that necessarily rests upon observational units or attitudes, the latter again being ascertained by means of questionnaires. In the literature on the theory of measurement, however, the quality of sociometry is discussed without a distinction being made as to the respective shares of error caused by attitude measurement or observation, respectively.

In summary, the central aspect in the treatment of the research methodology used in the subdisciplines of sport science were the causes of errors. These have been identified as follows:

- Errors caused by measuring instruments, including their handling
- Errors caused by test people
- Errors occurring when conclusions from indicators to theoretical constructs are drawn

The calculus of error for these three sources of error is based, as is generally known, on the test criteria of objectivity, reliability, and validity.

In case of an additive discipline, it is admissible that the calculi of error be performed separately according to the single disciplines to which the research methods or the characteristics to be measured, respectively, relate. For an interdisciplinary science, however, only one calculus of error can and need be performed. It has to take its point of departure in the causes of errors, not in the single subdisciplines (i.e., the calculus of error has to be problem-oriented and not discipline-oriented). In particular, the following has to be observed:

- Limiting the causes of error to measuring instruments and their handling is only justifiable in case inanimate nature is the object of investigation.
- If man is included in the object of investigation, then a trait fluctuation as a possible source of errors has to be taken into consideration, irrespective of the discipline that the used research method comes from.
- Biomechanical, sport-physiological, sport-motor, and sport-psychological test procedures differ for each characteristic in a different way as to the validity of indicators and as to the methods used to measure indicators. They do not differ as to the errors occurring on account of the working load.
- Testing the validity is unnecessary when directly observable and measurable data are collected and when the researcher desists from further interpreting the data. This likewise applies to biomechanical descriptions as well as to the description of interactions via observation and sociometry.
- The advantage of an interdisciplinary approach would be that there is not a multiplicity of differing calculi of error; only one calculus of error takes different sources of error into account according to the specific problem investigated.

The following brief excursus as an appendix intends to make obvious that this approach should by no means remain limited to so-called empirical research:

In an article on didactics published in 1962, Bernett tried to substantiate educational objectives by linking typically human needs with historical phenomena.

In the sense of Dilthey, the historical phenomena of sports, German gymnastics, rhythmical gymnastics, and the games movement are objective expressions of elementary kinds of action such as controlling, playing, fighting, and creating. Transposed into the language of test theory, the objective expressions (i.e., the phenomena) are the indicators for the latent (i.e., the not directly observable) elementary dispositions or elementary kinds of action. We then have to test the validity of these indicators. Thus one would have to examine or at least substantiate that German gymnastics is a valid indicator for controlling, and so on.

Final Remarks on Sport Pedagogy

As a conclusion, a few remarks will be made on sport pedagogy, which, in view of the brevity required here, will not be detailed or comprehensive. Doing so, three aspects of crucial importance will be analyzed.

First, is there a specific sport-pedagogical research methodology that in its contents goes beyond that which is claimed for sport science? This question can clearly be answered in the affirmative, because on the one hand, sport pedagogy is not only an empirical science, but it consists of, among others, the subdisciplines of philosophical anthropology and sport history. But also within the empirical domain, sport pedagogy contains, to a very high degree, structural elements that are only insufficiently covered by the research methodology of sport science hitherto described. In this connection, one can think, for example, of teaching and training programs, the contents of which cannot be derived from theories but which require creativity. No principal differences, on the other hand, exist in evaluation. Here the methods used are in keeping with the empirical research methodology described. The question of whether the special pedagogic responsibility implies consequences for empirical work within sport pedagogy will be deferred for the moment.

Second, what is the place held by sport pedagogy within or with respect to the system of sport science? The conceptions concerning the position of sport pedagogy within sport science differ. According to one view, sport pedagogy is seen as a coordinate subdiscipline of an interdisciplinary sport science and ranks equally with biomechanics, sport psychology, sport sociology, and so forth. According to a second view, sport pedagogy itself constitutes an interdisciplinary science. It is, so to speak, a duplicate of sport science, but this duplicate is like a photograph which has been made by means of a special filter mirroring the respective pedagogical responsibility.

Third, how rational is sport pedagogy, or what are the implications of pedagogical responsibility for scientific work, especially for empirical work within sport pedagogy? This question is the central philosophical-theoretical problem as to what is to be considered scientific and what is not. An extensive discussion on this problem cannot be led here. My position is the following: Pedagogic and scientific responsibilities are demands that are prior to any science and that go beyond any science.

Whoever gives pedagogic responsibility the appearance of scientific accuracy (i.e., the one who claims scientific accuracy for it without pointing to its value-judgment character) commits errors which, in most cases, will be considerably greater than those described above.

References

Bernett, H. (1962). Der Kanon der Leibeserziehung. *Die Liebeserziehung,* 9, 282–290.

Lazarsfeld, P.F. (1962). Philosophy of science and empirical social research. In E. Nagel, P. Suppes, & A. Tarski (Eds.), *Logic, methodology, and philosophy of science* (pp. 463-473). Stanford, CA: Stanford University Press.

Nixon, J.E. (1967). The criteria of a discipline. *Quest,* 9, 42-48.

Willimczik, K. (1983). A comparative analysis of theories of sport science. In H. Lenk (Ed.), *Topical problems of sport philosophy.* Schorndorf & Stuttgart, Germany: Hofmann-Verlag.

CHAPTER 5

Possibilities and Foundations of Comparative Physical Education and Sport Through Language and Terminology

Wolfgang Kneyer

Language and terminology are central areas of any scientific work. Terminology is called a constitutional criteria for the scientific acknowledgement of an academic field. Also, sport science as a young and partly not-yet-established scientific discipline depends on a clear and unique system of terms. If a person considers such a sport-specific system of terms, then he or she can see that a lot of work still has to be done within sport terminology. The uncertainties in the terminological clarification and the definition of sport-relevant terms are limiting factors especially for comparative scientific research. A comparative sport pedagogy depends on its quality and its amount of a clearly defined pool of terms, which, if possible, is unified across language borders. Because no such unified system of terms is available, neither in general education nor in sport pedagogy, research within comparative sport pedagogy is difficult; terminology must be within the comparative sport pedagogy.

So far, the necessity to deal with language and terminology within comparative sport pedagogy is easily understood. Before questions of terminology and language can be analyzed, however, the meaning of these questions for a comparative sport pedagogy should be defined in more detail in order to show the possibilities and limitations of comparative sport pedagogy in regard to language and terminology. This will be done in connection with further proposals within this analysis. On the basis of such a definition of the position it will be possible to develop and present possibilities.

The important definitions for this analysis will be clarified and defined in the following from the terminology point of view without dealing with a detailed analysis. The terms *linguistic, precoordination,* and *postcoordination* within language will be explained; the terms *terminology, synonym, homonym,* and *polysem* within terminology will be explained.

> The topic of linguistics is the natural language. Natural languages are systems of signs which originated by nature in order to regulate communication needs of men . . . . By the syntax the formally allowed connections of signs to larger

> units (regularly: sentences) are fixed. Within semantics the mean of signs and its combinations are analysed. The pragmatic is considering the intention and the knowledge outside of the language of the person who is producing and receiving the language signs. Maybe natural languages can be defined best by their pragmatic dimension. The human being is using language in order to get around by understanding and acting in this world. (Kuhlen, 1980, p. 676)

This very detailed definition of linguistics clearly shows the importance of linguistic questions, especially for comparative scientific work.

Precoordination, especially in connection with *documentation, linguistics,* and *terminology*, refers to the connection of several terms to a composed term or to the "system of indexing according to the combination of terms while indexing" (Neveling & Wersig, 1975, p. 68). Consequently, *postcoordination* mainly refers to the use of simple terms or "the indexing principle according to the combination of terms while searching for combinations of index-termini" (Neveling & Wersig, 1975, p. 67).

On principle, the totality of all terms and the teaching of terms is called *terminology*. Because these terms are based on terms or content of thoughts, and because terms are chosen more or less accidentally, difficulties in comprehension constantly arise within the (scientific) communication process; this makes further inquiries necessary.

> The possibly extended avoiding of such questions, i.e., the complete understanding right away and the avoiding of such misunderstanding within the languages, therefore can be regarded as the most important task of terminology. One is trying to reach this by defining every word (naming) exactly or at least by explaining that the term defined by a word has to be defined according to content (in certain cases, amount) from a language point of view in about the same way as a person who is fond of nature is defining an unknown plant with the help of a definition book. Such definitions of terms possibly should be valid for the whole field. (Laisiepen, Lutterbeck, & Meyer-Uhlenried, 1972, p. 101)

The importance of terminology for science is becoming even stronger by the openness and flexibility of the natural language (day-to-day language) because the clear relationship of a name to a term is not always given. Within this process, synonyms, homonyms, and polysems can appear. *Synonyms* are defined as "one or more different namings with almost similar meaning which are used equivalently" (Neveling & Wersig, 1975, p. 40). *Homonyms* can be defined as "namings with the same form and different meaning" (Neveling & Wersig, 1975, p. 40). *Polysems* can be defined as "namings with almost identical form of different meanings" (Neveling & Wersig, 1975, p. 40). For example, elevator and lift are synonyms; ball (sport equipment) and ball (dancing event) are homonyms; and cell (prison) and cell (body) are polysems.

This analysis comprises the aspects that are important in relationship to the foundations and limitations of comparative sport pedagogy within language and terminology. The first aspect will be to discuss the general theoretical foundations of linguistics and terminology. In dealing with this, especially the body of knowledge, the research activities, the relationships between terms and their naming within linguistics, and the definition strategies and the problem of synonyms, homonyms, and polysems within terminology will be discussed.

On the basis of this general theory, the second aspect is to discuss the language and terminology limitations of comparative sport pedagogy. Within language, the multilinguality and the connected difficulties of precoordination versus postcoordination, language structures, and problems of transferring will be mainly discussed. Within terminology, the variety of definitions in sport, which will be explained by an example, and the problem of advantage-naming and disadvantage-naming will be analyzed.

A possible solution for the discussed limitations of comparative sport pedagogy, the sport thesaurus, will be presented as the last part of this chapter. The structure and function of the sport thesaurus and the agreed-upon working guidelines and gained knowledge from the thesaurus are important.

Further aspects within information (e.g., language and terminology) cannot be analyzed in more detail in this investigation.

General Theoretical Foundations of Linguistics and Terminology

This second section introduces the scientific areas of linguistics and terminology. Thus limiting the subject area and presenting sport-related research activities are especially important. Furthermore, the relationship of "term-naming-name" within linguistics and the field of definition as well as the problem of synonyms, homonyms, and polysems within terminology should be discussed.

As defined earlier, the subject area of the science of language (i.e., linguistics) is the natural language. As a special discipline of semiotics, the general theory of sign linguistics deals with the syntactics, semantics, and pragmatics of language, which is defined as a system of signs. For this investigation, the semantic level (especially the word *semantic*) and the syntactic level are both important. Dealing with the word *semantic* shows us a basic difficulty that can be characterized with the words *term, naming,* and *name.* We give terms to represent certain items in our surroundings (i.e., cognitive constructs such as the construct or the imagination "table" or "didactics" or similar things). These units of thinking, or constructs, are connected to namings (i.e., certain signs—a name is a sign too); with the help of these namings we try to express our cognitive construct.

If, in a dialogue, Person A says *table* or *didactics* then Person B is expected to recognize Person A's cognitive constructs of "table" and "didactics." The naming 747 also has to be understood by the communication partner to mean an airplane like a Boeing 747 or Jumbo-Jet. The clear connection of the namings like 747 or names like *table* or *didactics* to the respective terms (i.e., the cognitive constructs) is the central problem of word semantics and the communication process in total. The name *table* probably will not lead to any misunderstandings, but the naming 747 might. Complex and manifold constructs like the name *didactics* are the most complicated to understand.

The terminology, understood as the vocabulary of the language and the teaching of this field, can be called applied language science. One of the most important tasks of terminology is the definition of names, especially namings, of terms. The definition of a naming has to be seen in relation to the term by describing the content of the term (intention) and the amount of the term (extension). If someone adds the sign *sport* to the term *teacher*, then the new term *sport teacher* has a larger content in regard to terminology than *teacher*, but a smaller amount in regard to terminology because *teacher of mathematics, teacher of languages*, and so forth are excluded. The classical form of a definition in the sense of a strong teaching of terminology is the content definition which has all signs that characterize the content of a term. Because this form of definition can be applied only seldom—indicating all signs of a term is difficult—often the second main form of definition is used (the so-called amount of definition), which indicates all objects that fall under one term. Another possibility of definition is the distinction of the terms from each other by an explicit presentation of their mutual relationships.

This means the indication of nets of terms. This form of definition that avoids the limitation of terms by language means is used mostly within thesauri.

Specific difficulties within the terminology are synonym, homonym, and polysem problems. Different namings for the same term (synonym), identical namings for different terms (homonyms), and formal identical namings for different terms with the same amount of meaning (polysems) [e.g., cell (prison), cell (biological), and cell (red)] lead to misunderstandings within the natural language. The solution to these problems, for example, defining a preferred naming with synonyms, and so forth, is one of the most important terminology tasks. For sport many variable terminological analyses are available within the national and international fields; in total, however, a clear and unique terminology has not been determined yet.

Language and Terminology in Sport

Adequately presenting the wide field of language and terminology in sport is not possible within this presentation. Therefore, in the following section sport language and sport terminology will be discussed as limiting factors of comparative sport pedagogy. By doing this within-language, multilinguality and different uses of pre- and postcoordination are stressed. For the area of terminology, it is especially important to present the variety of definitions in sport as a limitation of comparative sport pedagogy; it is also important to indicate the difference between the preferred and the nonpreferred naming.

Even if a scientist who is working in comparative sport pedagogy can speak foreign languages, he or she will still have difficulties with multilinguality. Knowing namings in his or her own and the foreign language is not sufficient; he or she must know the constructs of the terms that are behind the foreign language namings and must understand this to be able to work comparatively in an effective way.

In this connection, correct translated namings often have opposite terminological contents in a foreign language. Also, a fixed naming that does not have an equivalent in the other language poses a problem for the scientist who works comparatively. Thus the German word *Rückschlagspiel* (games in which the ball is constantly moved from one team or player to the other) does not have a corresponding English naming, and no German equivalent is available for the English naming *raquetsport*. Even the different uses of the pre- and postcoordinated namings in different languages are limiting factors of comparative research. While, for example, the German language tends to have precoordinated namings such as *Schulsport*, *Sportwissenschaft*, and so forth, the English language tends to have postcoordinated namings such as *school sports*, *sport science*, and so forth. These differences in the structures of different languages, besides pure language knowledge, pose a relatively high limitation for comparative sport pedagogy. This limitation can be effectively resolved only if it is possible to make the diverging structures of terms transparent and thus explainable.

Although terminology work began relatively early in the development of sport science, today a normed vocabulary exists neither in the national nor in the international areas. The nonexisting subject matter terminology is, without doubt, another limitation for comparative sport pedagogy.

Another consequence of this bad situation is the increase in the number of new namings for well-known terms and, in a linear way, in the number of new definitions. If a person considers a typical term for this case, namely *didactics*, then a very exacting scientist would have to spend a long time collecting all of the definitions of *didactics* and putting these definitions in order. Obviously, such a term as *didactics* is undergoing a constant social and scientific change; nevertheless, a comprehensive definition including all intentions and extensions of this term should be found. Also, it has to be seen that there is another terminological limitation for comparative research, namely the different usage of synonym namings for relatively clearly defined terms. This problem is clearly evident in the different terminologies of Western and Eastern Europe and can be exemplified by namings like *Leibeserziehung* and *Körpererziehung*. In this case, surpassing borders and ideologies, a unique and situative solution should be found in order to make better mutual understanding and comparative research possible.

Surpassing the Limitations of Comparative Sport Pedagogy by the Multilingual Sport Thesaurus

By developing a multilingual sport thesaurus, the aforementioned limiting factors of a comparative sport pedagogy can be surpassed. Even if the sport thesaurus developed by the international commission (The thesaurus of the International Association for Sports Information—IASI) has not been developed primarily for comparative research in sport but rather for information purposes, it still can contribute to comparative sport pedagogy, especially in regard to language and terminology. After defining the term *thesaurus* within this text, structure and function of the foundations of the IASI sport thesaurus and some work results are presented.

Beginning here, the word *thesaurus* is to be defined in accordance with the valid rules and norms as follows: According to its function, a thesaurus is a means of terminological control. *Terminological control*, in this context, means on the one hand, the translation from a natural language, used by authors, indexers, and users to a language that is restricted in its freedom of expression (language of documentation) and means, on the other hand, the translation back from this language to the natural language. According to its structure, a thesaurus is a controlled dynamic vocabulary of terms connected in meaning and gender that completely cover a specific field" (Wersig, 1978, p. 27). Also see ISO/DIS 2788 (1974); ISO/DIN 1463 (1976); and UNESCO/ISO/TC 46/WG5 (1976). According to DGD-KTS (1975), "a thesaurus is a natural language-based documentation language which strives for the clear and reversible coordination of terms and names of the natural language by using total terminological and vocabulary control and by describing the terms and the relations between them through presenting the relations between the names and, if necessary, using other aids" (Wersig, 1978, p. 27). According to these definitions, a thesaurus is a system of keywords (descriptors) that are terminologically controlled and have been put into connection with each other by relations. Therefore a thesaurus can be of great importance for the area of language and terminology of comparative sport pedagogy.

Tasks and Aims of the Sport Thesaurus

The tasks and aims of a thesaurus can be taken directly from the definitions discussed earlier.

> As aids in the field of information and documentation it is the task of the thesaurus to check and file the vocabulary used for the description of the contents of documents and in this way to make a reliable and money saving way of indexing, storing and researching. (DIN, 1983, p. 7).

According to this normed establishment, a thesaurus's task is to produce a link between special terms and names under terminological and vocabulary control and to file them by indicating the relations between the names.

> All precautions, that are suitable, ... to avoid the disadvantage of misunderstandings between participants of the communication due to non-standard usage of names, are to be understood as being under terminological control, which is an essential characteristic of a thesaurus. This is mainly a question

of being in control of the problem of synonyms and homonyms. (Laisiepen, Lutterbeck, & Meyer-Uhlenried, 1972, p. 275)

The second aspect that should be mentioned here (i.e., the presentation of the relations between the names) has two different intentions. Like the terminological control, these relations should be produced to make the connection of terms and meanings between objects, things, and ideas clear according to the natural language. Only through this clarification will the whole complex of terms, which becomes concrete in the wealth of special terms of a field, be made understandable and clear. This presentation of relations is essential, especially in multilingual thesauruses, because the supralingual compatibility can only be achieved through the interconnection of names. This already indicates the second intention that the presentation of relations aims at in a thesaurus.

In a certain way, a scope definition of the term in question is given by presenting the relations between the individual names. This terminologically interesting aspect leads to a network of names in a macrothesaurus which reflects the structure and the state of development of the field in question.

The enormous amount of theoretical and practical dissertations about sport have brought with them a great number of special terms. These may be terminologically controlled and put into relation to each other in a sport thesaurus. Thus the limiting factors formulated in the earlier section that are valid for comparative sport pedagogy can be taken away to a great extent.

Bases of Thesaurus Development

The two main bases of the development of the IASI-Sport thesaurus—(1) the relator model, which presents the different relations between the descriptors; and (2) the basic thesaurus, which was especially developed for the IASI-Sport thesaurus—are to be dealt with in the course of the present section:

The relator model. The system of relators shown in Figure 1 has been developed on the basis of the internationally normed relations between the descriptors and their names (i.e., relators) and based on the further development of these names by the IASI-commission thesaurus.

Semantic relations (i.e., synonymy) exist between terms with the same meaning (e.g., *elevator* and *lift*). A thesaurus shows which one to use. Logical relations (of similarity) refer to terms like *skiing* (as a broader term BT) and *skiing, alpine* and *skiing, nordic* (as a narrower term, NT). The two NTs are related terms. Ontological relations allot part terms (PTs) to a total term (TT). Part terms of one total are contiguous terms (CT). So the *Nordic Combination* (as a TT) consists of *jumping* and *cross-country* (as PTs). Functional relations, of which there are many, describe the relation between *skiing* and *winter sport discipline*. The term *skiing* belongs to *winter sport discipline*, but there are also functional relations like *cause-effect* and

Semantic	Terminological				Way of classification
	Logical	Ontological	Functional	Other	
	BT broader term	TT total term	FBT functional broader term		Upper level
	NT narrower term	PT part term	FNT functional narrower term		Lower level
Synonyms	RT related term	CT contiguous term		ASS association	Co = level
USE use	UF used for					

Simplification: BT + TT + FBT = BT
NT + PT + FNT = NT
ASS = RT

Figure 1. The IASI Thesaurus relator model.

precondition-result-context. Associative relations are terminological relations, which are not hierarchically classified. On the contrary, associative relations make it possible to connect descriptors logically with each other based on fact. Thus associative relations can connect the *player's role* (sociological term) with the *player's position* (sport-practical term).

The basic thesaurus. The science of sport must be called a very heterogeneous field, as it is orientated toward many different sciences. This means that several more-or-less clearly limited individual sections exist, which causes the problem of overlapping when producing a thesaurus. These difficulties became particularly evident when the facettes of the theoretical fields of sport science were produced. Therefore, a "metalevel" was created to fulfill two important tasks: (a) file all facettes, and (b) integrate every aspect of the theory of science.

Thus it is established that the limitation of the individual sections of sport science can be made pragmatically and that the polydimensional classification of individual phenomena, which are being dealt with under different scientific aspects, can be achieved. Starting from an analytic division of the forms of sport and the scientific work, there is a division into three groups according to the grade of complexity:

- The general conditions of sport, which contain the external structures that determine sport
- The fields of sport that give information about the internal structure of sport and sporting activities

- The sport disciplines that show in which form sporting activities take place

Although this basic thesaurus structures the field of sport systematically, there is no claim for its validity as a scientific taxonomy; however, when producing this thesaurus, we took care that all theoretical aspects of science were included, that specific terms of theory were filed, and that internationally differing developments were fitted in. Only in this way did it seem possible to produce a beyond-all-borders compatible thesaurus for the field of sport.

Figure 2 shows the supreme level of abstraction of the basic thesaurus. Even on this level, the earlier mentioned possibility of variable classification becomes clear. Using the example of *skiing*, this polydimensional classification is clarified once again in Figure 3.

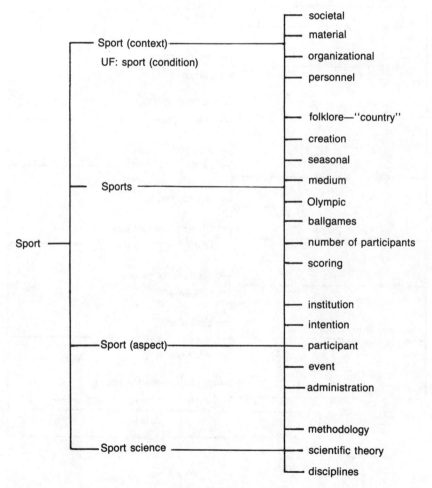

Figure 2. Supreme level of abstraction of the IASI thesaurus basic structure.

Via the broader terms *winter sport discipline, outdoor sport discipline, individual sport discipline, and quantifiable (c-g-s system)* as narrower terms to *quantifiable discipline* and *Winter Olympics* as narrower terms to *sport discipline (Olympic)*, the term *skiing* can be referred to in each case.

Just like a certain sport discipline can be allotted to certain groups of sport disciplines, theoretical or theory-related parts of thesauruses (facettes) can be integrated in the overlapping structure of the basic thesaurus. This guarantees that the user of the thesaurus will be lead to the descriptor that he or she is interested in via any arbitrary descriptor that he or she wants to start from. These possibilities make clear the ad-

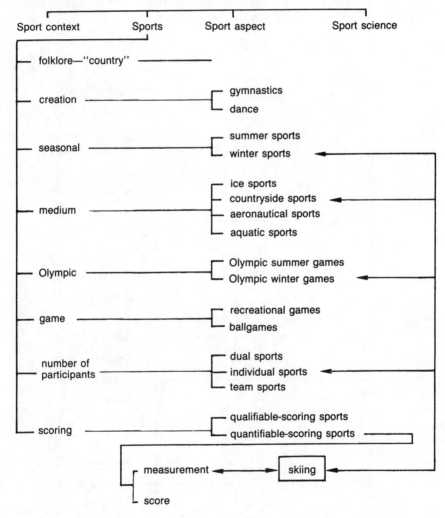

Figure 3. Example of basic thesaurus classification.

vantages of the general principle of a thesaurus as opposed to any other system.

Results and consequences of the thesaurus. The structural, terminological, and multilingual work with the IASI sport thesaurus has shown that the thesaurus principle can contribute to the unification of sport-relevant term definitions and to the terminological understanding across country and language borders. Working with the basic thesaurus has contributed to making the different concepts of sport in the countries and language groups presented in the thesaurus known and to finding surpassing possibilities for a solution.

The translation work of the defined source language (German) into other languages has brought the knowledge that the problem of precoordination versus postcoordination is other than structural divergencies, the real background for word-to-word translation. With the help of a flexible thesaurus principle, this difficulty can be solved within the presentation of synonyms.

In summary, the sport thesaurus is fulfilling functions beyond its primary and original task, namely the documentation of language. It is also aiding the development of the scientific investigation of sport, especially sport pedagogy.

Summary and Future Perspectives

In summary, language and terminology are main limiting factors of comparative research in sport, especially in sport pedagogy. This is the problem of multilinguality based especially on different language structures and different constructs of terms within language; this relates to a variety of definitions in sport within terminology.

The possibility for a solution is a multilingual sport thesaurus which is being developed right now. This thesaurus considers the different structures of languages, and provides clear relationships between terms and namings, provides a clear picture of the relationships between terms, and thus provides a content and amount definition.

It is hoped that the presented sport thesaurus will be published on the national and international level to contribute to a unification of sport-related subject matter terminology. Comparative research in sport (e.g., within comparative sport pedagogy) would become easier and thus scientists could contribute to a further scientific investigation of the worldwide phenomenon of sport.

References

DGD-KTS (1975). *Terminologie der information und Dokumentation*. München: Author.

ISO/DIN 1463 (1976). Richtlinien für die Erstellung und Weiterentwicklung von Thesauri. Berlin: Author.

ISO/DIS 2788 (1974). Documentation-guidelines for the establishment and development of monolingual thesauri. Genf: Author.

Kuhlen, R. (1980). Linguistische Grundlagen. In K. Laisiepen, E. Lutterbeck, & K.-H. Meyer-Uhlenried, *Grundlagen der praktischen Information einer Dokumentation* (pp. 675-732). München: Sauer K.G.

Laisiepen, K., Lutterbeck, E., & Meyer-Uhlenried, K.-H. (1972). *Grundlagen der praktischen Information und Dokumentation*. München-Pullach: Verlag Dokumentation.

Neveling, U. & Wersig, G. (Eds.). (1975). *Terminologie der Information und Dokumentation*. München-Pullach: Verlag Dokumentation.

UNESCO. (1976). *Guidelines for the establishment and development of multilingual thesauri*. Paris: Author.

Wersig, G. (1978). *Thesaurus-Leitfaden*. München-Pullach: Verlag Dokumentation.

CHAPTER 6

Limitations and Foundations of Comparative Physical Education and Sport Through Language and Terminology

Erich Beyer

Dietrich Kayser

Introduction (by D. Kayser)

These statements are an introduction to Dr. Beyer's analysis.

This paper is based on a project initiated and fostered by the Federal Institute of Sport Science that deals with "Sport Science Terminology—German, English, French." The development of this international project—the methodological procedure of which will be described in detail by Prof. Beyer—is almost as old as the Federal Institute of Sport Science (Bunderinstitut für Sportwissenschaft) (BISp) itself, and it certainly illustrates the possibility of reasonable cooperation in sport science on the international level. At the same time, it characterizes the developmental activities of the Federal Institute of Sport Science with a view to comparative physical education and sport.

As early as 1972, about 1 year after the foundation of the Federal Institute of Sport Science, first discussions on a trilingual dictionary of sport science terminology took place; these discussions were initiated by Prof. Dr. Rieder (Heidelberg), who was Director of the Institute at that time. This was certainly not by chance, because the decree on the foundation of the Federal Institute of Sport Science already contained a statement on the coordinative function of this Institute with regard to sport science activities on the international level. This function also is obvious in the support of this symposium. Anyone who frequently attends international conferences knows that terminological problems increase the difficulties in international communication. This is most obvious if we consider that, even in our own linguistic area, we often encounter communicative problems in a branch of science which develops from different scientific and practice-oriented sections. For this reason, any institution that becomes active on the international level has great interest in the improvement of linguistic communication.

This intention was supported by a second circumstance. In 1972, the sport science dictionary, "Sportwissenschaftliches Lexikon," was published for the first time. The sport science terminology dealt with in this dictionary far exceeded anything else that had been previously compiled in a German-speaking country. The development of this publication essentially influenced further discussion on the possibilities of an international comparative study in the area of terminology. The sport science dictionary quickly attained an important position in the field of sport science in the Federal Republic of Germany. This was primarily because the editors, under the effective direction of Prof. Dr. Peter Röthig (Frankfurt), constantly tried to improve the validity of the terminology by publishing revised and enlarged editions of the dictionary in rapid succession. Since 1976, when the third edition was published, this author also belonged to the editorial group. The work on the fifth edition of the dictionary (Röthig, 1983), which took about 4 years, was closely linked with the work of Prof. Beyer. Since autumn 1983, the fifth edition has been available on the market. With minor delays, the work of the editorial group and the international team under the direction of Prof. Beyer paralleled each other and, as far as the major issues are concerned, will be finished in the near future. Comments coming from English or French experts made it possible for one term or another to be modified because in many cases, the translation helps to elucidate ambiguities that are also inherent in the mother tongue but have not yet been realized in this way. Apart from that, questions resulting from a different theoretical understanding may provide useful ideas. In this way, comparative analysis is already possible and useful during editorial work.

Before dealing with the form of presentation and the validity of the terminology, one more statement about our starting point, which was "German sport science terminology," should be made. Basically, it would also be possible to approach this problem from any other language, under the condition that a similar dictionary is already available or would be prepared. Concerning the comparative analysis in the field of sport science or physical education, however, it is the great advantage of the German language, in general, and German sport science terminology, in particular, that theoretical approaches from sport science in the German Democratic Republic—and, with that, from all countries in Eastern Europe—as well as theoretical approaches from the Federal Republic of Germany and the Anglo-American countries have been taken and connected to our own approaches. This primarily applies to training, movement, and coaching theory as well as movement studies/motor learning/kinesiology.

The remarks referring to the different origins of sport science terms also show how difficult it is for a dictionary to present terminology in such a way that contradictions are more or less excluded. Because we have no uniform theory of sport science or theory of physical education as a whole or in different branches, it is also impossible to have a uniform terminology. Besides this, sport science with its branches still is a very dynamic mixture so that too narrow definitions cannot be maintained in the long-run. For this reason, the editorial group normally tried to define certain subject fields according to pragmatic aspects (relating to an interdisciplinary approach), such as consultation by sport students preparing their papers, and tried to put the individual subject fields under the responsibility of one author. The objective was to achieve at least a medium level of coherence. This became possible by selecting different articles on specific analytic terms for a series of subterms and pure definitions. Therefore, the different lengths of the statements made in connection with the individual terms also imply a certain evaluation of their importance.

To what extent can the statements of the meaning of the terms be considered as definite for sport science in the Federal Republic of Germany? Of course, the editorial group always tried to find competent authors for the specific terms. Nevertheless, only very few terms are not controversial in the area of sport science in the Federal Republic of Germany and the other German-speaking countries. For this reason, the definitions always imply, to some extent, the attitude of the respective author. We tried to ensure, however, that different approaches are at least mentioned. In case of an international comparison, be very careful not to jump to conclusions referring to the position held by German sport science. In any case, such a thorough discussion of explicit standpoints printed in such a dictionary of sport science is a basis for reasonable comparative study. This will also become obvious in the following statements of Prof. Beyer.

Main Analysis by E. Beyer

Trying to find out which possibilities we have to work with in the sense of comparative physical education and sport through language and terminology, we should bear in mind that terms are not pictures, but only symbols of the contents of imagination or reality in the mind. This is just as true for the simple things of everyday life as for terms at a higher level of abstraction. We should also take into consideration that the contents of imagination are shaped by historical tradition, social norms, religion, and forms of production. In other words, *house* does not necessarily mean the same thing to a Japanese peasant, an African Negro, an Eskimo hunter, an American farmer, or a New York citizen. This is also true for other terms of everyday life such as *window, wedding,* and *funeral* and for terms such as *sport, physical education, leisure-time sports,* and even *swimming* and *wrestling.* This paper will show how far language and terminology can help us in our comparative studies of physical education and sport and describe the limitations for such studies.

Before discussing the details of a project on which the author has been working with a team of international experts for several years, some remarks are in order concerning the different concepts and systematic approaches of some recent publications on sport science terminology in one or several languages. In this context, such a survey can be only very short without claiming to be complete. Details on the project that the author and a team of international experts worked on for several years are mentioned later in the text.

Texts of Terminology

Dictionaries and encyclopedias such as *Sportwissenschaftliches Lexikon* (5th edition, Röthig, 1983), written in German, *Contribution à un lexique commenté en Science de l'Action Motrice* (Parlebas, 1981), written in French, and the *Encyclopedia of Sport Sciences and Medicine* (American College of Sports Medicine, 1971), written in English, exist in only one language. Each of them offers excellent definitions of terms, but none of them can be a direct help for comparative studies of physical education and sport through language and terminology because each is available in only one language.

Other publications do exist in two, three, or more languages. An example is *Zum Begriff der Bewegung* (Bernett, 1966). This work is the result of an international conference of experts who worked on the terminology of movement and physical education. It contains translations of terms in German, English, and French and partial definitions that do not discriminate the differences of usage in those three languages.

A similar publication is the *Glossaire Scientifique et Technique.* (Institut provincial d'Education physique, 1962), translated in French, German, English, and Dutch. It was placed at the disposal of the participants of the International Congress of Physical Education in Liège in May 1962. It offers the translations of sport medicine scientific and technical terms in alphabetical order and in four languages without defining them.

In cooperation with the International Association of Sport Information (IASI) and the Scientific Society of Physical Education and Sport in Vienna, Fr. Tscherne published his *Modellfacette 'Leichtathletik'* (1976) in German, French, Polish, Portuguese, and Serbocroatian. Following a special systematic order of terms, this work only offers translations of terms without defining them, and the author does not give any reasons for his choice of languages—especially for his decision to leave out English.

A very interesting publication is the *Terminology of Physical Education and Sport* (Teodorescu, L., 1973). The definitions in six languages, namely Rumanian, French, Spanish, German, English, and Russian, begin from a Rumanian starting point. The material is subdivided into three parts according to a special order. The first part deals with general terms of physical education, sport, and sport science. The topic of the second part is human movement and motor activity and the third part is dedicated to training and coaching. Unfortunately the definitions are literal translations of the Rumanian texts without annotations or comments clarifying the differences in the terminology of the respective languages.

Under the auspices of the International Society of Sport Psychology, Epuran edited *63 Termes de Psychologie du Sport* (1972). This edition is the result of the work of the Scientific Committee of the European Federation of Sport Psychology in cooperation with national commissions in Rumania, Bulgaria, Hungary, Spain, and Czechoslovakia. Its concept is quite different from the others. All of the text is written in one language only, namely in French. There is no common starting point. The national commissions handed in their own definitions of the different terms of sport psychology. The editor also tried to formulate a synthesis of the different definitions for each term. Many terms were only defined by some of the national commissions. The concept of separate definitions gives the national commissions a chance to define the terms according to the terms in common usage in their commissions' countries. On the other hand, these separate definitions vary in content and length and do not refer to each other. This makes it very difficult for the reader to find the clear information that he or she is looking for. The choice of participating countries and even of terms seems to have been made more or less at random.

In 1975 the International Union of Psychological Science published a *Trilingual Psychological Dictionary* in English, French, and German. It is a pure dictionary without any definitions or annotations.

The most valuable of the aforementioned publications are encyclopedias in English, French, or German; unfortunately these do not offer any chances for comparative studies. On the other hand, some polyglottal publications are, on the whole, not very helpful for comparative studies either. They deal with one or the other area of sport science such as sport psychology or sport medicine, or they are restricted to a limited number of terms. Often the choice of languages seems to be unbalanced.

In the course of the rapid development of sport science research, many new technical and scientific terms have been created, and the steadily increasing differentiation of sport science terminology has caused considerable communication difficulties within international discussions of problems in the area of sport science. The younger a particular scientific domain is the less stable the scientific terminology is. This is particularly true for sport science and physical education.

The New Project

What are the aims and objectives of the new project?

- It is intended to give sport scientists, physical educators, and physical education students general information about sport science terminology in German, English, and French.
- It is meant to reduce international communication problems in sport science and to give easier access to the scientific literature published in these three languages.
- It is intended to facilitate international cooperation and offer material for comparative studies in the different branches of sport science.

Of course, languages other than German, English, and French (especially Spanish and Russian) should have been included in the project, but this was impossible. This does not mean, however, that such deficiencies might not be compensated for in the future.

From the very beginning, a kind of encyclopedia that provided definitions, not just translations, of scientific terms, was planned. To reach this goal, a procedure had to be agreed upon. The project group might have devised a thesaurus of terms of sport science and physical education and asked German, English/American, and French experts or teams of experts to define these terms. The group did not choose this way for many reasons. If several English experts were asked to define one term in their mother tongue, they would offer as many different definitions as the number of experts asked. These definitions would differ in style, form, concept, and perhaps even content. A similar, but possibly more confusing, result would occur if experts from different countries were asked to do the same thing. Such a procedure makes it extremely difficult to compare the definitions, because the authors do not refer in any way to the definitions given by the other authors in other languages. This is why the project group decided to use a single language (German) as a starting point.

Because German was the chosen language, we were able to use German definitions—some of them slightly altered—from the *Sportwissenschaftliches Lexikon* (Röthig, 1983). These definitions were and still are being translated and checked by American, British, French, German, and Luxembourg experts. The checking is being done to find out whether contents and linguistic formulations correspond to the term usage in the respective countries. Differences in English and French terminology are marked by symbols—one, two, three, or four asterisks— denoting the grade of deviation.

*   This term is a literal translation of a German term. The phenomenon is recognized and studied, but in English/American (or French) this special term is not used to describe it.
**   There is no such term in the English/American (or French) terminology. This is a typically German term in sport science.
***   This term is infrequently used, even in technical terminology.
**** This term has a different meaning in the English/American (or French) terminology.

If necessary, annotations or comparative explanations are added to clarify differences concerning single phenomena or entire scientific concepts. This procedure helps make the texts more concise and offers better possibilities for comparative studies.

The whole project is based on a long-term program. It can be carried out only because we have an extremely cooperative international team of sport scientists and translators from Germany, Great Britain, the USA, France, and Luxembourg.

The fact that this team has been working together for several years without substitutes is proof enough of the intense and enthusiastic engagement of the whole team. In total, about 130 sport scientists have cooperated in developing the German and trilingual dictionaries.

Many financial, personal, temporal, and technical difficulties have had to be surmounted to complete this dictionary. Besides such difficulties, other factors have influenced and limited the possibilities of the trilingual dictionary to provide objective information in comparative studies. One such disturbing factor is the choice of terms. Very often, separating sport science terminology from the terminology of the so-called mother sciences is almost impossible. Obviously the technical terms of general education, psychology, sociology, medicine, and physics are used in the special areas of physical education, sport psychology, sport sociology, sport medicine, and sport biomechanics. But whatever the case may be, defining the precise limits between technical terms of physical activities and technical terms of sport science also is difficult. Some terms are identical in spelling and content in the three languages. This is mostly the case with English terms that have been integrated into French and German, such as *bit, input, output,* and *feedback.* Regardless of slight differences in spelling, the medical terms are mostly identical in the three languages. On the other hand, some same terms in the three languages do not necessarily mean the same thing in these languages. This is discussed later.

The choice of authors in this project is at least as important as the choice of terms. This choice may also influence the results of the work. The authors, being expected to define the different terms, should be highly qualified specialists of their branches of sport science and should command a wide horizon of knowledge, experience, and thought. Nevertheless, an author tries to define a term in accordance with his or her own scientific concepts, making the project a team effort. Among the cooperators there are experts whose tasks are to check and recheck the translations. They, too, are highly qualified sport scientists who have to decide whether the definition of a term corresponds to its usage in their own languages. If it does not, they have to clarify the differences by adding comparative explanations.

A third important factor that might influence the quality of the work exists—the choice of translators. Beyond linguistic qualifications, translators need a profound knowledge of sports, physical education, and sport science. Ordinary translators normally cannot meet these requirements.

Attention should be drawn to a number of terms that raise specific problems. As mentioned before, some same terms in English, French, and German do not necessarily have the same meanings in these three languages. Here are a few examples:

Sport. This term is the same in English, French, and German, but it is used in quite a different sense in these languages. In English and French the word *sport* has a much more limited meaning than in German. In French and English *sport* is mostly restricted to competitive sports that are regulated by rules and regulations, and the meaning does not extend to physical education. The German expression *sport* includes areas of physical activities that would never be called 'sport' in English. This is why German word combinations with the word *sport,* such as *Ausgleichssport, Alterssport, Familiensport, Leistungssport, and Gefängnissport* are described by French, British, and American experts as terms that are not used in their languages to describe the same phenomenon. These terms seem to belong to a typically German terminology.

Pädagogik. Similar difficulties exist with the German terms *Pädagogik* and *Pädagogie.* The German term *Pädagogie* corresponds to the English word *education.* The annotation of the American expert says that in the U.S. the term *pedagogics*—the science of education—is seldom used. The word *pedogogy* is also used infrequently; it refers both to the practical and theoretical aspects of education. So the German term *Sportpädagogik* equals *Theory of Physical Education* in English. In French, *Pädagogik* and *Pädagogie* are translated to *pédagogie;* but the French experts say in their annotation that the classical distinction between *pédagogie pratique* and *pédagogie en général* can no longer be maintained because the development of the theory of education has created a different relationship between theory and practice.

Manager. The word *manager* exists in German, French, and English. These terms appear to be identical. But in reality their meanings are different. In German, a *Sportmanager* is a person who is responsible for the administration and organization of clubs, federations, or sport events. In American/English, the term *manager* is sometimes synonymous with *coach* or *head coach;* in French, a *manager* is often a person who trains a team or coaches it during a match. This means that in French and American/English, *manager* is synonymous with *coach* and *head coach* and not so much with *administrator.*

Most interesting are annotations that are made to clarify different trends or concepts. In the following a few examples are given:

Hermeneutics. The American expert comments, "Hermeneutics have hardly been applied in American sport science which has placed a premium on empirical scientific methods as a methodological monism. Lately, there have been considerations of methodological pluralism which acknowledge the validity of hermeneutics" (cf. Harris).

Action theory. The German definition of action theory describes four kinds of theories, namely philosophical explanations and interpretations of action, sociological theories of action, psychological action theories, and cybernetically oriented action theories. The American expert makes the following remark: "Action theory as defined above is generally unknown in American sport science. This is especially true for the philosophical explanations, phenomenology, hermeneutics, and certain psychological model-theoretical explanations. Symbolic interactionist and marxist interpretations do exist, and the area of motor control is guided basically by cybernetically oriented action theory. Action theory should not be confused with action research, the goal of which is to understand or solve social problems."

Identity. An additionally interesting comment is given by the American expert about the term *identity.* He writes, "With the exception perhaps of sexual identity, the term *identity* appears infrequently in the psychological and social research of sport and physical activity in the USA. Literature available on the development of self focuses especially on such topics as self-concept, self-confidence, self-esteem, and self-efficacy. Contrary to the German interpretation, social aspects of the self are deemed important. From a theoretical point of view, the older symbolic interaction writings (Cooley, Mead) have enjoyed resurgence and interpretation (mirror theory). Social learning theory (Bandura, Walters), however, is the dominant conceptual framework for research in the area of self-concept. Emphasis is given to processes of initiation and social reinforcement (model theory)."

Such annotations and comments are very essential for understanding trends in current or development situations for research in different areas of sport science in various countries. In this context citing other equally interesting and important annotations and comments is not possible. Plenty of these comments are of great value in the comparative studies.

Regarding the different branches of sport science, it can be said that the technical terms of sport medicine cause the least difficulties; differences in meaning in the three languages are almost nonexistent. The reason certainly is that medicine as such looks back on a long tradition of its terminology, which is derived from Greek and Latin and has already been internationally accepted for a long time. Nevertheless, some terms reflect intense efforts of research in different branches of sport medicine in one country or another. Seen from a German point of view, this is especially true for terms that are related to physiological effects of the load of training on the human organism. A few examples follow:

German	English
Leistungsmedizin	Performance Medicine
Sporttraumatologie	Sport Traumatology
Herzvolumenäquivalent	Heart Volume Equivalent
Kritisches Herzgewicht	Critical Heart Weight
Erholungspulssumme	Pulse-Sum during Recovery
Arbeitspulssumme	Pulse-Sum during Work
Herzleistungsquotient	Quotient of Cardiac Work Capacity
Arbeitsinsuffizienz des Herzens	Working Insufficiency of the Heart
Leistungspulsindex	Pulse Index during Work
Sportherz	Sport Heart
Sauerstoff-Dauerleistungsgrenze	Oxygen Endurance Performance Limit

These expressions are more or less literal translations of German terms of sport medicine. English/American and French experts denote them as purely German terms.

In the area of kinesiology, a similar comparison can be made with the following French expressions which are literal translations of German terms, but which are not accepted in the French terminology:

German	French
Bewegungsdrang	Désir impétueux du mouvement

German	French	(cont.)
Bewegungsmerkmale	Caractéristiques motrices	
Bewegungskombination	Combinaison du mouvement	
Bewegungskonstanz	Constance motrice	
Erwerbsmotorik	Motricité apprise	
Azyklische Bewegung	Mouvement acyclique	
Bewegungsverwandtschaft	Parenté des mouvements	
Bewegungsübertragung	Transmission motrice	
Azyklische Schnelligkeit	Vitesse acyclique	
Bewegungspräzision	Précision motrice	
Funktionsphase	Phase fonctionnelle	

In the area of physical education, French and English/American experts have similar difficulties with German technical terms: Pädagogik, Unterrichtsform, Lehrverfahren, deduktive-und induktive Lehrmethode, Neigungsgruppe, Kürturnen, Bewegungserklärung, Übungsreihe, Spielreihe, rhythmische Reihe, Stationsbetrieb. They mostly declare them to be typical German terms and say that the phenomenon is recognized, but that this special term is not used to describe it. This is also true for many terms referring to the theory of training.

Some other terms designate new areas of sport science; these terms are not yet used in English or French terminology, or the meanings of them are slightly different in these two languages. A few examples follow:

German	English
Sportanthropologie	Anthropology of Sport
Sportökologie	Ecology and Geography of Sport
Sportmeteorologie	Meteorology of Sport

Out of about 900 terms within the project, these are only a few examples; they already give an impression of the possibilities for comparative studies. On the other hand, they also show the danger of making conclusions as to the standard of research in one country or another. It cannot be forgotten that the dictionary takes the German teminology as a starting point, which means that, if the English/American or French terminologies would have been taken as starting points, the outcome would perhaps be different in one respect or the other. Maybe sport science research in other countries has laid more stress on other areas of sport science. Nevertheless, increasing differentiation of the already existing scientific terminology may give evidence of highly intensified research in a special branch of sport science.

Summing up, the terminology of sport science and physical education offers many possibilities for comparative studies. It is, of course, indispensable that any evaluation of language and terminology has to take care not to draw unwarranted conclusions.

In the course of this project the working group has always been aware of difficulties and possible disturbing factors; it is hoped that the results of the efforts will be of value to sport science in general and to comparative studies in sport science and physical education specifically.

References

American College of Sports medicine (Ed.). (1971). *Encyclopedia of sport sciences and medicine*. Madison: University of Wisconsin.

Bernett, H. (Ed.). (1966). *Zum Begriff der Bewegung* [The notion of movement]. Schorndorf: Hoffman.

Bandura, A., & Walters, R.H. (1963). *Social learning and personality development*. New York: Holt, Rinehart and Winston.

Epuran, M. (Ed.). (1972). *63 Termes de psychologie du sport. Le 3ᵉ Congrès Européen pour La Psychologie des Sports* [63 terms of sport psychology. Third European Congress of Sport Psychology]. Köln. Schorndorf: Hoffman.

Institut Provincial d'Education Physique (Ed.). (1962). *Glossaire scientifique et technique. Francais-Anglais-Allemand-Néerlandais* [Scientific and technical glossary. French-English-German-Dutch]. Unpublished.

International Union of Psychological Science (Ed.). (1975). *Trilingual psychological dictionary. English, French, German*. Author.

Mead, G.H. (1934). *Mind, self and society*. Chicago: University of Chicago Press.

Parlebas, P. (1981). *Contribution à un lexique commenté en science de láction motrice*. [Contributions to a commented dictionary of physical action]. Paris: Publications INSEP.

Röthig, P. (Ed.). (1983). *Sportwissenschaftliches Lexikon* [Dictionary of sport science]. Vol. 5. Schorndorf: Hofmann.

Teodorescu, L. et al. (1973). *Terminologia educatiei fizice si sportului* [Terminology of physical education and sport]. Editura Stadion.

Tscherne, F. (1976). *Modellfacette Leichtathletik* [Model facet of track and field]. Universitätssportzentrum Wien.

CHAPTER 7

The Object of Research and Methodological Principles of Sport Pedagogics in Some Selected Countries

Zofia Żukowska

Several concepts of sport pedagogics research are emerging. Some authors find it related to and rooted in general pedagogics (Ceausescu, 1976; Draganov, 1972; Fiala, 1963; Röblitz, 1961; Żukowska, 1969). Others identify it with the theory of physical education (Grössing, 1975; Matveev, 1972). Still other studies bring out the anthropological and didactic fundamentals of sport pedagogics (Grupe, 1969), elevating sport didactics to the leading object of research of sport pedagogics (Grössing, 1975; Haag, 1973); this is often linked with elaborate methodological problems that embrace, apart from the aims, contents, and analyses, the methods, means, forms, planning, and control of the physical education teaching process (Kalinowski & Żukowska, 1975).

The broadly conceived subject of research in sport pedagogics encompasses, along with sport didactics, questions related to the personality and work of the physical education teacher and trainer (Fiala, 1973; Svoboda, 1977; Widmer, 1974; Żukowska, 1979), the educational interactions between the student and the sport teacher, and the aims and place of sport in and out of school (Beyer & Röthig, 1976).

We are familiar with attempts at critically analyzing various models of sport pedagogics that exist in the literature (Meusel, 1976) and with the ensuing systematization of disciplines within sport pedagogics. Studies written by Birone (1971), Meusel (1976), and Widmer (1974), among others, are helpful in searching for the scientific foundations of sport pedagogics and in proving its relationship with both the pedagogics science in general and the sport science, including the practical implications of the theory so conceived. Additionally, one of the first pedagogical implications for sport activity arose out of Neumann's studies (1957) of the impact of sport on personality.

I believe that the object of research in sport pedagogics is education through sport and education for sport. Such broadly conceived research should take into account the whole array of psychosociological determinants of the pedagogical process in sport. I am against restricting research in sport pedagogics to sport didactics alone. I identify the didactics of physical education and sport with the broadly perceived methods of physical education and sport treated as scientific disciplines—the term traditionally used in many countries, including Poland, Bulgaria, and Romania. I can hardly subscribe to identifying sport pedagogics with the theory of physical education. I derive the theory of physical education from pedagogics and I perceive it on the one hand as a department of comprehensive education—a propaedeutic to the sport science—and on the other hand as the synthesis of this science with implications for practice.

The area covered by the sport pedagogics research is expanding along with the development and growing significance of physical education in the world today and with the development, besides physical education and sport, of new fields such as recreation through movement and motor rehabilitation.

This expansion is also inspired by modern educational tendencies for which sport is a particularly good basis for development. They are partnership, autocreation (self-realization), autosocialization, and autoeducation. Hence the interest in this area of research and its effects is growing.

In turn, this expands the methodological stratum of research. We can distinguish the following types of research: applied, initiatory, and interdisciplinary. Among these kinds of research there are single unitary, single cross-sectional, continuous, and sponsored. Continuous research is increasingly more common, and I especially appreciate its value to sport pedagogics.

A majority of works mentioned here are normative. Their authors deduce the object of research of sport pedagogics from the theories and knowledge existing in cognate fields. More and more often we have to use empirical research based on the purposeful, representative, stratified, or proportional sample. I believe that the development of empirical research carries prospects for the development of sport pedagogics. Seemingly obvious judgments in this field still need to be empirically verified.

The character of scientific papers in sport pedagogics evolves from descriptive and descriptive-analytical to descriptive-explicative, descriptive-analytical-evaluative and synthetic-theoretical. The most frequently used methods of research are diagnostic probe, document analysis, analysis of individual cases, pedagogical experiment and historical-comparative analysis. These methods involve various techniques, of which the most common are observation, questionnaire form, interview form, sociometrics, tests, and inventory.

As the object of pedagogics research becomes more and more defined, the methods and techniques of research proper to this discipline grow richer. In my view, the most specific method is the pedagogical experiment. This is the only method that conducted at a definite time and involving the behavior of experimental and control groups, can give us a thorough answer to the question about the impact of sport on personality, human attitudes, social bonds, and group integration. It will also give us a better insight into the motivation behind the pursuit of sport and the question of transfer of shaped traits and gained values. In our civilized world we can learn from this method about the revalidating and resocializing values of sport (Widmer, 1974; Żukowska, 1981, 1983) so they can be properly utilized in practice.

The findings of research involving the pedagogical experimental method, apart from their clear practical implications, constitute the basis for syntheses that enrich the theoretical foundations of sport pedagogics.

Six main problems are pursued in Polish research in sport pedagogy. First, we have a long tradition of research on the personality, which began in the 1950s. There was research on the personality of the physical education teacher and trainer; then came research on the destinies of graduates of higher schools of physical education; finally came a normative model of the graduate. Subsequent research empirically verified that model by pinpointing factors that conditioned the graduate's efficiency. Currently we carry out research into the efficiency of performance by the physical education teacher, trainer, and rehabilitation specialist.

Second, problems of educating the cadres for physical culture feature very broadly in the research. I only wish to outline the predominant questions. They concern the research on the optimal model for the student, systems of intramural and extramural studies in Poland and the world, problems involved in pedagogical practice, postgraduate education of specialists, the number and causes of failures during study, applied methods and techniques of teaching, research on the formal and informal structure of the higher school community, and finally the effectiveness of education with particular emphasis on the didactic-educational systems functioning in academies of physical education.

Third, the process of education through sport and for sport embraces the socioeducational determinants of physical education and sport in and out of school, the trainer's deontological code of conduct, the educational work with young people talented in sport, the correlations between the physical development, physical fitness, and mental fitness of young people—the optimal model of the student's growth—and the psychosociopedagogical factors behind the effectiveness of the trainer's work, with special account being taken of his or her pedagogical background.

Fourth, in the axiological categories, sport comes in for examination on the basis of the multifarious findings of empirical research which concern, in particular, the intellectualization of the process of teaching and improvement in sport, the educational consequences of the relationship between sport and the arts, the shaping of moral postures during sport activity, and the socioeducational and personality values of sport, allowing for the age, sex, and educational environments—school, sport clubs, culture centers, sociopolitical and educational-guardianship organizations.

The findings of this research have furnished the groundwork for analyzing the educational values of sport, among which we propose to distinguish the following:

• Perfectionist values
• Sociocentric values

- Allocentric values
- Intellectual values
- Aesthetic values
- Emotional values
- Pleasure values
- Prestige values
- Material values
- Health values

Fifth, we are working to verify these sport values that we have assumed in the educational categories in our research in order to identify the relationships and dependencies between the physical culture and the youth subculture. The research covers the peasant, the student, the worker youth milieux, and a group of highly qualified sportsmen.

Finally, research is underway on the physical culture at all levels of youth education. It covers the diagnosis of the state of affairs and the verification of new programmatic-organizational solutions allowing for the base and the cadres. This research is applied to preschool-age children, school youth, high school students, soldiers, young people deviating from the growth standards—special school system—and organizations that take care of the leisure time.

The outlined problems predominating in the sport pedagogics research in Poland reflect respective literature in which the research findings are given in detail.

The limited space of this scientific presentation allows me to outline only these questions. The authors and the topics of their research are provided in the enclosed reference list.

References

Beyer, E., & Röthig, P. (Eds.). (1976). *Beiträge zur Gegenstandsbestimmung der Sportpädagogik* [Contribution to the development of scientific basis in sport pedagogics]. Schorndorf: Hofmann.

Birone, N.E. (1971). *Sportpedagogia* [Sport pedagogics]. Budapest.

Ceausescu, N. (1976). *Pedagogia educatiei fizice si sportulùi* [Pedagogics of physical education and sport]. Bukarest.

Draganov, P. (1972). *Piedagogika* [Pedagogics]. Sofia.

Fiala, V. (1963). *Strucnè pedagogika* [Sport pedagogics]. Prague.

Fiala, V. (1973). *Cvicitél, trener—pedagog* [Instructor, coach—pedagogue]. Prague.

Grössing, S. (1975). *Einführung in die Sport-Didaktik* [Didactic studies in physical education]. Frankfurt/Main.

Grupe, O. (1969). *Grundlagen der Sportpädagogik* [Fundamentals in sport pedagogics]. Munich.

Haag, H. (1973). *Didaktische und curriculare Aspekte des Sports* [Didactic and methodological aspects of sport]. Schorndorf: Hofmann.

Kalinowski, A., & Zukowska, Z. (1975). *Metodyka wychowania fizycznego* [Methods of physical education]. Warsaw.

Matveev, L.P. (1972). Die Theorie des Sports als Wissenschaft und Unterrichtsfach [Theory of sport as science and specialized didactic discipline]. *Theorie und Praxis der Körperkultur*, pp. 875-884.

Meusel, H. (1976). *Einführung in die Sportpädagogik* [Introduction to sport pedagogics]. Munich.

Neumann, O. (1957). *Sport und Persönlichkeit* [Sport and personality]. Munich.

Röblitz, G. (1961). *Pädagogik* [Pedagogics]. Leipzig.

Svoboda, B. (Ed.). (1977). *Didactic studies in physical education*. Prague.

Widmer, K. (1974). *Sportpädagogik* [Sport pedagogics]. Schorndorf: Hofmann.

Zukowska, Z. (1969). Wybrane zagadnienia pedagogiczne w pracy trenera [Selected pedagogical subjects in the work of a coach]. Warsaw.

Zukowska, Z. (1979). Styl życia absolwentów uczelni wychowania fizycznego [Style of life of the graduates of the Academy of Physical Education]. Warsaw.

Zukowska, Z. (1981). Sport jako wyznacznik stylu zycia. Kulturowe wartości sportu [Sport as an indicator of lifestyle. Cultural values of sport]. Warsaw.

Zukowska, Z. (1981). Wzory osobowe sportu [Personal patterns of sport]. In *Sport i kultura* [Sport and culture]. Warsaw.

Zukowska, Z. (1983). Wartości wychowawcze współczesnego sportu. Sport w ksztaltowaniu kultury i osobowości [Educational values of modern sport. Sport in shaping culture and personality]. Warsaw.

CHAPTER 8

Comparative Research in Regard to Physical Education in Poland

Pawel Kudlorz

The almost 1,000-year-old history of Poland is no history of a splendid, isolated island. The contrary is true. Poland participated as a country of Europe very extensively in all cultural dimensions of our continent from the Renaissance to the Enlightenment and up to the present. This was not only done in a passive way. On the one hand, the advanced ideas were transformed and adapted to their own conditions; on the other hand, the fields of culture (Fryderyk Chopin, Krzysztof Penderecki) and knowledge (Nikolaj Kopernik, Marie Curie Skłodowska) were enriched.

For most of our history, scientists and intellectuals of the Enlightenment period followed advanced tendencies and trends out of inner necessity and desire. Unfortunately, the "Magistra Vitae" also shows a bad side: for more than 100 years—from 1795 until 1918—Poland lost its state sovereignty and was divided by three neighboring powers—Austria, Prussia, and Russia. During that time, the divided areas had to submit themselves to the rules and administrations of the occupied powers; this was true for almost all areas, including education, physical education, recreation and sport, and so forth. From this resulted the characteristic form of the Polish educational system and its physical culture which was rooted in national traditions and influenced by the impact of foreign powers in the 19th century on the one hand, and by willingly adopted foreign ideas, achievements, and solutions on the other hand.

At present, the previous interest in foreign educational systems, physical education, and sport has changed to a systematically scientific research. In this analysis the development of comparative research is presented in two areas of physical culture in Poland. In the first part of the analysis, the development of Polish comparative education (i.e., the "older sister" of comparative physical education) is analyzed. In the second part the research directions are presented in two areas of physical culture: physical education and sport in schools, and physical education teacher training.

The Development of Comparative Education

Comparative education is mentioned first in 1937. The next reference can be found only after World War II in 1946. At one time, some educationists felt that comparative education should not have its own name or should not be part of science; this is not true today. The meaning prevails that "the comparatistic, which is used to a different extent in the total field of education, is not excluding the development of an independent discipline called comparative education" (Wiloch, 1970, p. 29).

The affirmation of this statement, expressed in 1970, can be found in *The Pedagogical Dictionary*, published in 1981: "Comparative Education is a discipline which is dealing with the analysis and comparison of education systems in different countries in connection to its political, economical, and sociocultural development" (Okon, 1981, p. 224).

Wiloch worked hard to make comparative education an independent scientific discipline. He wrote many articles, but published the only existing book in Polish with the title, *Introduction to Comparative Education* (1970). Figure 1 shows a model in which the author tries to locate the place of comparative education within the system of educational sciences (Wiloch, 1970, p. 184).

Development of Comparative Research Within School Physical Education

In a written form, the term *comparative physical education and sport* was used for the first time in Poland in 1983 (Kudlorz, 1983). This, however, does not mean that no comparative research in regard to physical culture existed in our country up to that time. It simply was referred to by different terms such as *comparative analysis, problems of comparative research, historical-comparative studies*, and so forth. Jaworski defined the term *comparatistic* (in relation to research in the social-educational problems of physical culture) in the following way: "Comparatistic—a juxtaposition of facts and phenomena with the aim to find out and generalize the characteristic signs and the existing similarities, differences and their conditions" (Jaworski, 1976, p. 4).

Many publications that are related to the topic of this analysis in regard to other countries could be mentioned, but research was not coordinated and the publications were written ad hoc.

A planned comparative research was started at the end of the 1960s. First of all, it was decided to edit a series of summaries of selected articles that were published in foreign journals from 1961 to 1973. The series was intended especially to help researchers learn about critical meanings of the status quo and about new proposals. In 1975, the book company Sport und Touristik edited a collection of summaries of articles from 10 countries. Secondly, a team of authors was found that wrote a monograph, *The School Physical Education in Different Countries*. The book contains compact information on 22 countries (Jaworski, 1976). This

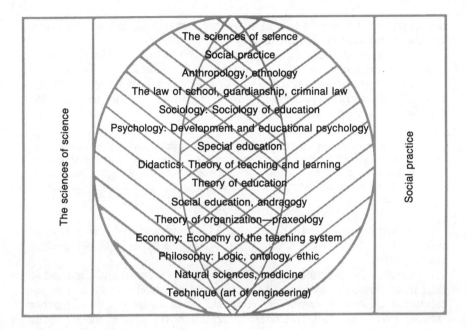

The sciences of science

Social practice

Anthropology, ethnology

The law of school, guardianship, criminal law

Sociology: Sociology of education

Psychology: Development and educational psychology

Special education

Didactics: Theory of teaching and learning

Theory of education

Social education, andragogy

Theory of organization—praxeology

Economy: Economy of the teaching system

Philosophy: Logic, ontology, ethic

Natural sciences, medicine

Technique (art of engineering)

The sciences of science

Social practice

 Object of education as science   Object of comparative education

Figure 1.   Position of comparative education within the system of educational sciences—A model.

Note.   From *Wprowadzenie do pedagogiki prównawczei* [Introduction to comparative education] (p. 184) by T.J. Wiloch, 1970. Warsaw: Państwowe Wydawnictwo Naukowe. Copyright 1970 by T.J. Wiloch. Reprinted by permission.

publication seems to be a valid one, especially in regard to the usage of a "comparative analysis scheme of models (systems) of physical education and sport of children and youth," which was developed by Polish scientists in an original and unique way. The scheme contains the following topics: aims and objectives; organizational forms of instructional units; content; methods; evaluation of the performance of pupils; teachers; and material conditions (Jaworski, 1976 pp. 6-17).

Comparative Research within Physical Education Teacher Training

Teacher training is one of the most important facets of every educational system. Its status is a result of many factors. In connection with our objective, we would like to stress two groups of factors: the home tradition and foreign influences.

In the following analysis, however, only the influence of foreign countries is discussed. Here is an example. In relation to the 30-year-anniversary of the Academy for Physical Education in Warsaw (started in 1929 as the Central Institute for Physical Education), the chronicler W. Gniewkowski (1960) wrote:

> Within the Teacher Training of Physical Education Teachers the experiences and designs of foreign countries were used. Patterns of interesting solutions were given by existing institutes and schools of higher learning in Sweden, France, Germany as well as Belgium, Denmark and the United States. (p. 33)

After World War II, many different articles on physical education teacher training for school physical education were published in Polish professional journals.

Unfortunately, no colleague in Poland and no team of authors tried to deal in a compact way with the problem of physical education teacher training in different countries as Wojtynski did in regard to general teacher training (Wojtynski, 1971). Certain information in regard to this topic can be found in the previously mentioned book, *The School Physical Education in Different Countries*, in which the problems in 22 countries were analyzed. However, in the chapters concerning Japan and Cuba, the problem of teacher training was not included.

In Poland, two international conferences were organized in which the development and present status of comparative research in regard to the inclusion of physical education in institutions of higher learning were discussed. The first one, "La Formation des Educateurs Physiques et Sportifs," was organized in 1970. The second one, "The Process and the Effects of Physical Education Teacher Training," was organized in 1980. Under the topic "Physical Education Teacher Training in the Light of Comparative Research," eight papers were given.

Poland is one of the few countries in which the graduate of a 4-year-study, the holder of a Master of Physical Education degree, has the right to gain the title of doctor and of habilitated doctor within sport sciences.

The 1980s show the character of comparative research not only in topics for dissertations (e.g., "The Cadre Education for the Necessities of Physical Education in the United States of America," Kudlorz, 1980), but also in habilitation works (e.g., "The Student Teaching in the Process of Physical Education Teacher Training," Mankowska, 1981 and "Studies of Higher Education on Physical Education," Jaworski, 1982).

The following milestone in the development of comparative research is a project of international research. Before the Olympic Games in Moscow, six socialist European countries decided for the first time to study comparative research within physical culture. The results were published in 1980 in the book, *Coaches and Physical Education Teachers Training in Socialist Countries* of the Central Committee of the Czechoslowak Union of Physical Education (1980).

The Inclusion of Comparative Physical Education and Sport within Sciences for Physical Culture

In 1982, Krawczyk, professor for sociology and philosophy in the Academy for Physical Education in Warsaw, published a scheme of sciences for physical culture. This is the result of scientific research in regard to the evaluation of the theoretical thoughts in the discussed area in Poland. According to Krawczyk, the term *physical culture* is a synthetic category unifying the above mentioned theory of middle range, meaning the theories on physical education, sport, recreation, and so forth. In this model,

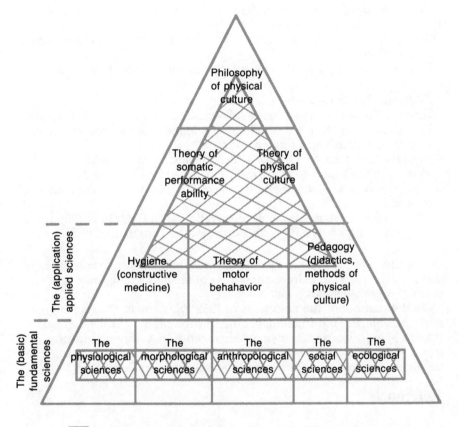

Subject of comparative physical culture

Figure 2. Inclusion of comparative physical culture into the system of physical culture sciences.

Note. From "Ksztaltowanie sie teorii kultura fizyczna w Polsce " [The development of the physical culture theory in Poland] by Z. Krawczyk, 1982, *Kultura Fizyczna, 9-10*. Copyright 1982 by Z. Krawczyk. Reprinted by permission.

the comparative field within physical culture or the object of comparative physical culture was introduced (Krawczyk, 1982, p. 1-4; see Fig 2.).

Final Remarks

In this analysis, the author mainly tried to give the development that was taken by the comparatistic in Poland in regard to two areas of physical culture: school physical education and physical education teacher training.

It seems that the general tendencies are in accordance with those all around the world. The author also tried to construct a model of comparative physical culture.

However, the question has to be raised about which perspectives are developed within the young subdiscipline in the sciences of physical education. According to our opinion the problem can be compared to communicating vessels.

From the Polish point of view, people should do the following:

- Continue comparative research in regard to other areas of physical culture. The research results, besides producing pure knowledge, will be fruitful in application possibilities of selected solutions that are examined in the practice of foreign countries;
- Introduce comparative physical education and sport as part of the study in the teacher training curriculum. This would be in accordance with the certain acknowledgement of this subdiscipline within the academic world;
- Initiate official relationships in cooperation with the International Society on Comparative Physical Education and Sport (ISCPES).

From the point of view of the ISCPES, the Polish research results from comparative physical culture should be published in the journal, *Comparative Physical Education and Sport*.

On the one hand, the objectives of ISCPES, namely the exchange of scientific data and information, should be promoted. On the other hand, readers should learn their own systems better by receiving information on other models and by analyzing foreign solutions (as in the case of the problems of physical culture and their solutions in Poland).

References

Central Committee of the Czechoslowak Union of Physical Education. (1980). *Coaches and physical education teachers training in socialist countries*. Prague: Charles University, Faculty of Physical Education and Sport.

Gniewkowski, W. (1960). Kronika. In *Akademia Wychowania Fizycznego 1929-1959*. Warsaw: Sport i Tunystyka.

Jaworski, Z. (Ed.). (1976). *Szkolne wychowanie fizyczne w rożnych krajach* [The school physical education in different countries]. Warsaw: Academy of Physical Education.

Jaworski, Z. (1982). *Wyższe studia wf* [Studies of higher education on physical education]. Warsaw: Academy of Physcial Education.

Krawczyk, Z. (1982). Kształtowanie sie teorii kf w Polsce [The development of the physical culture theory in Poland]. *Kultura Fizyczna,* **9-10.**

Kudlorz, P. (1983). Problematyka szkolnego wychowania fizycznego w publikacjach Miedzynarodowegeo Stowarzyszenia Porównawczego Wychowania Fizycznego i Sportu [The problems of school physical education in publications of the International Society on Comparative Physical Education and Sport]. *Kultura Fizyczna,* **9-10.**

Kudlorz, P. (1980). *Ksztalcenie kadr dla potrzeb wf w Stanach Zjednoczonych Ameryki* [The cadre education for the necessities of physical education in the United States of America]. Praca dokotorska/maszynopis. Warsaw: Academy of Physical Education.

Mańkowska, M. (1981). *Praktyki pedagogiczne w procesie kształcenia nauczycieli wychowania fizycznego* [The student teaching in the process of physical education teacher training]. Warsaw: Academy of Physical Education.

Okon, W. (1981). *Słownik pedagogiczny* [The pedagogical dictionary]. Warsaw: Państwowe Wydawnictwo Naukowe.

Wiloch, T.J. (1970). *Wprowadzenie do pedagogiki prównawczej* [Introduction to comparative education]. Warsaw: Państwowe Wydawnictwo Naukowe.

Wojtyński, W. (1971). *O ksztalceniu nauczyciela szkoly podstawowej w Polsce i świecie* [The education of the elementary school teacher in Poland and other countries in the world]. Warsaw: Państwowe Zaklady Wydawnictwo Szkolnych.

PART II

Comparative Research: Physical Activity Within Schools

CHAPTER 9

School Physical Activity in Comparative Perspective: Prospects and Problems

John C. Pooley

Any overview that addresses the status of a field of study or part thereof must, by necessity, be incomplete. This is because no matter how exhaustive the search, a variety of research will probably escape detection. For example, much research is not reported internationally, and some is written in a language in which the searcher is unfamiliar. Other problems include the variety of writing available and the availability of research. When preparing this paper, for example, the writer discarded brief one- or two-page statements headed "comparative." While this type of research varies greatly and spans the quantitative and qualitative spectrum, much of the writing is best described as anecdotal, depending as it does upon the opinion or knowledge of one person.

The status of comparative research in physical activity in schools is low; that is, very little research is reported. In contrast, comparative research in education is burgeoning and is reported in journals like *International Review of Education, Comparative Education,* and *Comparative Education Review.* In addition to our own, as yet, modest *Comparative Physical Education* journal, the *International Journal of Physical Education* and *FIEP Bulletin* address some comparative research; but most often these journals include a variety of issues not treated comparatively. No criticism is intended here; rather, it is merely stated that very little cross-national research is being conducted whether quantitatively or qualitatively. Literature searches using the *ERIC, SIRC,* and the *Review of Leisure and Sport Abstracts* support this. A personal contact made to approximately 25 international scholars considered to be sufficiently interested in the topic under scrutiny, either by being involved in research themselves or knowing of the work of others, revealed several studies. However, the few studies that were reported by these scholars further suggests that more work needs to be done.

Few cross-national studies are available. Thus presumably few have been completed on the topic of physical activity in schools. This contention is supported by the fact that, in the two chapters relating to the topic of physical activity in schools (physical education, and intramural and extramural activities in the schools) in the most recently published Western text by Bennett, Howell, and Simri entitled *Comparative Physical Education* (1975), only three studies that were cross-national or cross-cultural were cited. Furthermore, in the earlier seminars of the ISCPES held respectively in Israel, Canada, and the United States, only five papers focused on this topic.

Physical activity in school must be examined in the context of type (formal physical education classes; intramural sport; interscholastic sport; club activities; and informal play); time allotted or time available (formal class time; practice and competition time; and free time available before, during, and after school hours); facilities and their availability (indoor, outdoor, natural environment; and degree of restriction); objectives (educational outcomes; balance of opportunities for mass/elite; physical outcomes; social-emotional outcomes); and organizational responsibility (institution–physical education teacher, coach, other teacher; student).

Intramurals are "defined as a diversion primarily intended for fun, permeated by a spirit of moderation" (Kniker, 1984, p. 171). Hopkins (1978), writing in the *Canadian Intramural Recreation Association*, indicated that *intramurals* means "within the walls" and caters to mass involvement in physical activity. "[Intramurals] means a voluntary and varied program of physical activities that meets the needs, interests, and abilities of those within the [school] community" (Hopkins, 1978, p. 1). *Interscholastic sport* is used to describe contests in which individuals or teams from one school compete against those from another.

Having defined subconcepts of physical activity, the presence or absence of various forms of physical activity in schools must be recognized based on national, sex, or school-type differences. For example, at the secondary level, formal physical education classes are stressed in socialist countries; intramurals (in the form of house competition) are emphasized in British schools; interschool sport is emphasized in North America, especially in the United States; sport afternoons for all are a strong feature of Australian schools; games afternoons of up to 2 hours in duration are provided for most students of private schools in many parts of the world; and sport clubs (emphasizing participation for all, not competition for the few) are a feature of Swiss schools. Many models and variations exist within countries or even regions. In fact, in visiting schools in the countries highlighted, the author was struck by intranational differences that always make comparisons based on national differences problematic.

Status of Cross-National Research

One of the first studies that best fits the focus of this paper was completed in 1968 by Kenyon while he was at the University of Wisconsin in the United States. He compared the values held for physical activity by selected urban secondary school students in Canada, Australia, England, and the United States. While many findings are listed, Kenyon concluded that both primary and secondary involvement in physical activity by adolescents is a function of many past and present forces. A decade later, in 1978, Van Lierde and Van Dun compiled a document on school sport representing 18 European countries. This was followed by a survey on "the extra-curricular school sport" in European countries. Both documents are out of print and, although references are made to them in other papers, it is presently not possible to refer to them in detail.

It is significant, however, that the chapters on physical activity in schools in Bennett, Howell and Simri's 1975 and 1983 texts include very few references to comparative studies; most of the material used came from studies of a single country, leaving these authors to draw comparisons themselves. With few exceptions, therefore, those interested must rely on reports about physical activity in schools in single countries or, in rare cases, on a cluster of countries sharing the same ideology. Examples of the former include material by Anthony (1980), Kane (1974), McIntosh (1963), Johnson (1966), Hendry and Welsh (1981), Hendry and Thorpe (1977), Davidson (1977), Department of Physical Education, Republic of China (1980), Macintosh and King (1976), and Hardman (1980; 1981); examples of the latter are the text by Riordan (1981) on *Sport Under Communism* and the text by Demetrovic and Kostka (1980) on *Coaches and Physical Education Teachers Training in Socialist Countries*.

Professional physical education and interschool and intramural sport organizations in countries as far apart as New Zealand and Canada publish journals or newsletters regularly reporting or commenting on new or innovative ideas relating to their specific programs. The author is also aware of a number of theses or dissertations with a similar focus. Undoubtedly, many more lie hidden in university libraries throughout the world. The majority never surface beyond their defense. Finally, widely disparate journals do publish research relating directly or indirectly to contemporary comparative issues, examples of which follow.

In the United States, Duda (1984) completed research of achievement motivation in sport and in the classroom using a cross-cultural analysis of Navajo and Anglo students. She also joined forces with Allison to compare race and sex differences in sport and academic domains (Duda and Allison, 1984). Canadian researcher Vertinsky (1983) examined sex equality in physical education in England; some references are made to the United States and Canada. However, a second study, coauthored with Cuthbert, compared teaching preferences of physical educators in two national settings. They concluded that Canadian physical educators place emphasis on fitness and the development of skills for future lifestyles, while British teachers attach more importance to fun and the promotion of team spirit as major physical education goals (Vertinsky & Cuthbert, 1983).

Clumpner and Smith (1983) drew attention to the "conspicuous differences" between high school interscholastic programs in the same sport in Canada and the United States. The strength of national values is highlighted by this study in view of the adjacent geographical area selected: the province of Alberta in Canada and the state of Washington in the United States. However, this should not be surprising because Chandler (1981) found intranational differences in emphasis and focus of physical education and games programs in Canadian private schools and Fiander (1981) found marked differences in opportunities for and involvement in intramural and interscholastic sports within the *same* Canadian province as a function of size and location (urban or rural). Earlier, Macintosh and King (1976) also found variations of the proportion of students involved in interscholastic sports in another Canadian province.

Interscholastic Sport

By contrast to the Canadian situation, a measure of the enormous interest in American high school sport is that, even 15 years ago, 100 million spectators reportedly attended high school basketball games annually (Jennison, 1970). The figure is almost certainly higher now.

As with other extracurricular programs in schools, debate continues about the values that are gained from participation in interscholastic sport. In reviewing a conference on "Sport in American Life" held at Iowa State University in 1972, Kniker deduced these values to be control, competition, social security, physical well-being, and spirit; he also found that this level of sport is characterized by a spirit of dedication, sacrifice, and intensity (Kniker, 1984, pp. 170-171).

Interschool sport is increasingly taking on the role of the community representative, either in the school itself or in the wider community in which the school is located. Moreover, it is increasingly (in the international sense) being viewed as a successful representative to other communities in terms of the win-loss record of its team, rather than for other reasons such as playing well, playing enthusiastically, or playing fairly and demonstrating sportsmanship. As Snyder and Spreitzer state:

> Sport frequently serves as a symbolic representation of larger social groups, and this process serves as a means of collective identification, loyalty and pride, or conversely, of shame and in the embarrassment by members of the school or region represented by the team. (Snyder & Spreitzer, 1983, p. 113)

Physical Education

Physical education (i.e., formal classes that coexist with other subjects in the school curriculum) is widely criticized in many countries. Specific shortcomings are identified in the United States (Sage, 1981), England (Anthony, 1980), Finland (Silvennoinen, 1982), Canada (Carre, Mosher, & Schutz, 1979), and Hungary (Varpalotai, 1983). For example, physical education loses status when compared with interscholastic sport; it becomes an elective in many countries to the extent that as many as 80–90% of students beyond age 15 have no physical education at all; those who teach it lose interest, preferring to coach; and the materials taught are outdated, repetitious, and boring.

There is no question that, in some countries, the rift between physical education and interscholastic sport has become so very great that the two are unrelated. In a chapter devoted to sport within educational institutions in the United States, Snyder and Spreitzer conclude that "at all levels of education, sport has become progressively more detached from physical education, intramurals and play. In fact, the term 'player' is becoming an anachronism as heavily organized athletic programs move closer to the world of work" (1983, p. 122).

One reason why physical education classes and interscholastic sport are unrelated is that, in some countries like Canada and the United States, declining enrollments in the former and the high profile of the latter make competitive sport more appealing to physical education teachers, parents, and students. Moreover, when physical education teachers coach competitive school teams for 2 or 3 hours, 7 days per week and when sport has more status than physical education in school settings, teachers become casual and unenthusiastic about teaching, leading inevitably to a decline in standards. Consequently, students strive to be excused from compulsory classes or elect other school subjects when they have a choice. In a comprehensive cross-country tour of Canadian provinces in 1975, Martens concluded that "interschool athletics dominates the physical education program at the senior high level (aged 15-18) and perhaps also at the junior level (aged 12-14)" (1976, p. 31).

Intramurals

Intramurals often become the poor relation; they are admired in principle but squeezed out for lack of attention. For example, one male high school physical education teacher who visited my class recently, although having the responsibility for organizing the intramural program for 1,400 students, admitted that he was uninterested and preferred to coach the girls' basketball team; that was where he spent most of his energies and had the most interest. This is not atypical in North America.

The roles of national professional organizations representing physical education, interscholastic sport, and intramural sport are questionable. Whereas some organizations are effective in providing information and guidance, and in some cases are even inspirational to members, others are unable to identify with their constituents. Organizations whose mandates are to set standards, provide innovative ideas, and link communication between widely dispersed professionals often reach only a modest percentage of potential members. For example, one of the largest professional organizations in the world, the *American Alliance for Health, Physical Education, Recreation and Dance* (AAHPERD), has attracted less than 30% of potential members to join, in spite of a vigorous membership campaign in 1983-1984 (Hayward, 1984). However, ideally the 10 articles that constitute the "International Charter of Physical Education and Sport" provide guiding beacons to all people interested in "placing the development of physical education and sport at the service of human progress" (UNESCO, 1979, p. 27).

Summary

Having provided some examples from comparative research, as well as from case studies regarding the present status of physical education, interscholastic sport, and intramural sport, it seems reasonable to refer to some of the major conclusions from studies reported in the recent Bennett, Howell, and Simri (1983) text because theirs is the most comprehensive survey of material known. General findings are the following:

- The universal aim is to develop physical skills.
- The trend is to develop and cater to elite athletes.
- A seeming paradox exists because programs appear to develop a permanent personal interest in lifetime physical activity.
- The emphasis on fitness is either related to person health or to the benefit of the country as a whole.
- Physical education classes are often required in many countries but are not always offered because of financial, facility, or personnel constraints.
- Physical activity may be practiced in varying degrees outside the class timetable either in an organized way through intramurals, interscholastic sport, or sport clubs or through unorganized activity during planned breaks and lunchtime. These in turn are usually dependent upon available facilities, the climate, and cultural values.
- Other than in countries with strong central control, and even in those sometimes, individual school administrators often determine the degree of emphasis on physical activity in their schools. Consequently, many local variations of physical education emphasis exist.

In a more general sense, school sport is believed to contribute to educational goals; specific studies have shown that sport participation is related to higher academic aspirations and better marks (grades). (See Phillips & Schafer, 1971, and Spreitzer & Pugh, 1973, for example.) However, school sport may also subvert academic goals, especially when it becomes the most important activity for some students and coaches at school.

Strategy for Cross-National Research

Some examples of research have been identified so that others may learn from the methodologies used and subsequently choose to replicate existing studies or modify approaches as a function of methodological rigor or pragmatic consideration.

The overview of physical education in schools by Bennett, Howell, and Simri (1983) both provides a broad picture in cross-national perspective and underscores the need for comparative studies. Most of the papers used are based upon single countries; few actually compare one system with another. Moreover, most are descriptive; few attempt to be analytical.

Whereas descriptions of systems of physical education or elements of systems may have a place, authors would perform a greater service by explaining how the systems evolved. This ought to be followed by an analysis of the system under scrutiny to provide a much greater understanding of the phase of physical activity that then might be compared with the system, or part thereof, in another country, region, or district. Only then can valid comparisons showing similarities and differences be drawn. Studies are often superficial. Until comparativists actually compare, by applying the principles of scientific research (meaning the use of disciplined or ordered methods, the determination of a logical model to be applied, the absence of personal bias in the writing, and the drawing of conclusions based upon the data available), our field will not mature.

As previously indicated (Pooley, 1979), research may be quantitative or qualitative—both are acceptable; but until comparisons are made, we are not engaged in comparative research. This is not to say that individuals have no right to undertake case studies; as many of us have agreed, this is a first step which, for those either personally wishing or commissioned to examine systems in their own country, may be voluntary or mandatory. But we can only understand our own system when viewed in perspective with others; we can only see its strengths and weaknesses and finally determine what to leave untouched and what to change by comparing it with others. I therefore strongly advocate that we reserve our journal for comparative papers and not use it for case studies; otherwise, we perpetuate the myth that papers on a single system are comparative. If the editorial board decides to use some case studies, then these should be designated in an appropriate section.

A simple model for comparative researchers to use would be for two or more researchers to conduct the same research in different locations and compare results. This would be cheap and practical; it would only require finding colleagues who would be willing to share in the research process. The idea for the research would be individually chosen but the research methods to be employed—the population and sampling techniques, the instrument used for data collection, and the type of document to be written—would be a shared venture. Joint authorship would result. Such an enterprise would be heuristic, that is, one shared experience would lead to another. Undoubtedly, more comparative research ought to be done. It may be the easiest way to ensure material for our journal and ultimately the survival of our field of study.

This may be an appropriate time to address the issue of method in comparative physical education research. In a simplistic sense, two approaches are used by comparativists: these are variously named *quantitative* and *qualitative, empirical* and *humanistic,* or *verstehen* (understanding) and *erklären* (explaining). These three dyads do not have identical meanings, but they do represent general dichotomies of focus that scholars choose when they research a problem. Often the approach chosen reflects the preference of the scholar, based on his or her graduate education; however, problems to be solved may require a specific type of methodology. A variety of types of research are therefore acceptable.

Issues for Investigation

Many issues are related to research in physical activity. The following are some examples.

Status.   A fundamental question that needs to be addressed crossnationally is what determines the status of physical education and extracurricular
activities (relating to physical activity) in schools? Although their status
can be measured in terms of percentages of students involved—whether
required or elective, whether taught by specialists or nonspecialists,
whether used as a subject for entrance to tertiary institutions or not, and
so on—the actual status of physical activity programs in schools is difficult
to measure. Status may be low when compared with other subjects in
the curriculum. Status therefore is determined by teachers (including principals), educators in general, students, parents, and the society as a whole.
Although each variable listed may contribute to status, until these variables (and others) are measured, and until the perceptions of those populations are also measured, we will continue to make judgments based on
personal opinion and anecdotal information. Please note, however, that
because politically socialist countries stress physical activity in schools
more than capitalist countries and because central control prevails more
in socialist countries than in capitalist countries, programs are more likely
to be adhered to in socialist countries. Nevertheless, early attempts to
determine the status of physical activity in schools were not enough
(ICHPER, 1969).

Stated and actual programs.   A difference often exists between stated
and actual programs of physical education, including extracurricular activities in schools. This point is not only revealed through reading the
research of others; it also may be a problem when reviewing curricula
of school programs directly. What is written or stated about programs
from national to individual school levels may not be consistent with the
actual material taught. For example, many nations require physical education programs at a given age level; however, it is not infrequent to learn
that, either by accident or design, classes sometimes persistently are not
taught.

Separation of the sexes.   Although many countries emphasize the importance of social outcomes from physical activity settings that presumably
relate, in part, to healthy interaction between the sexes, programs are
often separated on the basis of sex from a young age. However, from
a physiological standpoint, this separation often is not justified. The principle of integrated programs should be considered at all levels; for
example, all activity classes at the author's own university are coeducational.

Female role models.   Many extracurricular activities for girls in schools
are often organized and coached by male teachers. When this persists,
girls lose the opportunity to interact with female role models, which may
be undesirable.

Other issues.   The General Secretary of the Physical Education Association of Great Britain and Northern Ireland identified the major problems
facing the physical education profession both nationally and regionally.
These were (a) the loss of curriculum time; (b) the selling of playing field

facilities; (c) the poor standard of primary physical education; (d) the lack of career structure; (e) the severe cutbacks in grant aid; (f) the variations in initial training and inservice provisions; and (g) the increase in the recreational 'nature' of curriculum time (*General Secretary*, 1983).

Other questions to be considered are the following:

- Should school physical education be evaluated on the basis of physical skill, cognitive skill, or attitudinal and behavioral dimensions?
- What impact do physical education teachers and school coaches have on students from different countries?
- Should physical education teachers be involved in preparing elite athletes?
- Are the values stressed by teachers in physical education classes or coaches in interschool sport programs in conflict with adolescent values?

The Value of Comparative Physical Education and Sport Research

The value of comparative physical education and sport research can be appreciated only when the results of applied research are used to illuminate the advantage of one method over another or of one curriculum over another. Comparative physical education and sport then can be seen as useful and necessary rather than as unimportant or frivolous.

Internationally, physical educators and coaches in schools are under pressure because of the following elements:

- Public confidence in physical education is decreasing.
- Established academic subjects are being reemphasized at all school levels, leaving "less important" subjects such as art, music, and physical education to compete for declining time in the weekly program.
- Declining enrollments are leading to fewer teaching positions and to fewer new physical education teachers entering schools.
- Given the previous three elements, teachers and coaches are often neither required nor encouraged to continue their educations by attending short-term courses or longer certificated or degree programs in colleges and universities. Even in extreme circumstances when professionals become incompetent, they are rarely dismissed. In fact, teacher/coach evaluations, after an initial probationary period of 1 or 2 years, rarely exist.

Reflecting upon these and other earlier shortcomings in physical education, interscholastic sport, and intramural sport, it is reasonable to conclude that school physical activity programs are in a situation of crisis. All who have a stake in these programs are urged to take action following analysis. The position of physical education classes, along with other facets, can be strengthened from within each school, university-based comparativists can describe, analyze, and compare programs (using the late George Bereday's terminology). Furthermore, research findings must be published and disseminated to people who are in positions to take action. Comparative research is therefore vitally important for the future vibrancy of physical activity in schools.

Conclusion

From reports about physical activity in many countries, it can be seen that many intranational, as well as international, variations exist. Moreover, within one region, state, province, or county, not all program emphases are likely to be the same; most people generally know that the power in many schools, whether formally permitted or informally assumed, lies with the principal. Though principals are more likely to be powerful people in Western or Third World countries, they also may have the same power in Socialist countries. This is not to say that principals in the Soviet Union or the People's Republic of China are given a broad latitude for individual initiative, but some flexible practices may exist depending on local conditions. In many countries also, a substantial minority of students attend private schools, almost all of which vary considerably in such elements as types of activities, allotment of time, program objectives, range of facilities, and basis of leadership when compared to state schools. Consequently, comparative studies must be approached cautiously and researchers must make careful appraisals of the territory under investigation; otherwise, concealed traps often await the unwary, which result in invalid comparisons.

When considering the responsibility of comparativists when examining physical education, interscholastic sport, and intramural sport in schools, it seems reasonable to turn again to the *International Charter of Physical Education and Sport*. Specifically, Articles 6 and 10 may have been addressed to us. They state that "research and evaluation are indispensable components of the development of physical education and sport" and "international cooperation is a prerequisite for the universal and well-balanced promotion of physical education and sport." The way ahead is clear. If we adhere to these articles, the place and importance of comparative study is assured. The challenge to comparativists is to plan systematic studies, whether narrowly or broadly focused, so that we or educational administrators, can make changes based on inductive or deductive rationales. This is a service we can and should provide in education. Our salvation may depend upon it.

References

Anthony, D. (1980). *A strategy for British sport.* London: C. Hurst and Company.

Bennett, B.L., Howell, M.L., & Simri, U. (1975). *Comparative physical education and sport.* Philadelphia: Lea and Febiger.

Bennett, B.L., Howell, M.L., & Simri, U. (1983). *Comparative physical education and sport* (2nd ed.). Philadelphia: Lea and Febiger.

Carre, F.A., Mosher, R.E., & Schutz, R.W. (1981). *British Columbia assessment of physical education.* Unpublished paper: University of British Columbia.

Chandler, T.J.L. (1981). *Physical education and games in Canadian private schools: A comparative analysis.* Unpublished master's thesis, Dalhousie University, Halifax, Nova Scotia.

Clumpner, R. & Smith, G.J. (1983). Interscholastic football: Comparisons in program administration between Canada and the United States. *Proceedings of the FISU Conference–Universiade '83 in association with the 10th HISPA Congress* (pp. 708-718). Edmonton, Canada: University of Alberta.

Davidson, S.A. (1977). *Current status of health, physical education and recreation.* Ottawa: CAHPER.

Demetrovic, E. & Kostka, V. (1980). *Coaches and physical education teachers training in socialist countries.* Prague: Central Committee of the Czechslovak Union of Physical Education.

Department of Physical Education, Ministry of Education. (1980). *Physical education and sports in the Republic of China.* Taipei: Department of Physical Education of the Republic of China.

Duda, J.L. (1984). *A cross-cultural analysis of achievement motivation in sport and the classroom.* Manuscript submitted for publication.

Duda, J.L. & Allison, M.T. (1984). *Variations in value orientations: Race and sex differences in sport and academic domains.* Manuscript submitted for publication.

Fiander, P.R. (1981). The role of extracurricular activities in public senior high schools in Nova Scotia as perceived by the principal. Halifax, Nova Scotia: M.Ed. Thesis, The Atlantic Institute of Education.

General Secretary. (1983, January-February) Action (editorial). *British Journal of Physical Education,* **41**(1), p. 1.

Hardman, K. (1980). The development of physical education in the German Democratic Republic. *Physical Education Review,* **3**(2), 121-136.

Hardman, K. (1981). The development of physical education in West Germany—General background: From occupation to full sovereignty. *Physical Education Review,* **4**(1), 44-60.

Hayward, H. (1984, April). Centennial year brings golden opportunity for membership growth. *Update,* p. 10.

Hendry, L. & Thorpe, A. (1977). Pupils' choice, extracurricular activites: A critique of hierarchical authority. *International Review of Sport Sociology,* **4**(12), 39-49.

Hendry, L.B., & Welsh, J. (1981). Aspects of the hidden curriculum: Teachers' and pupils' perceptions in physical education. *International Review of Sport Sociology,* **4**(16), 27-43.

Hopkins, P. (1978, September). A philosophy of intramurals. *CIRA Bulletin*, 4(1), 1-2.

International Council on Health, Physical Education, and Recreation (ICHPER). (1969). *Physical education in the school curriculum.* Washington, DC: Author.

Jennison, W. (1970). *The concise encyclopedia of sports.* New York: Watts.

Johnson, W. (Ed.). (1966). *Physical education around the world* (Monograph 1). Indianapolis: Phi Epsilon Kappa.

Kane, J.E. (1974). *Physical education in secondary schools: Schools counsel enquiry.* London: MacMillan.

Kenyon, G.S. (1968). *Values held for physical activity by urban secondary school students in Canada, Australia, England and the United States.* Report for the United States Department of Health, Education and Welfare.

Kniker, C.R. (1984). The values of athletics in schools: A continuing debate. In D.S. Eitzen (Ed.), *Sport in contemporary society: An anthology* (2nd ed., pp. 170-182). New York: St. Martin's.

Macintosh, D., & King, A.J.C. (1976). *The role of interschool sports program in Ontario secondary schools: A provincial analysis.* Ontario: Ministry of Education.

Martens, F.L. (1976). *Physical education across Canada.* Unpublished report, Canada: University of Victoria.

McIntosh, P. (1963). *Sport in society.* London: C.A. Watts and Company.

Phillips, J.C. & Schafer, W.E. (1971). Consequences of participation in interscholastic sports: A review prospectus. *Pacific Sociological Review*, 14, 328-338.

Pooley, J.C. (1979). Quantitative and qualitative analysis in comparative physical education and sport. In U. Simri (Ed.), *Proceedings of an international seminar* (pp. 83-93). Israel: Wingate Institute.

Riordan, J. (Ed.). (1981). *Sport under communism* (2nd ed.). Montreal: McGill-Queen's University Press.

Sage, G.H. (1981, April). On limited definitions of equality in sports. *Phi Delta Kappan*, 6(8), 583-585.

Silvennoinen, M. (1982, November 18-21). *On the similarities between the extra-curricular sport activities of Finnish comprehensive school children and the curriculum of physical education.* Paper delivered at the International Symposium on Research in School Physical Education, University of Jyväskylä, Finland.

Snyder, E.E. & Spreitzer, E.A. (1983). *Social aspects of sport* (2nd ed.). New Jersey: Prentice Hall.

Spreitzer, E. & Pugh, M.D. (1973). Interscholastic athletics and educational expectations. *Sociology of Education*, 46, 171-182.

UNESCO. (1979). International charter of physical education and sport. *FIEP Bulletin*, 49(2), 26-30.

Van Lierde, A. & Van Dun, H. (1978). *The sport at school: Survey of the situation in eighteen European countries.* Brussels: Clearing House for Council of Europe.

Varpalotai, A. (1983, July). *Physical education and amateur sport in Hungary: A comparative study.* Paper presented at the CAHPER Annual Conference, Toronto.

Vertinsky, P. (1983, October). The evolving policy of equal curricular opportunity in England: A case study of the implementation of sex equality in physical education. *British Journal of Education Studies, 31*(3), 229–251.

Vertinsky, P., & Cuthbert, J. (1983). Profiles of physical education strategies: A cross-national comparison of English and Canadian Teachers. *International Review of Sport Sociology, 2*(18), 67-81.

CHAPTER 10

Comparative Research in Regard to Physical Activity Within Schools— A View From the Beach

John E. Saunders

The subtitle of this paper is "A view from the beach" because the author perceives himself as a student of pedagogy with an interest in physical education and sport in schools rather than as a comparativist. The author was drawn to a major involvement in the UNESCO regional survey of physical education and sport in Asia and the Pacific from this background. This survey was undertaken during 1982 as a part of the preliminary work toward the third UNESCO interdisciplinary regional meeting of experts in physical education and sport. The meeting addressed the application of the "Sport for All" principle to the socioeconomic and cultural conditions of Asia and the Pacific region and attracted participants from 18 of the 29 member-states of that region. This paper, which addresses the issue of the comparative research in regard to physical activity within schools, will therefore focus on the context of Asia and the Pacific, and specifically the UNESCO survey data. It will first outline the nature and process of the survey itself. Then a necessarily selective view of school-based physical activity in the region will be presented through a descriptive analysis of some relevant data. A preliminary comparison of two selected variables will then be undertaken using the process of juxtaposition. Finally, in a general conclusion some brief reflections will be made on the nature of the comparative process and the present situation in the English language literature concerning comparative physical education and sport in schools, and finally on the pressures toward a separation of comparative physical education from comparative sport studies.

The UNESCO Regional Survey

The UNESCO region of Asia and the Pacific comprises 29 member-states in total. Of these, 21 participated in the regional survey.

Unit of Analysis

What is immediately clear is the immense range of traditions and cultures represented in this group. With such a large list, Stensaasen's (1979) plea for cultural settings roughly similar and/or similar in characteristics of particular significance to the problem under study becomes a wild fantasy. The unit of analysis, if we wish to seek comparisons from such a data base, includes the largest nation in the world (USSR), the world's most populated country (China), a highly urbanized modern city stage (Singapore), a largely rural community containing over one quarter of the world's languages together with people who have had virtually no contact with 20th century civilization (Papua, New Guinea), a huge island continent (Australia), and a collection of tiny coral atolls and islands (Maldives). It seems as if every dimension of every geographical and sociocultural variable must be represented in such a sample.

Validity of Data

Data for the survey were gathered by means of an extensive questionnaire mailed to the national UNESCO commissions of the member states. The questionnaire addressed four spheres of concern—primary schools, secondary schools, tertiary and further education, and the community—and sought information in four areas of inquiry about physical education and sport—its organization and administration, its planning and implementation of curriculum, its facilities and equipment, and its teacher (or coach/leader) preparation. Only selected data concerning primary and secondary schools are discussed in this paper. UNESCO national commissions were asked to identify appropriate experts to respond for each sphere of concern. The source of the data is thus the informed judgment and knowledge of leading spokespersons for each country's education system. As such, the data carry the authority of a semiofficial statement but are also subject to the weaknesses of official perspectives. For example, the data are likely to reflect the intended or stated curriculum rather than the actual transactions that occur. Also, the fact that a single perspective is presented of course compounds the unit of analysis problem of assuming homogeneity among a collection of states as rich and varied in heritage as those of the Republic of India, or within components of a nation as culturally diverse as the various coastal and highland people of Papua, New Guinea.

Existing Data Bases

Despite their patent limitations, the data generated in a "broadbrush" study such as this do have the advantage of allowing for simultaneous and balanced comparison in which information from one country can be matched with comparable information from the other countries in the study (Bereday, 1967). Data currently readily available in the English language concerning physical education and sport in the countries of this region were not of a comparative nature, but rather were of the kind referred to by Howell and Howell (1979) as *first order* or *primary studies* (i.e., studies of a particular country or culture that provide fundamental information concerning the practice of physical education and sport in that society). Unfortunately, such studies are not only asynchronous, but, for the most part, lack a common and systematic categorization of data as a basis for further analysis and comparison.

Descriptive Analysis

As a basic prerequisite to the most simplistic of interpretive analyses, a brief outline of each respondent nation was drawn up in terms of population, gross national product (GNP), geography, economy, and culture (Saunders & Jobling, 1982). Where precise quantification was sought, comparable figures were often difficult to find in this exercise, particularly, for example, for GNP that ranged on 1978 figures from Nepal's $120 per head (U.S. dollars) to Japan's $8,800 a head (U.S. dollars). The extent of some of the contrasts under the other headings has already been noted. Cultural and ethnic diversity is a feature of many nations in this group; the population of the USSR, for example, comprises over 200 different ethnic groups speaking up to 180 different languages and dialects. Yet at another end of the continuum, Japan has few local variants of the Japanese language and foreigners constitute less than 1% of the country's population. The great religions of the world—Hinduism, Buddhism, Muslim, and Christianity—all exist prominently and in various mixes in this region. These clearly have a considerable and varying influence on social and educational policy and attitude, not least in the area of sport and play.

Physical Education and Sport in the Curriculum

Aims and Objectives

Respondents were asked initially to indicate their nations' general aims for both primary and secondary education and then to detail aims for primary and secondary physical education and sport. Responses to these questions were far from complete. Iran, Singapore, and Western Samoa failed to complete their responses to either section, whereas China, Indonesia, Mongolia, New Guinea, Sri Lanka, Tonga, and the USSR failed to respond to the general aims section. Bangladesh failed to respond to the primary physical education and sport section.

It is interesting to speculate as to the reason(s) for this irregular pattern of response. The rational curriculum model (Taba, 1962) suggests that curriculum design starts from a broad statement of educational goals and develops through various operational divisions, such as subject areas, to more specific goals and objectives. If physical education and sport is to be seen as an integral part of the educational process, then its aims and objectives would need to reflect and be consistent with the general aims for education and schooling. Whitehead and Hendry (1976), writing in the United Kingdom (UK) context, have commented on the perceived marginality of physical education teachers. This feeling of being "separate" and "different" in the school curriculum by the teachers might, it appears, be pervasive (compare Nettleton's (1979) observations in his study of the role perceptions of physical education teachers in an Australian context). A marginal and peripheral role for physical education and sport in Bangladesh, for example, would seem likely, given the aim of primary education as being "to give the children the knowledge of reading, writing and arithmetic and help them to develop themselves as fruitful citizens of the country."

This might explain a nil response for the aims of primary physical education and sport. At the secondary level, education for citizenship is further emphasized: "To educate pupils to be worthy citizens of their country." Thus physical education and sport becomes merely an extension of general education with, it seems, no specific or intrinsic value or contribution, that is, "to educate pupils in general education keeping an eye on their physical, mental, emotional and social development, and to make them worthy citizens of their country."

Those general aims that were expressed varied from the broad-ranging and comprehensive (e.g., Australia, India, Japan) to the more concise and succinct (Bangladesh). Yet it is hard to surpass the honesty and directness of the Maldives response, "To pass the London GCE '0' level exam," which the reader suspects is closer to the actual curriculum than some of the more convoluted replies of the more "sophisticated" nations. Perfectly consistent with such a general aim is this country's response concerning the aims of physical education and sport—"There are no aims for physical education and sport in secondary schools"—because no London GCE "0" level exam exists in this subject. Again, the reader may have a suspicion that what is made explicit here is a reality of the hidden curriculum in some cases where the rhetoric of the intended curriculum would suggest otherwise.

Sifting through the general aims for primary and secondary schooling, three distinct emphases seem to reappear which can best be classified as education for citizenship, education for individual development, and vocational education. Some nations appear to have a single emphasis (e.g., Bangladesh and Turkey for education for citizenship; Australia and New Zealand for education for individual development), but more commonly, a combination of emphases are apparent (e.g., Japan, Korea, and Nepal for vocational education and education for citizenship).

In reviewing aims for physical education and sport, the most striking aspect is the almost universal emphasis on health as an outcome in its own right or specifically associated with physical fitness (Australia, Nepal). Bangladesh and Sri Lanka provide the only exceptions; the latter has purely skill-based objectives at the primary level and skill-, participation-, and knowledge-based aims at the secondary level. The development of skill in one form or another was identified as an aim by 58% of the respondents and was the next most popular category after health. Knowledge and understanding was mentioned almost as frequently, particularly at the secondary level, referring either to knowledge of games and sports or of bodily health and fitness. Other aims mentioned in several responses were concerned with, in order of frequency, attitude development, social outcomes, and creativity/expression. Physical education and sport as an aspect of the quality of life received mention from Japan and Korea.

In general terms as far as consistency between broad educational aims and the more specific aims of physical education and sport are concerned, the picture was somewhat mixed. Thus an emphasis on social and vocational outcomes is mirrored fairly well in the following example from Thailand:

Aims for Primary Education

- education for all
- children learn the basic tools and skills to earn their livelihood after they finish school
- education for national unity

Aims for Primary Physical Education and Sport

- to promote good health in school children
- to train essential and basic sports skills
- to enhance group relationships among children
- to train for desirable, social and mental values

However, the match in the next sample from Malaysia is not as clear:

Aims for Primary Education

Development of
- basic skills of communication
- civic competencies—attitude of responsibility and co-operation and a commitment in national unity and solidarity
- physical, intellectual and emotional development

Aims for Primary Physical Education and Sport

- satisfaction and joyful participation in activities that are stimulating and filled with opportunities for self expression
- the development of a healthy organism and physical qualities
- the acquisition of a useful vocabulary of locomotive and basic games skills as well as motor control through large body movements

This apparently "loose matching" is not uncommon. It might suggest the same sort of conceptual confusion previously suggested as a feature of the Australian context (Saunders, 1979); such conceptual confusion is both cause and effect of the subject area's frequently observed peripheral status in the school curriculum. A resultant hypothesis might be that the degree of match between general school aims and the specific subject aims is a good predictor of that subject's status in the curriculum. At the very least, the degree of match is likely to provide a far more powerful variable than only the identification of the specific subject aims, which "are often vague, all things to all men and pure rhetoric'' (Taylor, 1984, personal communication).

The Subject Matter of Physical Education and Sport Programs

Despite the breadth and variety of aims, a reviewer cannot but be struck by the commonality of the concepts of schooling and physical education and sport in schools that appears to exist across a diversity of contexts. This 'commonality' is at its most evident in describing the subject matter of physical education and sport in school programs. However, before passing on to a consideration of the listings of activities that were provided, it is illuminating to first consider subject matter as it is specified through aims. As observed above, subject matter in Bangladesh is observed only as an aspect of general education and is not identified in specific terms. In the survey as a whole at the primary level, the subject matter was specified most often as games, then as sports, but also as movement, athletics, physical exercises, practical skills, dances, and outdoor activities. At the secondary level the subject matter is more frequently characterized as sport or sports but still also as games, and also as movement recreation, athletics, physical culture, and exercise. This lack of consensus reflects not just diversity as a result of different traditions and needs and so forth, but it also reflects the confusion in many 'western societies' alluded to earlier as to how to characterize physical education in the school curriculum. Such confusion has been identified in Australia as arising in part from the tension between educational goals and the manifest problems of the highly visible world of modern day competitive sport (Saunders & Jobling, 1983).

However, when the actual list of activities providing the subject matter of the program is reviewed, support exists for the view that we have a semantic problem rather than a conceptual issue. At the secondary school level, Team Sports (of the familiar 'international' variety) dominates the lists, followed by Athletics (Track and Field), Gymnastics, and Individual Sports. Clearly sport education is the norm in substance if not in statement. A strong suggestion exists, however, that primary physical education is viewed as different in kind from the secondary program. This comes from the predominance of minor games (modified games/games skill activities). But the subsequent ranking of team sports, athletics (track and field), swimming, and gymnastics follows very much the secondary profile. If there is a difference, it would seem that the role of primary physical education is to lay the basis for an ongoing sport education. Movement, dance, and health, it seems, are at the periphery in the world of primary physical education, as are theoretical studies, recreation activities, outdoor pursuits, and health in secondary physical education.

Learning Experiences

Information concerning some organizational features of the learning experiences in physical education and sport was sought for both primary and secondary schools (see Tables 1 and 2). As far as the average number of hours per week devoted to this area of the curriculum is concerned, it is pertinent to observe that the 2 hr 12 min per week averaged for both primary and secondary students is less than the minimum allocation of a daily period necessary for the achievement of even modest objectives and less than the target sought by the international professional organizations (ICHPER, 1984). The figures for both primary and secondary schools are very similar, although the primary figures vary more. There is a mixed pattern; some systems allocate more time in the primary schools, others allocate more in the secondary schools. A similar picture emerges as far as class sizes are concerned. The primary and secondary means are identical at 39 and there is a pattern of both increasing numbers in secondary classes vis-a-vis primary and the reverse. Class sizes

Table 1   Some Features of Primary School Physical Education and Sport Learning Experiences

Country	Average no. of hrs/wk.	Average class size	Co-educational	Provision for disabled	Provision for superior performers
Australia	2.25	30	Yes	Yes	Yes
Bangladesh	5	*	No	No	No
China	2	45	Yes	No	No
India	4	30-40	Yes	No	Yes
Indonesia	.75	45-50	Yes	No	No
Iran	2	40	No	Yes	Yes
Japan	3	34	Yes	Yes	No
Korea	3	60	Yes	Yes	Yes
Malaysia	2.25	50	Yes	Yes	Yes
Maldives	1	34	No	No	No
Mongolia	2	25-30	Yes	Yes	Yes
Nepal	1.5	50	Yes	No	No
New Zealand	1.5	30-35	Yes	Yes	Yes
Papua, New Guinea	2.5	40	Yes	No	No
Philippines	.75	30	Yes	No	No
Singapore	2.5	35-40	Yes	*	*
Sri Lanka	5	40-50	No	No	Yes
Thailand	2	40	Yes	Yes	Yes
Tonga	1.75	30	No	No	No
Turkey	1	30-40	Yes	No	No
USSR	2	*	Yes	Yes	Yes
Western Samoa	1	*	*	*	*

Note.   * = No response to this item.

Table 2 Some Features of Secondary School Physical Education and Sport Learning Experiences

Country	Average no. of hrs/wk.	Average class size	Co-educational	Provision for disabled	Provision for superior performers
Australia	2.5	25-30	Yes	No	Yes
Bangladesh	5	*	No	No	No
China	2	45	No	No	Yes
India	2	30-40	No	No	Yes
Indonesia	1.5	45-50	Yes	No	Yes
Iran	2	40	No	Yes	Yes
Japan	3	*	Yes	Yes	No
Korea	3	60	Yes	Yes	Yes
Malaysia	3	45	No	Yes	Yes
Maldives	1.5	*	No	No	No
Mongolia	2	25-30	Yes	Yes	Yes
Nepal	1	50	Yes	No	No
New Zealand	3	30	No	Yes	Yes
Papua, New Guinea	2	40	Yes	No	No
Philippines	1	50	No	Yes	Yes
Singapore	3.5	35-40	Yes[a]	*	*
Sri Lanka	2	20-50	No	No	Yes
Thailand	2	35-40	Yes	Yes	Yes
Tonga	2	30	No	No	No
Turkey	2	30	Yes	No	No
USSR	2	*	Yes	Yes	Yes
Western Samoa	1	*	*	*	*

Note. * = No response to this item.
[a]In some schools and at "A" level (matriculation age app. Grades 11-12).

indicate the need for considerable equipment if adequate learning time is to be offered to pupils in the skills of the various activities.

In considering the remaining aspects of learning experiences, it can be seen that a tendency toward coeducational physical education and sport is firmly entrenched at the primary level (16/5), but at the secondary level the situation is evenly divided (11/10). The likelihood of there being provision for disabled children is slightly less than even, but the talented secondary child is more likely to have provision made for him or her to develop his or her special talents.

Facilities and Budget

The most noble of aims, however, can be brought back to the hard ground of reality when the availability of resources needed to do the job is limited or nonexistent. The survey was able to underline the limited nature of human resources; specialist physical education knowledge was found to be available to primary children in the region only very rarely. Even at the secondary school level, only six nations suggested that the appointment of specialists to schools was a universal practice (Australia, Iran, Japan, Korea, Mongolia, USSR).

Information concerning the availability of "capital" facilities for the majority of schools must of course be a generalization of the greatest order. However, responses indicated that, in the majority of situations, the only thing that pupils could hope for in their physical education classes was for a 'grassy field' or other open area. Even this would be unavailable in a significant number of cases. Covered areas of any description were generally restricted to Japan, Korea, Mongolia, Singapore, and the USSR together with Australia and New Zealand (at the secondary school level only). Swimming pools were generally available in Australia, Japan, Korea, and New Zealand (primary only) and Singapore (secondary only).

For purposes of comparison, an attempt was made to assess the average annual budget for physical education and sport facilities and equipment for schools. This only proved to emphasize the difficulties of real accounting in this area. However, as a rule-of-thumb measure, respondents were asked to identify the number of balls a teacher might normally expect to be able to use if he or she were teaching an activity such as soccer to a class. In over 50% of the responses, one ball per class of 40–50 children was the answer at the primary level. What price the "opportunity to learn basic physical skills" with such a level of provision? At the secondary school level, however, one ball per five children was the mode, providing a further example of the generally superior provision at the secondary school level. This is despite the fundamental importance of the primary years for skill and attitude development. However, in general inadequate funding for physical education and sport programs, or, at the very least, low-priority funding within school budgets remains a common concern of administrators throughout the region, irrespective of their countries' relative financial status.

The Organization of Interschool Sport

Sport education can occur as a curricular activity, characteristically with an emphasis on instruction and frequently as part of a physical education program. It can also occur as a part of the extracurricular activity of a school; in such a context it can involve intramural activity or more formally organized activity between schools. In Australia there has been a growth in recent years toward a more formalized and structured interschool sport system—the foundation of a National School Sports Council in 1975. In Europe, a European School Sport Federation has been in existence since 1963 and was absorbed into the International School Sports Federation in 1972 (Bennett, Howell, & Simri, 1983). It was thus determined to investigate the current status of interschool sport in the region; the results are summarized in Table 3 for primary schools and in Table 4 for secondary schools. From these tables it can be seen that, at both

Table 3 Organization of Interschool Sport (Primary)

Country	Opportunity for inter-school sport	Approximate % children given opportunity	Approximate number of sports offered	Approximate number of school sporting associations	Nat'l/Dist. championships in majority of sports
Australia	Most schools	57	10	10	Yes
Bangladesh	Few schools	2	3	None	Yes
China	Few schools	5	2	None	No
India	Few schools	1	1-2	None	No
Indonesia	Most schools	15	2	2	Yes
Iran	Most schools	15-20	1	1	Yes
Japan	All schools	0.6	20	None	*
Korea	About half	(very few)	2-3	None	Yes
Malaysia	All schools	11	9	9	Yes
Maldives	None	None	None	None	No
Mongolia	All schools	60	6-8	6-8	Yes
Nepal	None	None	None	None	No
New Zealand	Most schools	15-20	10	10 (plus)	No
Papua, New Guinea	Few schools	5	*	None	No
Philippines	None	None	None	None	No
Singapore	All schools	80	5	*	Yes
Sri Lanka	Most schools	10	10	18	Yes
Thailand	About half	*	2-3	None	Yes
Tonga	Few schools	65	3	None	No
Turkey	About half	30	9	9	Yes
USSR	*	20-25	*	up to 10%ᵃ	Yes
Western Samoa	Few schools	*	9-10	*	No

Note. * = No response to this item.
ᵃAnswer was given in percentage rather than number.

Table 4 Organization of Interschool Sport (Secondary)

Country	Opportunity for inter-school sport	Approximate % children given opportunity	Approximate number of sports offered	Approximate number of school sporting associations	Nat'l/Dist championships in majority of sports
Australia	Most schools	58	12-18	12-17	Yes
Bangladesh	Few schools	10-15	5-6	5-6	Yes
China	About half	5	5	5	Yes
India	Most schools	3	10	10	Yes
Indonesia	Most schools	30	8	8	Yes
Iran	All schools	10-15	12	12	Yes
Japan	All schools	21	30	30	Yes
Korea	Most schools	5	10	10	Yes
Malaysia	All schools	20	16	16	Yes
Maldives	None	None	None	None	No
Mongolia	All schools	60	12	12	Yes
Nepal	Few schools	10	3	None	Yes
New Zealand	Most schools	30	20	10	Yes
Papua, New Guinea	Most schools	20	6	1	No
Philippines	About half	10	5	None	No
Singapore	All schools	80	18	18	Yes
Sri Lanka	Most schools	10	24+	18	Yes
Thailand	Most schools	30	4-5	*	Yes
Tonga	Most schools	40	6	6	Yes
Turkey	Most schools	30	9	9	Yes
USSR	All schools	25-30	*	*	Yes
Western Samoa	All schools	80	5	5	Yes

Note. * = No response to this item.

primary and secondary levels, interschool sport is almost a universal phenomenon, although it is present in varying degrees in the different countries. The Maldives, Philippines, and Nepal alone have no interschool sport at the primary level and the Maldives alone have none at the secondary level. Both the breadth of participation and the extent of involvement is clearly greater at the secondary level. Virtually all of the sports offered at the secondary level have a superordinate school sporting association, created presumably to administer competitions and so forth. National championships are the norm in the majority of sports. When it comes to an estimate of the actual number of children involved in the process, however, this varies considerably from the 80% suggested by Singapore and Western Samoa to the 3% suggested by India. The status and practice of extracurricular sport in schools is clearly one of a number of areas inviting more careful study and documentation in their own right.

Juxtaposition of Data and Preliminary Comparisons

In presenting the information so far, a tabular approach has been used to place data in juxtaposition on a country-by-country basis. Bereday (1967) described *juxtaposition* as ''the preliminary matching of data from different countries to prepare them for comparison'' (1967, p. 171). It may be seen then as an initial step toward simultaneous comparisons. In a multinational study such as this, however, the purpose is to seek general trends from the comparisons rather than to make detailed and ecologically sensitive comparisons. Thus a correlational matrix was extablished to identify possible relationships between four general factors, namely per capita GNP, population size, and two measures of commitment to education—school leaving age and percentage of involvement in tertiary education—and selected measures from this study. The measures selected had to be at an interval or ratio level of scaling and were the following: opportunity for interschool sport on a school-by-school basis, approximate percentage of children given the opportunity for interschool sports, number of sports offered, number of school sporting associations (for both primary and secondary levels), and average hours per week spent in curricular physical education and sport (primary and secondary).

Population size demonstrated no relationships of magnitude (i.e., more than .5) with any of the variables describing school physical education and sport programs. A similar picture emerged for school leaving age. Percentage of involvement in tertiary education, however, showed relationships of .50 with opportunity for secondary school interschool sport, .54 with opportunity for primary school sport, .66 with the number of sports offered at secondary level, and .58 with GNP. GNP demonstrated the greatest relationships with a correlation of .63 with opportunity for primary school sport, .83 with numbers of secondary school sports offered, .66 with numbers of primary school sports offered, and .72 with numbers of secondary school sport associations. Other results in the matrix showed a strong tendency for school sports offered in secondary schools to be governed by appropriate school sporting associations. This was less likely to be the case at the primary school level. Table 5 shows

Table 5   Juxtaposition of GNP with selected features of school physical education and sport practice

Country	GNP $US per capita 1978/1979 figures	Opportunity for inter-school sport (Primary)	Approximate no. of primary school sports offered	Opportunity for inter-school sports (Secondary)	Approximate no. of secondary school sports offered	No. of secondary school sports associations	Average hours of primary school sport and P.E./week
Japan	8,800	All schools	20	All schools	30	30	3
Australia	7,920	Most schools	10	Most schools	15	15	2.25
Singapore	6,515[a]	All schools	5	All schools	18	18	2.5
New Zealand	4,790	Most schools	10	Most schools	20	10	1.5
Iran	2,024	Most schools	1	All schools	12	12	2
Malaysia	1,825	All schools	9	All schools	16	16	2.25
Korea	1,308	About half	3	Most schools	10	10	3
Turkey	1,210	About half	9	Most schools	6	9	1
Mongolia	940	All schools	7	All schools	12	12	2
Philippines	620	None	None	About half	5	None	.75
Papua, New Guinea	560	Few schools	No response	Most schools	6	1	2.5
Thailand	463	About half	3	Most schools	5	No response	2
Tonga	430	Few schools	3	Most schools	6	6	1.75
Indonesia	360	Most schools	2	Most schools	8	8	.75
Western Samoa	350	Few schools	10	All schools	5	5	1
China	260	Few schools	2	About half	5	5	2
Sri Lanka	211	Most schools	10	Most schools	12	18	5
Maldives	200	None	None	No	None	None	1
India	140[c]	Few schools	2	Most schools	10	10	4
Nepal	120	None	None	Few schools	3	None	1.15
Bangladesh	60[b]	Few schools	3	Few schools	6	6	5
USSR	No figures available	No response	No response	All schools	No response	No response	2

[a]1980 figure.
[b]1970 figure.
[c]1974 figure.

the data in juxtaposition with countries listed in order of the GNP figures obtained.

Data were obtained at the nominal level only for the following aspects: physical education and sport learning experiences and curriculum planning procedures for physical education and sport. The variables considered are listed here:

Learning experiences

- Coeducational
- Provision for disabled
- Provision for superior performers

Curriculum planning procedures

- Existence of stated aims at system level
- Existence of stated aims at school level
- Existence of syllabus at system level
- Existence of written work program at school level

The relationship of these variables with the opportunity for interschool sport was examined by use of chi-square contingency tables. Relationships were identified in order of strength, between opportunity for primary interschool sport, and the following:

- Provision for the disabled ($p > .001$)
- Existence of school-based work program ($p > .001$)
- Coeducational learning experiences ($p > .01$)
- Provision for superior performers ($p > .01$)
- Existence of a syllabus at the system level ($p > .01$) (though not with the existence of stated aims at the individual school level!)

Relationships were identified, in order of strengths, between opportunity for interschool sport at the secondary level and the following:

- Existence of syllabus at system level ($p > .001$)
- Provision for the disabled ($p > .001$)
- Provision for superior performers ($p > .01$)
- Existence of written work programs ($p > .01$)
- Existence of stated aims at the school level ($p > .01$)
- Coeducational learning experiences ($p > .05$)

The data are reproduced in juxtaposition in Tables 6 and 7, with countries categorized according to provision of opportunity for interschool sport.

Such comparisons as those identified earlier represent an ordering of the data to seek for relationships. Statistics are a tool for determining the strength of such relationships. This level then is descriptive-analytical, but it cannot attempt to explain the relationships observed. This must

Table 6 Juxtaposition of Opportunity for Primary School Sport with Selected Learning Experiences and Curriculum Planning Procedures

Opportunity for interschool sport (primary)	Country	Provision for disabled	Existence of written work programs (school level)	Coeducational learning experiences	Provision for superior performers	Existence of syllabus (system level)	Existence of stated aims (school level)
All Schools	Japan	Yes	Yes	Yes	No	Yes	Yes
	Malaysia	Yes	Yes	Yes	Yes	Yes	Yes
	Mongolia	Yes	Yes	Yes	Yes	Yes	No
	Singapore	*	Yes	Yes	*	Yes	Yes
Most Schools	Australia	Yes	Yes	Yes	Yes	Yes	Yes
	Indonesia	No	No	Yes	No	Yes	Yes
	Iran	Yes	No	No	Yes	Yes	No
	New Zealand	Yes	Yes	Yes	Yes	Yes	Yes
	Sri Lanka	No	No	No	Yes	Yes	Yes
About half	Korea	Yes	Yes	Yes	Yes	Yes	Yes
	Thailand	Yes	No	Yes	Yes	Yes	*
	Turkey	No	No	Yes	No	Yes	No
Few schools	Bangladesh	No	Yes	No	No	No	No
	China	No	No	Yes	No	*	*
	India	No	No	Yes	Yes	Yes	No
	Papua, New Guinea	No	Yes	Yes	No	Yes	No
	Tonga	No	No	No	No	No	No
	Western Samoa	*	*	*	*	*	*
No school this item	Maldives	No	No	No	No	No	No
	Nepal	No	No	Yes	No	Yes	No
	Philippines	No	No	Yes	No	No	Yes
	USSR	Yes	Yes	Yes	Yes	Yes	Yes

Note. * = No response to this item.

Table 7 Juxtaposition of Opportunity for Secondary School Sport with Selected Learning Experiences and Curriculum Planning Procedures

Opportunity for interschool sport (secondary)	Country	Existence of syllabus (system level)	Provision for the disabled	Provision for superior performers	Existence of written work programs (school level)	Existence of stated aims (school level)	Coeducational learning experiences
All Schools	Iran	Yes	Yes	Yes	No	*	No
	Japan	Yes	Yes	No	Yes	Yes	Yes
	Malaysia	Yes	Yes	Yes	Yes	No	No
	Mongolia	Yes	Yes	Yes	Yes	No	Yes
	Singapore	Yes	*	*	Yes	Yes	Yes[a]
	USSR	No	Yes	Yes	Yes	Yes	Yes
	Western Samoa	*	*	*	*	*	*
Most Schools	Australia	Yes	No	Yes	Yes	Yes	Yes
	India	Yes	No	Yes	No	No	No
	Indonesia	Yes	No	Yes	No	Yes	Yes
	Korea	Yes	Yes	Yes	Yes	Yes	Yes
	New Zealand	Yes	Yes	Yes	Yes	Yes	No
	Papua, New Guinea	Yes	No	No	Yes	No	Yes
	Sri Lanka	Yes	Yes	Yes	No	No	No
	Thailand	Yes	No	No	No	No	Yes
	Tonga	Yes	No	No	No	Yes	No
	Turkey	Yes	No	No	No	No	Yes
About half	China	No	No	Yes	No	*	No
	Philippines	Yes	Yes	Yes	No	Yes	No
Few schools	Bangladesh	No	No	No	Yes	*	No
	Nepal	Yes	No	No	No	No	Yes
No school	Maldives	No	No	No	No	No	No

[a]In some and at 'A' level

Note. * = No response to this item.

await the collection of further, more ecologically complete data which may be used to test the hypotheses that have been generated from broad-based quantitative data such as this.

Conclusion

The following section consists of some concluding remarks on the international status of comparative research in regard to physical activity in schools. First, the nature of the comparative task is intimidating. After a brief trespass on the beach, that awareness of the daunting nature of the task is certainly not diminished—rather it is enhanced. Yet the author feels a sense of uplifted spirit from the experience rather than the more usual sense of despondency at having overreached oneself. In seeking to explain this, the reason must lie in the reformist perspective and impulse that is so much a part of the history of comparative education (Koehl, 1977). Educators, by their very nature, have an interest in examining good practice and becoming aware of what others do. In short, the very process of comparison involves a reevaluation of one's own perspective and an increased awareness of the conceptual framework through which one interprets reality.

It is precisely this tradition which makes the comparative studies area so empathetic for the student of pedagogy. Lauwerys (1965) put it in more contemporary terms when he talked about comparative education as an "action research" form. By all means, comparativists and researchers should seek for truth and more exact scientific methods in the classroom; but both groups of scientists should be prepared to glory in, rather than eschew, their reformist tradition. It is hard to argue with Stretton even today when he says, "Comparison is strongest as a choosing and provoking, not a proving, device: a system for questioning, not for answering" (1969, p. 247). While we can appreciate the forces that drive us to justification through the scientific method, might it not be time for a little more honesty and realism in this area?

As to the existing status of the field, Pooley (1979) lamented 6 years ago that it was rare to find truly comparative papers. The situation is little changed today. As far as physical activity in schools is concerned, however, there has emerged over the last few years a number of studies in the English language alone which invite secondary analysis for comparative purposes. Macintosh and King (1976) in Canada, Hendry (1978) in Scotland, Williams (1981; 1982) in New Zealand, and Saunders and Jobling (1983) in Australia have all produced empirically based studies in the area of sport in schools. In addition, 1982 saw the publication of a 25-nation study on extracurricular school sport undertaken by the Council of Europe in collaboration with the International School Sports Federation (Van Lierde, 1982).

Also, in classroom research on the teaching of physical education, there is growing evidence of a wealth of primary data that can lay the basis for increased comparative study. Empirical data relating to teaching behavior, learning behavior, and teaching/learning interactions have been reported in English from a number of cultural settings. Comparable and sometimes even identical coding systems have been used and comparisons already drawn concerning the commonality of research findings in this area between Belgium and the U.S. (Pieron, 1980). As far as methodology is concerned, "meta-analysis" or "techniques for the formal analysis of analyses" (Glass, 1976) offer a promising means for the further statistical treatment of such studies in a specifically comparative framework.

Finally to the future—the author would like to conclude with a plea and a prediction, each linked to the other. The plea is for greater attention to pedagogical studies. The impetus for comparative studies in physical education and sport has come from the historical/narrative approach. Even in comparative education itself it seems that the emphasis has been on the comparative sociology, the comparative politics, and the comparative economics of education (Koehl, 1977). While the study of the curriculum and the focus on teaching have become the centralizing component of education itself, now is surely the time to return to "the (true) discipline base." For potentially there may be a large number of trespassers to the shore of comparative study. As argued earlier, researchers into teaching are already adopting a comparative pose as they compare classrooms, teachers, and pupils not only from Florida to Massachusetts, from Gloucester to Yorkshire, and from Liège to Ostend, but also across national borders.

This leads to the prediction. Failure to reestablish pedagogical paradigms at the heart of research in comparative sport and physical education could lead to a dichotomizing of the field. Such a prediction is based on the perceived development of the subdiscipline model for physical education (Henry, 1964) over the last 20 years. Lewy (1979) made an important observation in describing the state of the art 6 years ago:

> Research in Physical Education established its own conceptual and organisational framework and emerged as an enterprise detached even from the umbrella protection of the loosely organized educational research community. . . . Research in physical education is concerned with the school and the school life too, but the frame of reference is not the school. Its focus became the phenomenon of sport with all its manifestations. (p. 7)

Those researchers who remained involved with physical education in schools became increasingly concerned at this diverging focus and in recent years have been reestablishing their links within the education discipline. Those whose major concern has been sport studies, however, increasingly have adopted the paradigms of the "mainstream" social sciences and journeyed increasingly further from their former colleagues. The message may be unduly pessimistic, but comparative sport studies seem to better describe the majority of comparative studies in our joint field, particularly in recent times (Bennett, 1982). Yet a significant value for comparative physical education has been identified—a fertile ground already tilled for future sowing and reaping. The landscape beyond offers considerable temptation for the visitor to the beach to stay and explore.

Let us work for continued strong links between education and sport, and the comparative process.

Acknowledgments

This paper was written while the author undertook a special studies program at the School of Education, University of Exeter, United Kingdom. Grateful acknowledgment is therefore made of the support of the School of Education and its director, Professor Ted Wragg. Particular thanks are due to Vic Ambler, Dr. Bill Taylor, and Dick Fisher (of West London Institute of Higher Education) for their comments on an earlier draft of this paper; thanks also to Sally Williams for her skill and patience in preparing the manuscript.

References

Bennett, B.L. (1982). What's new around the world in comparative physical education and sport. *Comparative Physical Education and Sport,* **11**, 7–12.

Bennett, B.L., Howell, M.L., & Simri, U. (1983). *Comparative physical education and sport* (2nd ed.). Philadelphia: Lea and Febiger.

Bereday, G.Z.F. (1967). Reflections on comparative methodology in education 1964-1966. *Comparative Education,* **3**, 168-187.

Glass, G.V. (1976). Primary, secondary and meta-analysis of research. *Educational Researcher,* **5**, 3–8.

Hendry, L.B. (1978). *Three dimensions of adolescence: School, sport and leisure.* London: Lepus Books.

Henry, F.M. (1964). Physical education: An academic discipline. *Journal of Health, Physical Education and Recreation,* **35**, 32-33.

Howell, M.L. & Howell, R.A. (1979). Research in comparative physical education and sport. In U. Simri (Ed.), *Comparative physical education and sport* (pp. 94–118). Netanya, Israel: Wingate Institute of Physical Education and Sport.

International council for Health, Physical Education and Recreation (1984). *Resolutions—XXVI Anniversary World Congress.* Netanya, Israel: Wingate Institute of Physical Education and Sport.

Koehl, R. (1977, June/October). The comparative study of education: Prescription and practice. *Comparative Education Review,* 177–194.

Lauwerys, J.A. (1965). The place of comparative education in the training of teachers. In *Physical education yearbook.* London: P.E.A.

Lewy, A. (1979). Research in physical education and its place within the framework of research on school learning. In U. Simri (Ed.), *Comparative physical education and sport* (pp. 7–13). Netanya, Israel: Wingate Institute of Physical Education and Sport.

Macintosh, D., & King, A.J.C. (1976). *The role of interschool sports programs in Ontario secondary schools.* Toronto: Ontario Ministry of Education.

Nettleton, B. (1979). Role perceptions of physical education teachers. In J. Emmel, D.D. Molyneux, N.R. Wadrop (Eds.), *Values into action* (pp. 73-79). Kingswood, South Australia: ACHPER.

Pièron, M. (1980). *From interaction analysis to research on teaching effectiveness: An overview of studies from the University of Liège.* Unpublished manuscript, Ohio State University, Columbus.

Pooley, J.C. (1979). Quantitative and qualitative analysis in comparative physical education and sport. In U. Simri (Ed.), *Comparative physical education and sport* (pp. 83-93). Netanya, Israel: Wingate Institute of Physical Education and Sport.

Saunders, J.E. (1979). Teacher preparation—Introduction and position statement. In J. Emmel, D.D. Molyneux, & N.R. Wadrop (Eds.), *Values into action* (pp. 159–160). Kingswood, South Australia: ACHPER.

Saunders, J.E. & Jobling, I.F. (1982). *The current status of physical education and "sport for all" in the region of Asia and the Pacific* (Report to UNESCO, Contract no. 515.809). Australia: University of Queensland.

Saunders, J.E. & Jobling, I.F. (1983). *Sport in education.* Kingswood, South Australia: ACHPER.

Stensaasen, S. (1979). Problems of method in comparative physical education. In U. Simri (Ed.), *Comparative physical education and sport* (pp. 51-58). Netanya, Israel: Wingate Institute of Physical Education and Sport.

Taba, H. (1962). *Curriculum development, theory and practice.* New York: Harcourt Brace and World.

Van Lierde, A. (1982). *The extra-curricular school sport.* Brussels: Clearing House for Council of Europe.

Whitehead, N. & Hendry, L.B. (1976). *Teaching physical education in England: Description and analysis.* London: Lepus Books.

Williams, L.R.T. (1981). *Attitudes of selected New Zealand school pupils towards physical education.* Wellington: Department of Education.

Williams, L.R.T. (1982). *Teachers of physical education: Their attitudes and perceptions.* Wellington: Department of Education.

CHAPTER 11

Physical Education in Schools in the Federal Republic of Germany: A Challenge for Planning Comparative Research

Erhard Rehbein

After a brief outline of the school system and the historical development of physical education in German schools is presented, the following aspects of physical education in the schools of the Federal Republic of Germany will be discussed: aims and objectives, program, time allotment, facilities and equipment, teaching methods, grading, competition, physical education teachers, administration, trends, and tendencies. Some videotape recordings will be presented to provide some glimpses into what is going on in the sport facilities of German schools.

Because of the scarcity of reliable data available for comparative studies, some suggestions are made about how to do research by international teamwork. Some problem topics of physical education in the schools of the Federal Republic of Germany are presented as a challenge for comparative research.

The School System

Except for the 12 years of Hitler dictatorship, Germany has never been a unitary state. Accordingly, legislation in cultural matters including education is the prerogative of the federal states. Each has a large measure of autonomy in organizing its school system. Some school curricula and graduation levels vary from state to state. The necessary leveling-out in regard to the general educational system is provided by joint agreements concluded by the Federal States; for deliberation of issues of common concern, a Permanent Conference of Länder Ministers of Education is regularly convened.

In the Federal Republic of Germany, school attendance is compulsory from the ages of 6 to 18 (i.e., for 12 years); full-time attendance is required for 9 years and part-time attendance at vocational schools is required thereafter. In some Federal States a 10th year of full-time compulsory attendance is required. Attendance at all public schools is free.

At the age of 6, children enter primary school (Grundschule). In general, primary school lasts for 4 years; in West Berlin it lasts for 6 years. All children attend primary school together. Thereafter their ways separate when they choose between several vocational or educational possibilities. About half of the age group subsequently attends a short-course secondary school (Hauptschule). Most students who leave secondary school at the age of 15 go into vocational training.

The intermediate school (Realschule) takes 6 years from the 5th to the 10th grade and leads to a graduating certificate at intermediate level.

The 9-year "Gymnasium" (5th to 13th grades) is the traditional grammar or senior high school in Germany. Its graduation certificate, the so-called "Abitur," entitles the student to study at the university. In recent years most federal states have introduced comprehensive schools with equal status along with the traditional schools.

In general, classes used to be scheduled 6 days a week; the tendency now is to reduce school to 5 days a week.

Each type of school has specially trained teachers. Academic study is obligatory for all, but its content and duration vary.

The student/teacher ratio fluctuates from state to state and from school type to school type. In the state of Schleswig-Holstein, for example, in the school-year 1982/1983 at the primary school, the ratio was 21.6 students per teacher. At the intermediate and senior high school level it was 26.7 students per teacher (Kultusministerium Schleswig-Holstein, 1983, p. 14).

The History of Physical Education

The history of physical education in German schools began in the late 18th century with Basedow and Salzmann making physical training an integral part of their educational institutions—the Philanthropinum in Dessau and the Schnepfenthal Institute. In 1842, physical education for boys was accepted as a regular subject in Prussian schools (Überhorst, 1980, p. 331). Fifty-two years later in 1894, physical education for girls was introduced as a regular subject (Überhorst, 1980, p. 500).

Since then, physical education in German schools has undergone a broad range of changes in regard to aims and objectives, content, time allotment, facilities, and general status. Germany's division into two politically and economically separate units after World War II—the Federal Republic of Germany and the German Democratic Republic—caused development in physical education in German schools to split into two sections. The following description of some aspects of physical education in schools will be confined to the conditions in the Federal Republic of Germany.

Aims and Objectives

The official policy of state autonomy for education results in a certain diversity of programs in the Federal Republic of Germany. National uniformity to a certain extent, however, is guaranteed by the Joint Committee for the Coordination of Educational Regulations.

Consider, as an example, the aims and objectives of physical education as described in The Basic Teaching Plan of the State of Schleswig-Holstein, issued in 1978. It states a number of general aims of physical education in schools and describes a sequence of basic functional movement and motor skills from the 1st to the 13th grades. The teacher selects the specific aims and the exercises to suit the need of the students, the season, and the facilities available.

The ultimate aim of physical education at school is to build permanent interest in physical activity and to endow individuals with motivation and the ability to actively, regularly, and intelligently participate in sport after school (Kultusministerium Schleswig-Holstein, 1978, p. 4). The objectives for this aim are the following:

- To teach the individual a broad variety of sport skills at school so that he or she is able to select the type of sport for life-long sport activities that is most suitable for his or her special capacities and needs
- To develop motivation for regular and active participation in sport

In more detail, the 12 following objectives are stated for the grades 7–10 (Kultusministerium Schleswig-Holstein, 1978, p. 5–7):

- To maintain and develop the natural need for movement and play
- To experience and improve rhythmic movement
- To learn, improve, and stabilize various motor skills
- To recognize the importance of psychomotor abilities for achievement and improve the latter
- To acquire many movement patterns that will improve the individual's motor performance in everyday life and at work
- To gain knowledge of how to act independent of the teacher in sport
- To know how to describe and evaluate one's own and others' motor performance
- To know how to assist others and to prevent accidents in sport
- To know how to practice sport outside the school and, for example, to know how to select a sport club according to one's needs
- To recognize the relationship between health and sport activities
- To be able to take part actively in the organization of everyday physical education and competitive events
- To be able to critically approach and understand the various forms and problems of sport in our society

Some rather striking characteristics of this enumeration appear at first glance:

- Leisure time use and lifetime physical activity are stressed.
- Students tend to be made ready to assume initiative and responsibility in planning and practicing physical activities.
- Military connotations (defense, patriotism) are totally absent.

- Explicit connections to moral and civic education (fairplay, order, leadership) are absent.

The aims and objectives mentioned so far were drawn from official documents. The aims realized at school, however, may deviate considerably from the aims stated in official documents because little control and supervision of teachers exists once they gain the status of a state official. Obviously there is no scientific evidence about the correlation between officially stated aims of physical education and the aims actually pursued and achieved by physical education teachers in the Federal Republic of Germany.

Program

In the elementary school, the following activities are offered: tumbling; free movement with and without apparatus; games; swimming; and fundamental movements such as running, jumping, and throwing.

On the secondary school level, apparatus gymnastics, dance, track and field, swimming, soccer, team handball, basketball, and volleyball form the core of the curriculum. In recent years, a variety of further activities has been introduced to German schools. The Basic Teaching Plan of the State of Schleswig-Holstein, issued in 1978, for example, includes the following so-called supplementary sports: badminton, hockey, judo, canoeing, roller skating, ice skating, rowing, sailing, skiing, tennis, and table tennis, some of which physical education teachers are supposed to offer on the secondary school level depending on environmental conditions and the teacher's competency to do so.

The majority of students tend to favor games such as soccer, volleyball, basketball, team handball, and badminton at the expense of the traditionally dominant apparatus gymnastics in the winter season, and track and field in the summer season. Boxing and wrestling are not in the physical education curricula in the Federal Republic of Germany because of the health risks. Many schools presently organize ski courses, usually held for 7-10 days at some mountain area, because most of the schools' local areas do not offer opportunities for skiing.

The successful claim of sport as an elective subject equal to science and foreign languages in the framework of the reform for the senior classes of the German high school has led to the theoretical study of sociological, psychological, biological, and biomechanical aspects of sport on the high school level. Each school that offers this special course first needs the special permission of the school authorities. Permission is granted or refused depending on the availability of competent staff and outstanding facilities.

Time Allotment

Physical education at all German elementary and full-time high schools is compulsory. The time requirement of three periods of physical education per week is uniformly applied to all grades and types of full-time schools except for the first and second grades of the elementary schools, which have a time allotment of only two periods per week.

Periods of physical education are scheduled to last 45 min. The average time for practicing sports is considerably lower, though, because changing clothes before and after class is frequently done within this time. Besides, the time requirements of three periods per week may not always be observed because of the shortage of staff in some schools.

Before 1982, not enough teachers were available at a school because of insufficient budgets; weekly physical education lessons tended to be dropped first because physical education suffered and still suffers from a lack of status and prestige in comparison with other subjects. Complaints of the sport organizations and Physical Education Teachers Association in the State of Schleswig-Holstein caused the state government in 1982 to issue a regulation stating that physical education, if necessary at all, may only be reduced in due proportion to the reduction of other subjects.

In addition to the mandatory lessons, some schools offer special courses designed to serve the special needs of the less-skilled boys and girls as well as the especially talented ones. In 1956, the Ministers of Educational Affairs of the 11 Federal States recommended daily physical activity for the first 2 years of the elementary school and three periods of physical education plus 2 hr of voluntary sport from the third grade upward, including vocational schools. Almost 30 years later, only a minimum of these recommendations has been realized. Here are some statistical data on the average of weekly lessons of physical education in the different types of schools in Schleswig-Holstein in the school year 1982/1983 (Kultusministerium Schleswig-Holstein, 1983, p. 14):

Elementary school	2.3 lessons per week
Short-course secondary school	2.7 lessons per week
Intermediate school	2.8 lessons per week
Gymnasium	2.6 lessons per week

Facilities and Equipment

During World War II, most of the indoor sport facilities were either destroyed or used for emergency housing. During the first postwar building and reconstruction period, the provision of adequate housing was the foremost aim. Therefore, a survey of the German Olympic Society in the late 1950s revealed that most of the schools in the Federal Republic of Germany had extremely poor sport facilities or none at all. At that time in the Federal Republic of Germany, there was a lack of 31,000 children's playgrounds—more than 14,000 general and school sport grounds, more than 10,000 gymnastics and sport halls, and 3,000 indoor and outdoor swimming pools. In 1960, the Federal Republic of Germany launched the so-called "Golden Plan," a long-range plan to raise the money for the necessary sport facilities.

The funds for this project came from three sources—the federal government provided about two-tenths, the states provided about five-tenths, and the communities provided about three-tenths. The demands of the ambitious "Golden Plan" were realized by the mid-1970s.

The Federal Institute for Sport Science in Cologne has a section doing research and advising on facilities and equipment. Today the majority of the schools have adequate facilities, which, after school hours, are used by sport clubs. The standard size of the sport halls being built in recent years is 27 × 45 m, which can be divided into three sections of 27 × 15 m.

The availability of equipment is adequate, in general. The standard, not reached by all schools, is at least one ball or shot for every two pupils in physical education classes, for example. The indoor facilities are primarily equipped for apparatus gymnastics and indoor games.

Considerable additional improvement for the sport facility/pupil ratio is under way because of the decrease in the school-age population: The Federal Republic of Germany has been holding the record of the lowest birth rate in the world for many years now.

Teaching Methods

A quotation may be given first (Bennett, Howell, & Simri, 1975):

> Generalization of teaching procedures for a country is hazardous indeed. It is well to remember that much depends on the individual teacher . . . . The teacher's enthusiasm, his experience and training, his energy, his initiative and creativity, his sense of humor, his love for children all make a difference (p. 57).

Besides, because of various reasons, empirical-analytic research about educational interaction in physical education is getting under way very slowly in the Federal Republic of Germany. Actually, scarcely any objective evidence about teaching methods and procedures applied to physical education classes is available. However, some characteristics of teaching methods and procedures in physical education in the Federal Republic of Germany are obvious and have been agreed upon by professional experts.

Whereas coeducation in physical education lessons used to be limited to grades 1-6, the tendency in the Federal Republic of Germany now is to extend coeducation in physical education to all grades.

The Basic Teaching Plan of the State of Schleswig-Holstein, for example, states that coeducation in physical education is the rule, but exceptions to the rule are permitted. Male and female teachers are permitted to teach physical education for boys and girls of all grades.

Varying according to the objectives, the physical education lesson *is divided usually into three periods:* (a) about 10 min for warming-up, (b) about 20 min for practicing skill techniques or developing physical and motor capacities, and (c) about 10 min for playing games or taking part in some relaxation activities. Some lessons are totally devoted to games.

The organizational pattern of physical education classes varies. Whereas in the warming-up period the entire class usually does the same activity under the supervision of the teacher, in the second and third periods classes are frequently divided into small groups with each group working on its own. If a new skill is introduced by the teacher, there is usually no grouping.

Formal exercises done in unison are extremely rare in physical education in the Federal Republic of Germany today. Strict class control and order for order's sake are stigmatized as being premilitary.

Especially in the lower grades, the problem-solving method is preferred to the deductive method because it is supposed to challenge initiative and creativity. In the upper grades, the students are expected to participate in organizing physical education without expressed leadership of individual students.

Grading

The teacher in the Federal Republic of Germany grades the performance of the individual student in physical education by assigning a number, 1 through 6, as in any other school subject. The grading is done on the basis of the progress the student shows during a course. According to the Basic Teaching Plan of Schleswig-Holstein, for example, the results of measurements, the individual's readiness to learn, and the individual's aptitude have to be taken into consideration.

The grade for physical education, however, does not have the same status as the grade in the academic subjects such as mathematics, languages, and so forth. The grade in physical education does not affect promotion, except for the students of the senior classes of the high school who have chosen physical education as a required subject for graduation; only in that case does the grade in physical education have the same status as the grade in any other academic subject.

Competition

Most of the physical education teachers in the Federal Republic of Germany stress many-sided training to work toward average-level performance. Specialization with the emphasis on achievement in sport contests is uncommon. As a rule, very little effort is made to increase students' interest in competitive sport. Several reasons are possible: the educational philosophy that cooperation is more important than competition, the unwillingness of physical education teachers to spend extra time on coaching and organizing intramural and interschool contests, or the inability of teachers and pupils to identify with the class or the school they are competing for. And of course there is the elaborate system of sport clubs that attract boys and girls who are interested in competitive sports.

So far, a general trend that applies to the majority of pupils and physical education teachers has been described. This may be an injustice to many teachers and pupils in the Federal Republic of Germany who do make great endeavors and spend a lot of time preparing for and organizing intramural and interschool competition. They receive very little publicity, and next to no spectators.

Both educators and sport club officials have an interest in expanding interschool competition in the Federal Republic of Germany. A nationwide competition of school teams in 10 sports, therefore, was set up in 1969 under the name of "Jugend trainiert für Olympia." After the preliminaries on the district and state levels, the finals are held in West Berlin. The State Ministries of Cultural Affairs and the German Sport Youth are in charge of this increasingly popular event. Last year more than 500,000 boys and girls took part in the events.

Another type of nationwide sport competition within schools is the so-called "Bundesjugend-Spiele" (Federal Youth Games), held twice a year, which includes apparatus gymnastics plus floor exercises in the winter and track and field and swimming events in the summer. Once a school has decided to participate in this contest, which is sponsored by the President of the Federal Republic of Germany, all pupils of the school, up to grade 10, have to take part. Everyone reaching a certain achievement set up for his or her age group in advance receives a document signed by the President. This contest aims at broad participation and average achievement, not at top performance.

Physical Education Teachers

In the first two grades of elementary school, physical education is taught by the classroom teacher, who also teaches all of the other subjects. All teachers of the elementary school are graduates from the teacher-training colleges. But only some of them are specially trained in physical education because physical education is only an elective in most of the teacher-training colleges.

All other grades are supposed to be taught by qualified physical education teachers who have graduated from the Departments of Sport and Sports Sciences at the universities or at teacher-training colleges.

Very few teachers in German schools teach physical education exclusively. If a teacher wants to gain the advantageous status of a state official, and more than 90% do so, he or she has to major in two subjects and pass academic examinations in these subjects. Four to 6 years of professional preparation are required, depending on the type of school or teacher seminar. So the vast majority of teachers in German schools teaches another subject besides physical education.

Physical education teachers carry the same work load as teachers of other subjects and they receive the same salary. An interesting discrepancy exists between the fact that the professional and economic status of the physical education teachers at schools is exactly the same as the status of teachers of other subjects, yet the status of the physical education class is rather low as compared to other subjects. The low status of the physical education subject is indicated by the fact that physical education is irrelevant for pupils' promotion.

Administration

No central federal agency administers either education or physical education in the Federal Republic of Germany. Education and physical education are administered by the Ministries of Cultural Affairs in the 11 Länder. The major responsibility of the states, however, is limited to the preparation of syllabi for the various levels of schools and the supervision of the training of physical education teachers. The guidelines provided by the administration are recommendations. The teachers are free to follow or not follow the guidelines. No state control means that no inspectors visit the schools.

Because there is no compulsory inservice training for teachers in the Federal Republic of Germany, the quality of teaching almost totally depends upon the teacher's personality and his or her professional ethics.

Trends and Tendencies

Nothing excitingly new and revolutionary in regard to methods, contents, or aims of physical education exists in the schools of the Federal Republic of Germany. But some considerable changes have occurred in physical education in schools. They have come about slowly but steadily, without anybody noticing the change as being very exciting or revolutionary.

The following statements have the qualities of hypotheses. Because of the absence of research in the following areas, no data are available to back the statements up.

One of the changes in school physical education is the *trend toward coeducation* in all grades. Reasons have been presented for and against coeducation. Before the argument had come to a conclusion, the change had come about in schools. At least in the northern part of Germany the majority of pupils practices sport in coeducational physical education classes. The initial change caused serious problems for some of the teachers because they had not been trained to teach coeducational classes in physical education. Besides, there was the problem that female teachers were frequently not accepted by boys of the upper grades whereas the male teachers usually were accepted by both boys and girls. The autostereotypes and heterostereotypes of boys and girls and of male and female teachers, as far as sport and physical education were concerned, had to be adjusted. Many questions still have not yet been answered, and many problems of coeducation in physical education have not yet been solved. Research in this field is needed.

Another trend is the *tendency to discuss and reflect on the problems* concerned with sport and learning sport instead of merely exercising and practicing sports in physical education classes. This trend, of course, is closely interwoven with the tendency to stress initiative and creativeness instead of obedience and subordination.

A Challenge for Joint Comparative Research

On several occasions of this presentation it had to be admitted that no data were available to back up the statements about physical education in the Federal Republic of Germany.

Changes in the national system of physical education frequently are brought about without more than vague expectations about the consequences. Glimpses over the fences of national borders may be able to provide some valuable information for reform decisions to be made.

Without any unrealistic expectations about the scope and the limits of the outcomes, here are some suggestions on how to do research in comparative physical education on a limited scale via international teamwork.

In Figures 1 and 2, two problem topics of physical education in the schools of the Federal Republic of Germany are put forward as a challenge for comparative research. This limited research (confined to a small geographical area such as a city or state) could be carried out in two stages. The first stage would deal with the status quo; the second would trace the historical development and predict the future development and consequences as well.

Basic Question 1   How many boys and girls of each grade and what type of school have coeducational physical education lessons? How many are non-coeducational?

Method: either use available statistical data or a questionnaire administered to schools in cooperation with the school authorities

Basic Question 2   What is the attitude of

(a) pupils
(b) parents
(c) physical education teacher
(d) school authorities

in regard to education in physical education?

Method: questionnaire

Basic Question 3   What are the arguments put forward in favor and against coeducation in physical education by

(a) pupils?
(b) parents?

Figure 1 (cont.)

(c) physical education teacher?
(d) school authorities?

Method: questionnaire

Basic Question 4   Are there differences between autostereotypes and heterostereotypes of boys and girls whose physical education classes are coeducational and whose lessons are noncoeducational?

Method: questionnaire

Basic Question 5   Is there any difference in the social-emotional atmosphere of coeducational and noncoeducational physical education classes?

Method: systematic observation

Basic Question 6   What is the legal basis for coeducational physical education in schools?

Method: content analysis of documents

Figure 1. Problem topic 1: Coeducation in physical education.

Basic Question 1   How many schools organize intramural sport contests and participate in interschool sport contests?

How many boys and girls participate in the various competitions?

Method: either use available statistical data or a questionnaire administered to schools in cooperation with the school authorities

Basic Question 2   What is the attitude of
(a) pupils
(b) parents
(c) physical education teachers
(d) school authorities
in regard to competition in school sports?

Method: questionnaire

Basic Question 3   What are the arguments put forward in favor and against school sport competition by
(a) pupils?
(b) parents?
(c) physical education teachers?
(d) school authorities?

Method: questionnaire

Basic Question 4   Do those pupils who participate actively or passively in school sport competitions show a higher degree of identification with their school than those who do not?

Method: questionnaire

Basic Question 5   How are coaching and competition financed?

Method: content analysis of documents

Basic Question 6   What is the publicity of school sport competitions like?

Method: content analysis of documents; systematic observation

Figure 2 Problem topic 2: Competition in school sports.

References

Bennett, B.L., Howell, M.L., & Simri, U. (1975). *Comparative physical education and sport*. Philadelphia: Lea and Febiger.

Kultusministerium Schleswig-Holstein (Ed.). (1978). *Lehrplan Realschule Sport*. Kronshagen.

Kultusministerium Schleswig-Holstein (1983). *Bericht zur Lage des Sports in Schleswig-Holstein*. Kiel.

Überhorst, H. (1980). *Geschichte der Leibesübungen*. Berlin.

CHAPTER 12

School Physical Education: Cross-National Issues to Be Researched

Margo Gee

In most countries, schools are assigned the role of providing some form of physical activity for children and youth. Although the manner in which physical activity is offered varies cross-nationally, one of the most common forms is in the physical education class. This class would seem to be an obvious and popular topic of study in comparative research; however, this is not the case. Very little current literature pertains to cross-national research on physical education classes in schools.

Therefore, the purpose of this presentation is two-fold: (a) to identify comparative studies in this area, and (b) to suggest cross-national issues in physical education that might be considered for research projects. This presentation begins by pointing out comprehensive comparative works on physical education classes, and then it examines specific investigations. Moreover, some case studies of single countries are mentioned for their applicability to comparative research in terms of common issues and themes that arise. In the second section these issues are analyzed in greater detail.

Physical education classes of primary- and secondary-level institutions are examined. Institutions of higher education are excluded. Furthermore, *physical education classes* are defined as those periods of formally structured physical activity provided for in the curriculum and class timetable. This does not include short breaks for recess, exercise, or physical culture.

Major Studies

The most comprehensive work to date is included in the text *Comparative Physical Education and Sport* by Bennett, Howell, and Simri (1983). The fourth chapter, "Physical Education in Schools," provides an excellent framework for comparing physical education classes. The authors discuss general aims and objectives, time requirement, curriculum, facilities and equipment, teaching, administration and supervision, and provision for special populations.

Other chapters in the text provide further comparative details of physical education classes. For example, the professional preparation of both specialist and nonspecialist physical education teachers is discussed. A chapter entitled "Sport and Physical Education Legislation" provides insight into various acts and laws concerning all aspects of classes, particularly the equality of opportunity aspect. The final chapter, "Comparative Physical Education and Sport: An Appraisal," puts forth 10 statements regarding characteristics of the international scene which the authors believe will have an impact on physical education and sport in the future. Many of these characteristics are applicable to physical education classes. Some examples are the increase of professional preparation, the growth of physical education in schools, and the goal of mass participation.

Seurin (1982) took a different approach to comparative physical education and sport. He grouped all countries into six different types of civilizations and analyzed common elements of sport provision, including physical education classes in many instances. Like Bennett et al. (1983), Seurin devotes a section to physical activity in the future. He lists motivations for participation in sport, many of which could be satisfied at younger age levels in physical education classes. Furthermore, he discusses the role of the school in the "Sport for All" movement.

Two other comprehensive studies exist which, although outdated, deserve mention. First, the "Physical Education Around the World" monographs of Phi Epsilon Kappa Fraternity provide a base for comparative analysis. The articles examine one country at a time in a very general way. Therefore, the reader must make his or her own cross-national comparisons from the brief overviews presented. Perhaps the monographs' most utilitarian purpose is to acquaint the beginning student with the concept of national differences and introduce him or her to other forms of physical education provision.

The other study is the ICHPER's *International Questionnaire Report* (1969). Part I, "Physical Education in the School Curriculum," is a survey report of physical education throughout the world. In this study, 81 countries report on aspects of physical education classes such as major objectives of physical education, activities in the program, and physical performance examinations. Part II, "Teacher Training for Physical Education," is actually a separate report in which 80 nations participated. By examining the professional preparation of specialist teachers, a clearer picture emerges of expectations for physical education classes in schools.

Both Parts I and II make longitudinal comparisons with a similar ICHPER study conducted in 1963. Again, the data for cross-national studies is provided, but the reader must draw comparisons. A major criticism of these reports and those of the Phi Epsilon Kappa Fraternity is that they rely on the knowledge and experience of only one respondent from each country. Consequently, validity of findings must be questioned.

All of these studies have tremendous scope; many nations throughout the world were examined. So few studies exist because amassing the amount of data required is difficult; therefore, one would expect to find more comparative studies of physical education classes which focus only on a small number of countries. The next section examines studies of this nature which have emerged during the past 5 years.

Small-Scale Comparative Studies

Once more, a paucity of research exists on comparisons of physical education classes in the current English literature. Studies might have been written in German, French, or Japanese, for example, but they have not been covered by this author.

The *International Journal of Physical Education* refers to aspects of physical education in other countries. The *British Journal of Physical Education* seems to have the most common occurrence of short cross-national comparisons. Some examples of these studies are "One Englishman's View of American Physical Education and Sport" (Fox, 1982) and "Greek Physical Education, Recreation, and Sport" (Rustage, 1982). These typically brief reports provide commentary on the physical education system of one nation through the eyes of a physical education practitioner from another. Comparisons are not empirically based. They are descriptive, subjective, and not extensive. Comparison is not the major focus of the articles. Nonetheless, their utility lies in the perceived cross-national differences that emerge through the author's commentary. This may give incentive to others to test these observations empirically.

Similarly, Mukhin (1974) and Tomkins (1983) offer analyses of physical education classes in countries other than their own; they examine Finnish and East German programs respectively. These studies are more scholarly. Again, comparisons arise not as part of the study, but rather as subjective descriptions and informal comments. Hardman (1980) has provided a case study of physical education development in East Germany. A cross-national comparison with the Soviet Union arises when he parallels development and delivery systems and clarifies a difference in the German approach.

Sabirov (1974) investigated gymnastics lessons in the German Democratic Republic and Japan. Although a complete description of each program is prepared, it becomes the reader's responsibility to make comparisons. Beran (1980) has written on physical education in Nigeria and the Philippines; he compares the primary level classes in the two developing countries.

Some researchers have published a number of articles on different nations which could easily be utilized in comparative studies. Some journals, such as the Journal of Health, Physical Education, and Recreation (JOHPER), present case studies of single nations on a regular basis. Although they do not necessarily use an identical format, comparisons of particular concepts in physical education are still possible. The strength of this type of analysis would lie in its up-to-date information, as opposed to information on single nations provided in the previously mentioned monographs of Phi Epsilon Kappa Fraternity. Finally, do not exclude texts written about sport in various countries. Sometimes they provide the most intensive, in-depth, and insightful illustrations available.

In summary, current literature pertaining to cross-national research on physical education classes is very scant. Given this situation, many areas and issues in physical education probably have not been studied in a comparative way. In the next section, literature regarding some of these issues is identified as a possible starting point for further comparative research on physical education classes.

Issues in Physical Education: Suggestions for Comparative Research

Many of the ideas for research are a direct result of investigations undertaken in various parts of the world. Others were derived after having examined current global situations. Therefore, some issues may appear more unique than others. Those that are more obvious have been included because of a dearth of research in the area.

Beginning with the area of aims and objectives of physical education curricula, a need exists to examine those that are suggested in the original UNESCO "International Charter of Physical Education and Sport" and the more recent UNESCO "Draft Medium Term Plan (1984-1989)." They are intended to be used as guidelines in physical education for all United Nations members. Further research might examine the degree to which these goals and objectives are implemented in practice.

It has been suggested that physical education programs are becoming more prevalent throughout the world (Bennett et al., 1983). Many countries now require physical education, but because of resource shortages, particularly among developing nations, offering a balanced program is impossible. Therefore, the existing gap between theory and practice could be investigated in a comparative study. Additional problems of physical education as a required but not implemented subject could also be included in this type of research.

Issues and controversies surrounding physical education as an examinable subject merit cross-national attention. The value of physical education might be analyzed as an examinable subject to the student in terms of academic achievement. This could then be juxtaposed alongside countries where physical education is perceived as a lower status, nonessential course because it is nonexaminable in those nations.

Differences between physical education classes in urban and rural settings at the primary level have been studied by Finnish researchers (Halopainen, 1982). Differences could be investigated at the secondary level as well. In a comparative study, one might wish to determine if the margin of difference between rural and urban schools is consistent among various countries. This could be based on geographical position, ideological stance, or state of development.

There is potentially a vast area of comparative research to be realized in nations with special populations. Programs, approaches, and facilities for these groups are in great need of cross-national study. Additional select groups, such as gifted children, are experiencing an even greater lack of research pertaining to physical education. This applies both to case studies and comparative investigations. A study examining attitudes and special programming between countries of different ideological positions might uncover some interesting and useful facts.

Bennett et al. (1983) state that research is increasingly focusing on elitism. An issue arising from this emphasis is the effect that it will have on the rest of the population. In physical education classes the elite are offered the best resources at the expense of other children. A cross-national study could compare the degree to which athletically gifted children are encouraged and their less athletically inclined peers are ignored. Variance among nations might occur according to the emphasis placed on international sport achievement and mass sport participation.

The current global economic crisis has seriously affected educational systems in all parts of the world. Because physical education, along with the arts, is considered to be peripheral to the academic curriculum in many nations, budget restraints will be felt more severely in these subjects. A comparative study of a very practical nature would be to examine different methods of coping with severe financial constraints and examine the central concerns of physical educators in this situation.

Luke (1983), and Duda and Allison (1984) have addressed the topic of multiculturalism and physical education. Along with other immigrants, many countries have accepted a great number of refugees in the face of international conflict. They often become established in ethnic enclaves and host nations emerge as pluralistic societies. The impact of multiculturalism on traditional physical education programs is enormous. Teachers must be able to recognize values and attitudes that each immigrant child brings with him or her and try to adapt the curriculum accordingly. A comparative investigation could examine the differences and effectiveness of various approaches to multiculturalism.

Sex role stereotyping in physical education has become an increasingly common focus of debate, especially among developed nations. Vertinsky (1983) and Sherlock (n.d.) have examined the issue in Britain and provided some insightful observations. By assessing the Sex Discrimination Act of 1975 in the United Kingdom, comparisons could be drawn to equal opportunity legislation in other countries, for example, Title IX in the United States. Vertinsky points out that in British physical education classes, "equal was seen to be equivalent rather than the same" (1983, p. 231). One might ask to what extent sex-segregated physical education classes offer stereotypic activities rather than identical activities. Furthermore, this issue may be applied to the teachers themselves: Does cross-national research reveal any major differences in sex-role stereotyping of physical education teachers during teacher training and in on-the-job expectations?

During recent years, lifetime sport activities have received considerable attention. Much of the credit for this phenomenon is because of "Sport for All" movements throughout the world. Increasing societal interest is reflected in the curricula of physical education classes in many nations. Therefore, comparative research might be undertaken to determine both the status and prevalence of lifetime sport in the curriculum. The concept of "education for leisure" also deals with physical education activities that could be extended to recreational time. Silvennoinen (1982) has studied similarities between the physical education curriculum and extracurricular activities of Finnish school children. This type of research easily lends itself to crossnational investigation.

Approaches taken to teaching physical education vary greatly between countries. Researchers in the United States (Mancini, Wuest, Cheffers, & Rich, 1983) have studied shared decision-making between teachers and students in physical education classes and have made comparisons to those classes completely organized by the teacher. They found that shared decision-making helped promote involvement, stimulate interest, and develop positive attitudes toward physical education. Similarly, formally structured physical education classes, such as those in Japan or the Soviet Union, could be compared to the more informal approach of movement education, which is common throughout Great Britain and many parts of the United States.

On a global basis, the majority of primary-level physical education classes are taught by nonspecialist teachers. Most often this occurs in less-developed nations where shortages of equipment and facilities are common as well. Given the lack of specialized training for physical education and scarcity of resources, one might ask what type of curriculum is utilized and to what extent it meets objectives of the national education department. Not only can this be examined crossnationally, but it is also applicable to pluralistic societies where great discrepancies exist between the dominant societal group and various minorities. Archer and Bouillon (1982) have already explored this situation within South Africa where apartheid is responsible for huge inequalities in physical education and sport among different racial groups.

Teachers in all disciplines are accepted as role models for their students to a certain extent. It seems, however, that the physical education teacher occupies a special position in this regard. His or her adherence to the subject matter in the form of personal health and fitness habits that he or she teaches is especially important if he or she expects students to adopt a similar lifestyle. Of course not all physical educators place the same emphasis on this role. It would be an issue for comparative research to determine how important it is for physical education teachers at primary and secondary levels to represent positive role models.

Parental involvement in physical education varies cross-nationally. Khripkova (1980) has revealed that parents take an active role in physical culture in the Soviet Union. Not only must they provide for physical culture breaks during the evening, but they also must maintain an ongoing liaison with their children's teachers. Snyder and Spreitzer (1983) investigated adult perceptions of physical education in schools in a study confined to the United States. Generally, there was a rather critical and negative attitude toward these programs. It may be assumed that parental attitude has a great impact on a child's perception of an activity. Therefore, if the parents are encouraging and supportive, then the child will view physical education in a positive light; if not, the opposite will be true. A comparative study could be conducted to determine the extent of involvement and determine the attitudes toward physical education classes of the students' parents. This might have practical value in the promotion of mass participation and healthy lifestyles through physical education curricula.

Another issue in physical education is political indoctrination. In Socialist bloc countries it is overt. Comparing this with covert political indoctrination occurring in Western nations might be possible. For example, one might look at the incidence of political values taught through sport at the school level. Measures could include the use of symbols such as flags, anthems, or posters during class activities.

Finally, daily physical education classes have been the object of concern in several case studies (Sinclair & Appleby, 1979; Bean, 1983). Cross-national comparisons would be useful in supporting or refuting their value. Classes could be measured in terms of promotion of physical fitness, influence on attitudes toward physical activity, and effect on the child's self-concept.

Conclusions

By perusing the current English literature on comparative research of physical education classes, it is glaringly apparent that this area of study has been largely ignored. A few major works do exist, but they are based on a composite of single nation studies or on the views of single respondents. Several case studies exist, but they are largely descriptive in nature, and comparisons generally lack a sound empirical foundation.

Although the current status of comparative research appears less than encouraging, it serves the purpose of pointing out areas in need of investigation. Several suggestions have been presented for research. Although these are by no means exhaustive, they present some key issues in need of study. Perhaps this will encourage some social scientists to carry out these studies and to think of other issues pertaining to physical education classes that would lend themselves to comparative research. Physical education is a primary means of socialization into sport and physical activities. Through the generation of a substantial body of knowledge in this area, it will enable practitioners to make physical education a more positive, meaningful, and enjoyable experience for youth throughout the world.

References

Archer, R., & Bouillon, A. (1982). *The South African game: Sport and racism.* London: Zed.

Bean, D. (1983). Daily physical education. From dream to reality. *British Journal of Physical Education,* **14**(4), 93–118.

Bennett, B.L., Howell, M.L., & Simri, U. (1983). *Comparative physical education and sport* (2nd ed.). Philadelphia: Lea and Febiger.

Beran, J.A. (1980, September 23-28). Primary school physical education in the Philippines and Nigeria. In J.C. Pooley & C.A. Pooley (Eds.), *Proceedings of the Second International Seminar on Comparative Sport and Physical Education* (pp. 163-171). Halifax: Dalhousie University.

Duda, J.L., & Allison, M.T. (1984). Variations in value orientations: Race and sex differences in sport and academic domains. Manuscript submitted for publication.

Fox, K. (1982). One Englishman's view of American physical education and sport. *Action,* **13**(1), 13.

Hardman, K. (1980). The development of physical education in the German Democratic Republic. *Physical Education Review,* **3**(2), 121-136.

Halopainen, S. (1982, November 18-21). Rate of development of physical and motor fitness, abilities and skills of comprehensive school pupils and differences in development between urban and rural pupils. In R. Telama et al. (Eds.), *Research in school physical education. Proceedings of the International Symposium on Leisure in School Physical Education* (pp. 265-272). Jyväskylä, Finland: ICHPER.

Khripkova, A. (1980). Physical education and the intellectual development of children. *Prospects: Quarterly Review of Education,* **10**(1), 3-12.

Luke, M.D. (1983). Multiculturalism and physical education. *Multiculturalism,* **7**(1), 15–16.

Mancini, V.H., Wuest, D.A., Cheffers, J.T.F., & Rich, S.M. (1983). Promoting student involvement in physical education by sharing decisions. *International Journal of Physical Education,* **20**(3), 16–23.

Mukhin, V.I. (1974). In the schools of Finland. *Soviet Education,* **16**(4), 57–63.

Physical education in the school curriculum. (1969). *ICHPER international questionnaire report.* (Part I, 1967-68 Revision). Washington: ICHPER.

Rustage, A.F. (1982). Greek physical education, recreation, and sport. *Action,* **13**(6), 174.

Sabirov, I.A. (1974). Gymnastics lessons in the G.D.R. and Japan. *Soviet Education,* **16**(4), 108–114.

Seurin, P. (1982). Sport and physical education. *International Social Science Journal,* **34**(2), 291-301.

Sherlock, J. (n.d.). *The female physical educator in Britain as cultural product and as cultural producer.* Bedford, England: Bedford College of Health Education.

Silvennoinen, M. (1982, November 18-21). *On the similarities between the extracurricular sports activities of Finnish comprehensive school children and the curriculum of physical education.* Paper delivered at the International Symposium on Research in School Physical Education. Finland: University of Jyväskylä.

Sinclair, G., & Appleby, J. (1979, November 30). Physical education pilot project: Final report, September 1977–June 1979. Vancouver, British Columbia: Vancouver School Board.

Snyder, E.E., & Spreitzer, E. (1983). Adult perceptions of physical education in the schools and community sport programs for youth. *The Physical Educator, 40*(2), 88–91.

Teacher training for physical education. (1969). *ICHPER international questionnaire report* (Part II, 1967-68 Revision). Washington: ICHPER.

Tomkins, M. (1983). Physical education and sport in East Germany. *British Journal of Physical Education, 14*(5), 143–144.

Vertinsky, P. (1983). The evolving policy of equal curricular opportunity in England: A case study of the implementation of sex equality in physical education. *British Journal of Educational Studies, 31*(3), 229–251.

CHAPTER 13

Is There Anything to Learn From the American "Experiment" in Coeducational School Physical Education?

Nanda Fischer

Because problem-solving in educational research in many situations cannot be done through experiments, problem-solving approaches in a foreign educational system can be seen "as adding perspective in order to enable more appropriate reform of one's own system" (Henry, 1973, p. 231). The problem at issue is coeducational physical education versus single-sex physical education. This problem is common to everyone because in most major nation's educational systems, coeducation is practiced in all subjects except physical education.

When the Health, Education, and Welfare (HEW) comprehensive regulations concerning Title IX took effect on July 21, 1975, barring discrimination on the basis of sex in the nation's schools and universities, all physical education classes except those in contact sport were to be integrated by sex. This seems to have been the beginning of a huge experiment in coed physical education in which approximately 16,000 school systems and 40 million students were affected. Even though secondary schools were given 3 years to cope with the regulations, most teachers and students were caught unprepared. This study was undertaken to observe and analyze this fascinating process and learn from the results.

Because of the dynamic process of this development, the study has been conducted over a period of 7 years, starting in 1978. To get more valid results, three phases had to be distinguished: Phase I (1978), the innovative phase; Phase II (1982), the routine phase; and Phase III, 1985 to the present, where students hardly ever experience single-sex physical education.

Research Design

Within the framework of this short paper, only a brief summary of the research design and some preliminary results can be given without tables or figures.

Hypotheses

In a first step the following hypotheses had to be evaluated:

1. Coeducation has the same meaning in both educational systems.
2. Sex-role typing in sport in the U.S. is similar to sex-role typing in sport in West Germany.
3. School physical education in the U.S. and in West Germany are similar.

Hypothesis 1.   Most often the term *coeducation* refers to an organizational pattern in an educational institution meaning joint education, especially the education of both sexes, and consequently in physical education meaning joint physical education classes of girls and boys. Scholars and legislators in the U.S. and in West Germany fully agree up to here. However, opinions differ as to whether only coinstruction is described. Coeducational classes must show additional criteria to be truly coed, such as boys and girls being admitted to the programs on equal terms (Dejnozka & Kasel, 1982). But what are equal terms? Answers given to this question show the differences: (a) instruction should be sex-independent (Kröner, 1976; Wawrzyniak, 1958), and (b) reorganization of the instructional process and all of its factors is absolutely necessary because in the present situation where sex-typing is still very strong, desexualization has to be an issue in physical education on which students have to work (Brodtmann, 1979; Jost, 1977; Kugelmann, 1980; Odey, 1976; Kretschmer & Ziegelitz, 1975). However, a definition for coeducation gained this way is only valid for a phase of transition and is too narrow a concept to describe the phenomenon in general. Therefore, the more general description given above, which is also used by Pfister (1983), is relevant to this study. Consequently, Hypothesis 1 holds.

Hypothesis 2.   The three most important factors in sex-role typing in sports were found to be (a) history and tradition of women's participation in sports, (b) family background, and (c) mass media.

Four historical eras of women's participation in sports in the U.S. can be distinguished: the first female sport activity era (until 1917), the first female athletic era (1917-1936), the feminine reaction to the athletic era (1936-1960), and the female athletic revolution (since 1960) (Boutilier & Lucinda, 1983). In West Germany the history of female sport participation is very similar; the main differences are that the second era ended in 1933 with Hitler coming into power and the fourth era started in 1945 after the end of World War II and was rather an evolution than a revolution, so that by 1960 German women were far ahead of American women in terms of sport participation; but since then, the American women have made up the difference and even went ahead of the Germans with the help of Title IX in amateur sports. On the level of professional and semi-professional sports, since the 1960s, everything has become so international that the situation is similar everywhere.

The family provides the foundation of the socializing process. The study of the research literature from the U.S. as well as from West Germany leads to the conclusion that the family still transmits to children a sex-typed ideology of play, physical activity, and sport (For a comprehensive summary of recent research compare Greendorfer, 1983, for the U.S. and Pfister, 1983, for West Germany). Because fathers and mothers behave differently toward children of different sexes in the vast majority of cases, an insidious form of discrimination in sports exists for girls. In early childhood discrimination is done by not reinforcing or even punishing non-adequate gender behavior and by labeling toys and games. Later on it is done by reinforcing participation in organized competitive and team sports for boys, but encouraging only participation in light rather unorganized physical activities for girls. Because patterns for sport participation seem to have stabilized before children enter secondary school, the influence of this sex-typing process in sport for children is evident in both countries.

Present mass media are extremely powerful forces that leave no person or social process uninfluenced. The impact of mass media is especially great on children because they cannot judge the validity of media content. The extent of coverage in men's and women's sports in the media in the U.S. and in West Germany clearly shows an underrepresentation of women in sports (Boutilier & Lucinda, 1983; Chafetz, 1975; Gerber, Felshing, & Wyrich, 1974; Miller, 1975; Pfister, 1983). The type of coverage in both countries is sex-stereotyped. Women in sport get a gender-role treatment—physical attire and appearance dominate—rather than a sport-role treatment (Boutilier & Lucinda, 1983; Bröker, 1982; Buschmann, 1982; Gerber, Felshing, & Wyrich, 1974; Molotch, 1978; Pilz, 1982). Sex-role typing through media in the U.S. and in West Germany is very similar.

Hypothesis 3. School physical education within the educational system in both countries is left to state or local authorities. Because local funding in the U.S. can be up to 55% of all funding, the quality of education depends mostly on the local conditions. In the following summary the conditions described resemble those in existence in middle income class neighborhoods. In West Germany the quality of education in the Gymnasium (only attended by 25% of the population) is almost the same in all places. After comparing the essential criteria for physical education in the earlier-mentioned institutions in the U.S. and West Germany, the following statements can be made:

- Social significance of physical education in both countries is rather low.
- Average time spent in physical education classes amounts to one extra period for U.S. students.
- Facilities in the U.S. are much more spacious.
- The organization is—with the exception of junior high schools—courses rather than classes in the U.S., with one physical activity per period, whereas the typical German Sportstunde consists of three elements: warming up, teaching/learning process, and games.
- A greater variety of subjects is available in American school physical education, but all of the subjects taught in Germany are also taught

in the U.S., with the addition of football, baseball, and dance.

- The two countries' curricula are similar in their most important criterion of aims and objectives: preparing students so they are fit to engage in physical activity after school age and exposing them to various dimensions of physical activity such as the fitness and health dimension, socializing dimension, and achievement dimension. However, very different curricula are designed. In the U.S. most often the teachers who teach physical education design the curricula and thus make the curricula very flexible because the curricula are only valid for one school. In West Germany a curriculum revision takes years because it is done by a committee of scholars, administrators, and teachers and concerns all schools in a state.
- In the U.S. only 25-50% of the physical education grade is based on achievement, while in West Germany grades are a mirror of a student's achievement.
- Teaching behavior depends on teacher training, tradition, and teacher personality. Teacher training in West Germany is more intensive in theory and practice. The teaching behavior in the U.S. traditionally depends on grade level and subject. In American junior high school teaching behavior is more similar to that of a German physical education teacher; in high school the teacher is more of an organizer and activity leader than a teacher. This does not hold for swimming and dance, in which a lot of instruction is done also on the high school level.

Despite the above mentioned differences, physical education in West Germany and the U.S. are fairly similar because they have the most important criterion in common: aims and objectives. Some differences in criterion are made up by differences in other areas (e.g., less time), but on the average more sophisticated teaching. Therefore Hypothesis 3 generally holds.

Field Work

The practice in physical education often is different from its theory. So even after Title IX, physical education is not coeducational for all. Even though HEW regulations clearly state that physical education courses must be integrated by sex, not all states interpret Title IX the same HEW way. Some states felt they were in compliance with the law when their program was equal for girls and boys but also segregated. School physical education was not given that much attention anyway because Title IX also affected athletic programs in which much more money was involved and programs gained more public attention. Besides, no case is known where a school lost federal funding because of noncompliance with Title IX (Boutilier & Lucinda, 1983).

Field work was employed for all three phases of my investigation of the practice of physical education after Title IX. It was done in Illinois (Chicago area), in California (Los Angeles area), in Florida (Tampa area), in the American DODDS schools in the south of West Germany, and in

German high schools in Bavaria (Munich area). All of the schools surveyed were secondary schools because the impact of Title IX was felt most strongly there.

Various techniques were used for the field work: classroom observations, questionnaires, group discussions, interviews, videotaping, filming, and photographing. The technique of group discussion, especially, was assumed to be an adequate technique to learn about group opinions and opinion-forming processes because the situation of a group discussion provokes spontaneous uncontrolled reactions that allow interpretation of stated opinions (ecological validity).

Preliminary Results

Because the investigation of Phase III is not yet completed, only some preliminary results and conclusions are summed up in this context without giving any figures or tables:

- Aims and objectives have not changed in coed physical education classes.
- Changes have taken place on the organizational level: Courses in dual sports often are being offered as mixed doubles courses. Team teaching has increased, which has solved lockerroom supervision problems. Grouping within courses in team sports has been left up to the students for practice purposes. It is evident that, independent of age or subject, besides single sex groups, coed groups have formed mostly on the high ability level in all courses. For competition, teachers have demanded the same boy/girl ratio on a team as in the course.
- Changes also have been observed on the subject level: Football has been replaced by flag football or touch football; baseball has been replaced by softball. Subjects that didn't seem to fit the needs of boys and girls equally have often been dropped from the regular program and left for the athletic program (e.g., gymnastics). On the other hand, sports from outside the American sport tradition, like soccer or team handball, have entered the picture. The skill levels of boys and girls have been equal since the professional way of playing the sport is not well known, so coed classes have been satisfying to all.
- Students' attitudes toward physical education in general have not changed (see also Alpers, 1977).
- Students have rated the social/emotional level in coed classes more positively than in single sex classes.
- Attitudes toward coed classes in individual and dual sports have been positive.
- For team sports, a majority of boys prefer separate classes, but soccer and volleyball have been rated as perfectly fit for coed classes by all (see also Montemayor, 1974).
- Teachers' attitudes seem to be age-, sex-, and race-related; the young black female teacher favors coed classes the most.

I would like to try to answer the initial question in discussing just one aspect of the results. The example of soccer being described by students and teachers alike as working well in coed classes (and classroom observation proves this) in the U.S., and on the other hand being described as an unfit subject for coed classes by students and teachers in West Germany, seems to show that it is not the subject that does or does not fit for coed classes. It is the label we put on it. If everyone who participates in the socializing process could de-label sport and physical activity, then an individual could choose the physical activity and the approach toward it (e.g., more or less competitive) that fits him or her the best. That could and should mean that now and then, only girls or only boys will gather in an activity group.

References

Alpers, P. (1977). *The effects of coeducational physical education on the expressed attitude of ninth grade boys and girls towards physical education as a physical activity.* Unpublished master's thesis, University of Kansas, Lawrence.

Boutilier, M.A., & Lucinda, S.G. (1983). *The sporting woman.* Champaign, IL: Human Kinetics.

Brodtmann, D. (1979). *Unterricht und Schulsport* [Instruction and school sport]. Bad Heilbrunn: Klinhart.

Bröker, A. (1982). *Gesellschaftsrollenklischees in der Sportberichterstattung. Eine exemplarische Untersuchung der Bildzeitung* [The community role in sport coverage. An illustrated study of magazines]. Unpublished master's thesis, Bochum.

Buschmann, C. (1982). *Sportlerinnen zwischen Leistung und Weiblichkeit. Untersuchung zur bildlichen Darstellung der Frau in der Sportberichterstattung der Bildzeitung* [Women athletes between performance and femininity. Study of pictorial depictions of women in sport coverage in magazines]. Unpublished master's thesis, Bochum.

Chafetz, J.S. (1978). *Masculine, feminine or human?* Itasca, IL: Peacock.

Dejnozka, E., & Kasel, D. (1982). In *American educator's encyclopedia.*

Gerber, E.R., Felshing, B.P., & Wyrich, W. (1974). *The American woman in sport.* Reading, MA: Addison-Wesley.

Greendorfer, S. (1983). Shaping the female athlete: The impact of the family. In M.A. Boutilier & S.G. Lucinda (Eds.), *The sporting woman* (pp. 135-155). Champaign, IL: Human Kinetics.

Henry, M.M. (1973). Methodology in comparative education. An annoted bibliography (1954-1972). *Comparative Education Review, 17,* 231-244.

Jost, E. (1977). Zum Problem der Koedukation im Sportunterricht [On the problem of coeducation in sport instruction]. In D. Brodtmann (Ed.),

Koedukation im Sportunterricht (pp. 2-13). Materialien zum Seminarthema Zeitschrift für Sportpädagogik, 1 (Beiheft).

Kaplan, J. (1979). *Women and sports.* New York: Viking Press.

Kretschmer, J., & Ziegelitz, M. (1975). Einstellungen von Sportlehrerin zum koedukativen Sportunterricht [Attitudes of physical educators toward coeducational sport instruction]. *Sportunterricht,* **24**(8), 263-267.

Kröner, S. (1976). *Sport und Gesellschaft* [Sport and society]. Ahrensberg: Cwalina.

Kugelmann, C. (1980). *Koedukation im Sportunterricht* [Coeducation in sport instruction]. Bad Homburg: Limpert.

Miller, S.H. (1975). The content of news photos: Women's and men's roles. *Journalism Quarterly,* **52**, 70-75.

Molotch, H.L. (1978). The news of women and the work of men. In G. Tuchman, A.K. Daniels, & J. Benét (Eds.), *Hearth and home: Images of women in the mass media.* New York: Oxford University.

Montemayor, R. (1974). Children's performance in a game and their attraction to it as a function of sex typed labels. *Child Development,* **45**, 152-156.

Odey, R. (1976). Zur Praxis koedukativen Sportunterrichts [On the practice of coeducational sport instruction]. *Sportunterricht,* **25**(1), 8-13.

Pfister, G. (1983). *Gesellschaftsspezifische Sozialisation und Koedukation im Sport* [Socially specific socialization and coeducation in sport](Sportsoziologische Arbeiten 8). Berlin: Bartels & Wernitz.

Pilz, G.A. (1982). Wandlungen der Gewalt im Sport [Power changes in sport]. Ahrensburg: Cwalina.

Wawrzyniak, K. (1958). Grundlage der Koedukation [Foundations of co-education]. Munich: Reinhardt.

CHAPTER 14

Some Elements of the Conception of Physical Education in Schools of European Socialist Countries

Zygmunt Jaworski

The information provided in this report is drawn from the results of comparative studies published in Poland in 1976 (Jaworski, 1976).

School physical education is understood here in a very broad sense that embodies different goals and forms of physical activity that are organized at school for pupils.

Taking this broad sense of school physical education into consideration, its organizational forms in European socialist countries can be divided into three basic groups of class types:

- Classes for pupils in good health
- Classes for pupils revealing special sport interests and talents
- Classes for pupils with low physical ability or general health problems

In the first group, the most popular form of class teaching is the so-called lessons of physical education. They are included in the curriculum as obligatory classes for pupils of all school grades, both primary and secondary. Usually 2 or 3 hr a week are given to these classes; more hours of physical education are offered to younger pupils if possible. These classes are usually held in 45 min, sometimes 90 min, methodological time units. The classes are provided for class groups. On the elementary level of teaching, which is usually completed when the pupils are 10-11 years old, the class groups are almost exclusively coeducational. On the other hand, segregated class groups prevail in the later stages (i.e., classes consist of pupils of the same sex). Younger and younger pupils tend to have segregated physical education classes.

Obligatory exercises for all pupils may be given before class or during the regular classes. They are supposed to counteract the negative effects of the pupils' prolonged sitting during school classes and to eliminate the inevitable symptoms of their weariness. In practice, this form of school activity has not yet become common.

The second group of classes—assigned for pupils with special sport interests and talents—is characterized by a great variety of organizational forms. These classes are usually facilitative. Their main purpose is to produce champion skills in pupils on a higher and higher level. The classes also fulfill other functions such as recreation, compensation, and so forth.

In this group of classes, sport competitions, through school and interschool contests, have the greatest popularity. However, the greatest role in preserving and developing sport interests and talents is achieved by classes in the sport sections of sport organizations acting in the schools.

Within the system of selecting sport talents and providing the talented youth with appropriate conditions for development, sport class groups and sport schools are organized; apart from the general program of education, specialist sport classes with an increased number of class hours are held.

The third group of classes includes the special classes whose common feature is accommodating physical education to the needs of pupils with lower physical abilities or health conditions. Classes of this type are provided for a relatively long period of time and on a large scale, especially in the Soviet Union, Czechoslovakia, and Hungary.

Obligatory physical education curricula are worked out centrally; specialized material is taught according to each school grade. Generally, the curricula include both types of subject matter: obligatory, for all schools; and optional, chosen by the physical education teacher. A tendency exists to enlarge the teacher's prerogatives in choosing the class material according to the conditions of the school and to geographical and climatic conditions.

The problem of evaluating the results for pupils' activities and achievements in the field of physical education produces controversy. The prevailing tendency is to determine measurable effects of physical ability. Usually the arrangements in this matter are settled in the curriculum or in a form of separate, centrally issued instructions.

For several years in some countries, mainly in the Soviet Union and the German Democratic Republic, homework assignments for physical education have been given. They have been regarded as a good way to individualize physical exercise and strengthen links between the school and the parents in the process of physical education of school children and youth.

This tendency is intensified by special physical education manuals for pupils. In the late 1960s, such manuals, worked out in an interesting way, were published in Yugoslavia. In recent years, a series of physical education manuals was published in Hungary. The manuals are also being published in Poland.

There occurred a tendency, worthy of mention, to unite physical education with hygiene, recreation, and tourism. This has been observed in all European socialist countries.

In projects concerning concepts of the future for school physical education in Poland, even full integration of physical education with hygiene is postulated.

Among the basic difficulties in school physical education development in European socialist countries is a serious lack of fully proficient physical education teachers in less-urbanized regions; another problem is the lack of ample sport buildings, supplies, and equipment. This is especially true in primary schools.

Reference

Jaworski, Z. (Ed.). (1976). *Szkolne wychowanie fizyczne w róznych krajach* [Physical education in schools of various countries]. Warsaw: Akademia Wychowania Fizychznego.

CHAPTER 15

Comparative Study of the Analysis of Objectives Within Sport Curricula From 1945-1984 Between the People's Republic of Poland and the Federal Republic of Germany

Annette Krüger

Pawel Kudlorz

One motivation for developing a comparison analysis of foreign countries is at least a wish to discover new and different things. Despite the fact that foreign education has a long tradition, only limited knowledge on certain countries exists (compare Krüger & Kudlorz, in press). This pilot study was started to help diminish the deficit of knowledge between the People's Republic of Poland (PRP) and the Federal Republic of Germany (FRG); the study compares the aims and objectives of physical education instruction between the PRP and in the FRG.

Because aims and objectives for school instruction are generally bound to historical processes, these historical processes must be analyzed in regard to their historical development. A pure status quo investigation easily could lead to superficial interpretations. To avoid this, the development of aims and objectives of both countries from 1945 until 1984 are analyzed.

This pilot study is supposed to be a first step of a planned large project; it will try to analyze content methods, evaluation forms, and so forth of school physical education and sport.

Rationale

If every school subject should prepare its pupils for the requirements of the respective society, then the hypothesis seems to be justified that aims and objectives of school physical education are different in different countries. But if the historical-geographical conditions of the PRP and the FRG are considered, both of which are continuing the English heritage of sport of the beginning 20th century, then the hypothesis should be differentiated. If the internationality of the modern top-level athletic sports is being considered, then the hypothesis seems to be justified that commonalities exist between the PRP and the FRG despite their different political and economical systems.

If one differentiates the genuine aims and objectives of physical education instruction (i.e., the aims and objectives that are mainly strived for in school physical education) and the nongenuine sport-specific aims and objectives (i.e., those that can be achieved within other subjects) then the two opposite hypotheses can be integrated. It can be assumed that commonalities exist in regard to the genuine sport-specific aims and objectives and that, in regard to nongenuine aims and objectives, differences exist between the aims and objectives of physical education instruction in the PRP and in the FRG. If one considers the federal structure of the FRG and the autonomy of the states in regard to school politics, it can be assumed that differences exist between the different federal states within the FRG, and therefore that there is only a high degree of commonality between Poland and one of two German federal states.

The aims and objectives of physical education instruction can be differentiated according to their degrees of concreteness. For instance, there are both general and sport-specific aims and objectives. The general aims and objectives normally are part of the introduction to the curricula and serve to legitimize sport content within school instruction. The more concrete sport-specific aims and objectives (often called *rough objectives*) are related directly to the objectives that should be reached through physical education instruction. Even more concrete are the theme-specific objectives (named *fine objectives*) that are supposed to be reached during the last years in the FRG with the help of special sport-disciplines such as specific, sport-related training and game forms of selected topics.

Because gaps exist between the different levels of concreteness—general sport-specific aims (rough objectives) and theme-specific aims (fine objectives)—this pilot study limits itself to the sport-specific aims and objectives. The analysis of general theme-specific aims and objectives and their relationships to each other must be done in other investigations.

The already-mentioned federal structure of the educational system in the FRG makes it necessary to present the curricula of all German federal states. To include the consequences of the respective ruling parties that govern the states in regard to aims and objectives, the data bases are the curricula of the federal states Nordrhein-Westfalen and Schleswig-Holstein (which are exemplary for Social Democratic Party of Germany and Christian Democratic Union governed states in the Federal Republic of Germany).

The Investigation

The investigation concentrated on the general schools, especially grades 1–4 of primary school and grades 5–13 of the "Gymnasium" of the FRG, and on grades 1–8 of primary school and grades 9–12 of the general lyceum in the PRP (compare Krüger & Kudlorz, 1984).

After a very extensive search of the respective curricula, 10 curricula of Schleswig-Holstein and 12 curricula from Nordrhein-Westfalen were analyzed. Because receiving information within the FRG on school problems in Poland was not possible and because this pilot study originated with a guest professorship of Dr. Kudlorz at the Kiel-University, the work of A. Lubowicz (1976) is the basis on which eight curricula from Poland from 1946–1966 are analyzed. This analysis was added to the new curricula available from Poland from 1978, 1983, and 1984. (The last Polish curriculum developed in 1984 for the general educational lyceum will be in effect in 1986.) Furthermore, open interviews were held with Professor Dr. Zukowska, Educational Researcher and Dean, and Professor Dr. Jaworski, Chairman of the Humanistic Institute of the Warsaw Academy of Physical Education, to get information about the development of pedagogy and sport pedagogy.

Results of the Curriculum Analysis

First the curriculum differences between Poland and the FRG are presented; then the commonalities of the PRP, Schleswig-Holstein, and Nordrhein-Westfalen are presented, as well as the commonalities of the PRP and Schleswig-Holstein and the PRP and Nordrhein-Westfalen. Data are taken from Kultusministerium des landes Nordrhein-Westfalen (1948, 1949, 1960, 1963, 1969, 1972, 1973, 1974a, 1974b, 1975, 1980, n.d.) and Kultusministerium des landes Schleswig-Holstein (1949, 1950, 1955, 1961, 1972a, 1972b, 1974, 1975, 1978a, 1978b, 1978c). The basis for differentiation of the differences or commonalities within the PRP and between Poland and the FRG primarily is the number of times the aims and objectives appear. Only in the second line is the time of appearance considered. *Commonality* means the difference of three or less objectives, while *difference* is the difference of more than three objectives.

Differences Between Aims of the People's Republic of Poland and the Federal Republic of Germany

Table 1 clarifies the differences in aims between the PRP and FRG.

Table 1 shows that only one nongenuine sport-specific aim, "Experiences and knowledge of the home country and the surroundings" is available. All other aims, which are either typically Polish or typically German, are genuine sport-specific aims. Interestingly enough, all aims, with the exception of "Promotion of development" (PRP) and of "Promotion of talent" (FRG), are included in the curricula only after 1970.

Table 1 Differences Between the Aims of the People's Republic of Poland and the Federal Republic of Germany

Aims	Frequencies		
	PRP	NRW	SH
PRP			
Promotion of development	10	2	4.5
Development of skills for recreation, daily life, profession, and defense	3[b]	0	0
Usage of the city for movement and sport	3[b]	0	0
Development of joy in movement and play	9	5.5	5
Experiences and knowledge of the home country and the surroundings[a]	5	0.5	0
FRG			
Promotion of talent	0	8.5	3
Experience of body, material, and risk	0	8	1[b]
Orientation for profession	0	3[b]	0
Development of fantasy and creativity	3[b]	8	7.5

Note. PRP = People's Republic of Poland. NRW = Nordrhein-Westfalen. SH = Schleswig-Holstein. FRG = Federal Republic of Germany. Half namings occur because some aims and objectives were restricted to only boys or only girls.
[a]This is the only nongenuine sport-specific aim; all others are genuine.
[b]Named for the first time after 1970.

Commonalities Among the Aims of the People's Republic of Poland, Nordrhein-Westfalen, and Schleswig-Holstein

Table 2 displays the common aims of the People's Republic of Poland and two German states.

All three areas have a high amount of agreement on these aims, which are oriented toward optimizing and toward developing other aims such as "Development of feeling and space," an aim not mentioned very often in all three areas. The nongenuine sport-specific aim "Attitudes for social integration" is mentioned almost equally as often.

Table 2 Commonalities Among the Aims of the People's Republic of Poland, Nordrhein-Westfalen, and Schleswig-Holstein

Aims	Frequencies		
	PRP	NRW	SH
Genuine sport-specific aims			
Promotion of general physical performance	10	10.5	8.5
Learning and improvement of movement skills	10	10.5	7.5
Development of feeling for rhythm and space	3	4	5
Ability for organizing sport	3	2	2
Sport-specific attitudes	3	3	3
Theory beyond sport disciplines	5	7	6
Critical understanding of movement and play	3	8	5
Nongenuine sport-specific aims			
Attitudes for social integration	5	5	6
Emancipative values	3	5.5	8
Working attitude	5	8	10

Note. PRP = People's Republic of Poland. NRW = Nordrhein-Westfalen. SH = Schleswig-Holstein. Half namings occur because some aims and objectives were restricted to only boys or only girls.

Commonalities Between the Aims of the People's Republic of Poland and Schleswig-Holstein and Differences with Nordrhein-Westfalen

Table 3 compares the People's Republic of Poland and the two German states to show similarities with Schleswig-Holstein and differences with Nordrhein-Westfalen.

The commonalities between the aims of the PRP and Schleswig-Holstein occur mainly because of the later recognition of aims in Schleswig-Holstein than in Nordrhein-Westfalen.

The first exception is the development of movement aesthetics; in Nordrhein-Westfalen this is only mentioned in the specific aims for special sport

Table 3 Commonalities Between the Aims of the People's Republic of Poland and Schleswig-Holstein and Differences with Nordrhein-Westfalen

Aims	Frequencies		
	PRP	SH	NRW
Genuine sport-specific aims			
Development of movement/aesthetics	3	2	0
Lifelong sport engagement	3	3.5	9.5
Recreational sport within and outside of school	3	2	7
Nongenuine sport-specific aims			
Introduction to scientific work	4	4.5	8
Development of character	5	6	1

Note. PRP = People's Republic of Poland. SH = Schleswig-Holstein. NRW = Nordrhein-Westfalen. Half namings occur because some aims and objectives were restricted to only boys or only girls.

disciplines. The second exception is development of character, which is equally often named in the PRP and in Schleswig-Holstein. This aim was named in Schleswig-Holstein mainly before 1956 for boys, while in the PRP it appeared for the first time in 1959 for both sexes.

Commonalities Between the Aims of the People's Republic of Poland and Nordrhein-Westfalen and Differences with Schleswig-Holstein

Table 4 shows the differences and similarities among the three areas on two genuine sport-specific aims.

One of the commonalities of the PRP and Nordrhein-Westfalen is the high-ranking aim "Prophylaxis, compensation, and recreation." In the PRP this appears in all catalogues for general aims from 1945 until 1984. In Schleswig-Holstein this aim does not have the priority that it does in Nordrhein-Westfalen and the PRP. The same is true for the aim "Multiple ability for movement."

Analysis in Regard to the Hypothesis

The fact that only one nongenuine and eight genuine sport-specific aims are mentioned in all three areas equally often, and that, in total, there are

Table 4 **Commonalities Between the Aims of the People's Republic of Poland and Nordrhein-Westfalen and Differences with Schleswig-Holstein**

Aims	Frequencies		
	PRP	NRW	SH
Prophylaxis, compensation, and recreation	11	11	6
Multiple ability for movement	11	8.5	2

Note. PRP = People's Republic of Poland. NRW = Nordrhein-Westfalen. SH = Schleswig-Holstein. Half namings occur because some aims and objectives were restricted to only boys or only girls.

four nongenuine sport-specific and six genuine sport-specific aims in common between the PRP and only one federal state of Germany proves the third hypothesis, namely that differences exist between the different states within the FRG.

After analyzing all sport-specific (rough) learning objectives of physical education and sport in the available Polish and German curricula (with no less than 97 objectives in Nordrhein-Westfalen and Schleswig-Holstein), the aims and objectives were differentiated into "genuine," "nongenuine," "single objective," and "summary" categories; this occurred after language barriers and related different content meanings of termini were discussed and solved.

The first hypothesis can be considered to be proven, because there are commonalities between the genuine sport-specific aims of the PRP and of the FRG. From 21 genuine sport-specific aims, 15 aims, including those that are in agreement with only one state of the FRG, are common. Considering that many commonalities between the aims of the PRP and of Schleswig-Holstein only exist because these aims were included in the Schleswig-Holstein curricula after they appeared in the Nordrhein-Westfalen curricula, the consideration of the commonalities between the PRP and only one of two states of the FRG seems to be justified. In spite of this fact, almost one quarter of sport-specific aims are different, and the commonalities of the sport-specific aims are not geared toward optimization; these observations require interpretation.

The second hypothesis, which says that because of the economic system and political state form, nongenuine sport-specific aims are different, can be considered to be wrong because five of the six nongenuine sport-specific aims are named by the PRP and the FRG almost equally frequently. In regard to commonalities and differences, factors other than politics or economics have to be considered (e.g., the influence of the pedagogy in Poland in relation to physical culture).

Interpretations of Selected Results

Because all results cannot be discussed within this limited space, one genuine sport-specific aim of the FRG—development of talent—is taken and analyzed according to the reasons for consideration of this aim. Reasons for commonalities and differences between the aims of the PRP and the FRG also are discussed.

Consideration of the Aim "Development of Talent"

The development of talent can be regarded as a specifically German aim which has been included in the Nordrhein-Westfalen curriculum since 1969 and in the Schleswig-Holstein curriculum continuously only since 1975, because no new curricula were developed for primary or secondary school in this state between 1969 and 1975. This fact has to be interpreted with some historical remarks. The poor showing of the German Gymnastics Federation team at the Olympic trials in 1964 (more athletes participated from the German Democratic Republic than from the Federal Republic of Germany within the German Olympic teams), the decision to have the 1972 Olympic Games in Munich, and the birth of the German Democratic Republic's own Olympic team in 1968 supported a comparison of the systems in regard to athletics. The development of talent was introduced as an aim within the FRG school sport curricula to produce Olympic athletes. Because the PRP has independent sport schools that promote pupils' talents in sport, this aim did not appear within the schools for general education.

Commonalities and Differences Between Aims of the People's Republic of Poland and the Federal Republic of Germany

The status of pedagogy at the end of the 1960s and the beginning of the 1970s could be a possible explanation for the commonalities between aims, especially the new aims in the PRP and the FRG such as "Developing emancipative values" and "Introducing scientific work."

In 1970, the third phase (1970–1984) of Polish pedagogy replaced the second phase (1956–1970), which had followed the first phase (1945–1955) (cf., Krüger & Kudlorz, in press). The starting point of the third phase was a report, published in 1973, on the status of education in Poland. Tendencies of pedagogy in Western European countries are also considered in this report. This led to the fact that Polish pedagogy made the theories of permanent education (lifelong learning) a basis of the third phase, which was developed in the late 1960s in France. Therefore school instruction was no longer considered the only possibility for education of individuals. School education was considered as only one aspect of total education, which either at the same time or later could be supplemented by other educational situations and possibilities and other educational institutions.

Three major aims are valid for school instruction in the PRP since that time: (a) the preparation for life in the given society, (b) the preparation for a profession, (c) and the preparation for participation in cultural life. A manifold personality must be developed to reach these aims. Three aims are understood under the term *manifold personality education*: the transmission of a basic motivation for lifelong learning, of techniques and methods for independent learning (introduction to science), and of the ability to participate in the social and cultural life. From a content point of view, such education is intended to affect knowledge, motivation, and emotion. These aims lean toward development of new educational forms of interaction, of process methods, of installment of voluntary learning units outside of school, and of increased freedom of the teacher to select a variety of topics for instruction.

Physical education and sport have been recognized as part of the social cultural life, as noticed in the changing of the terminology, to *physical culture*. Based on the aim "Preparing for participation in culture," more people had to be attracted to instruction in physical education and sport (not only those who had fun in sport according to international rules). Therefore the aims "Development of feeling for rhythm and space," "Development of fantasy and creativity," "Development of movement aesthetics," and "Recreational sport within and outside of school" were included under the aspect of lifelong engagement in sports. At the same time, pupils were to learn to engage in sport independently, without instruction. In connection with this, sport safety had to be increased to avoid accidents. This increased understanding can be seen in the general aims "Development of psychomotor and movement aesthetics" and "Individual, social abilities and attitudes." In opposition to the second phase, in which the educational and transfer value of attitudes acquired in sport was questioned (therefore the nongenuine sport-specific aims, except character development, were not appearing anymore in sport curricula), in the third phase the educational values are accepted and included again. However, the aims are supplemented with an introduction to science, which is equivalent to the educational aim of transmitting techniques and methods for independent learning and the promotion of "emancipative values," without which independent learning is not possible.

In regard to physical education instruction in the FRG, the connection of education and sport curricula did not exist in the FRG as it did in the PRP. Nevertheless, sport curricula could not be completely untouched by educational developments (cf., Krüger & Kudlorz, in press).

In the early 1960s the dominant educational direction since World War II (called Bildungstheorie) was criticized. Positivists said that the Bildungstheorie didn't sufficiently address the realities of school. The "Critical Theory" School (Frankfurter Schule) attacked the Bildungstheorie for its insufficient consideration of social influences. Because of these criticisms, the Bildungstheorie representatives asked whether this educational theory might be at the end of its period. Because of its basic theory, the educational theory for practice had to be written afterward; thus developing a value system to evaluate successful education and to offer solutions for available social requirements was not possible.

In the mid 1960s the cry "in regard to the future educational catastrophy" could be heard; this meant that the FRG compared to other industrial nations, fell back and had too few scientific technologically qualified young people (Blankertz, 1982). Furthermore, it became clear that the speed of social, technical, and economic development and the change in living conditions and working relationships had surpassed the knowledge that pupils had acquired in school. Therefore schools had to "awake the joy for constant further learning" and prepare the pupils for lifelong learning (cf. Deutscher Bildungsrat, 1970 p. 33). A comprehensive school reform was intended on the basis of the basic law (recognition and security for the dignity of man, free development of the personality, and free choice of profession), on the basis of the replacement of a static understanding with a dynamic understanding of talent (understanding learning processes independent of social classes), on the basis of the replacement of formal equality of chances with material equality of chances and on the basis of recognition of lifelong learning (cf. Deutscher Bildungsrat, 1970).

Because of the difference of cultural values, a certain catalogue of school subjects in the general education could not be reduced anymore. Therefore pupils were to be able to choose their individual educations themselves. The unity of education was guaranteed through the scientific orientation of all learning or through an introduction to science. With the introduction of the differentiated upper level of the gymnasium in 1972, the pupil could choose two "Leistungskurse" under the conditions in which he or she received 5 or 6 hours, instead of 3 hours, of instruction per week. This led to an equal position of sport with other subjects. On the other hand, the sport didactics had to integrate the orientation for the profession and introduce science into the curricula (i.e., introduce a critical understanding of movement, play, and sport theory beyond sport disciplines as well as emancipative values).

In the mid 1970s, the aims of sport, which so far were mainly geared toward optimizing sportive performance, were enlarged because until this time, the development of talent dominated. Therefore the following aims were included: "Organize sport," "Experience of body, material, and risk," and, as far as not yet realized, "Recreational sport within and outside of school."

When considering both developments, it becomes clear that the changes in the educational understanding (despite different theoretical foundations) in the FRG and in the PRP in the beginning of the 1970s are leading to a major alteration in physical education instruction. It is to become an "introduction to science," concentrating on lifelong learning and sport-specific aims that are not geared only toward optimization of sport played by international rules.

Final Remarks

As mentioned in the introduction, these results and interpretations are only a first step in a more comprehensive comparison of aims in the PRP and in the FRG. Many questions could not be considered in this analysis, such as: Is there really a direct relationship between education and sport curricula as there seemed to be in the 1970s? Are there other intervening factors such as the German Sport Federation in the Federal Republic of Germany that are not expressed in the interpretation?

References

Blankertz, H. (1982). *Geschichte der Padagogik* [History of Pedagogy]. Wetzlar.

Deutscher Bildungsrat. (1970). *Empfehlungen der Bildungskommission* [Recommendation of the educational committee. Structure scheme for the educational system]. Stuttgart: Author.

Krüger, A., & Kudlorz, P. (in press, a). The deplorable state of comparison of German-Polish and Polish-German physical education at school-demonstrated by the publications concerning physical education at school in the Federal Republic of Germany and the People's Republic of Poland. *Journal of Comparative Physical Education*.

Krüger, A., & Kudlorz, P. (in press, b). An analysis of aims and objectives of curricula of physical education (1945-1984). A comparative study between the People's Republic of Poland and the Federal Republic of Germany. *Journal of Comparative Physical Education*.

Krüger, A., & Kudlorz, P. (1984). *Der Sportunterricht in der Volksrepublik Polen und Ansätze zu einer vergleichenden Untersuchung zur Bundesrepublik Deutschland* [The physical education in the People's Republic of Poland and first start of a comparative study to the Federal Republic of Germany]. Paper presented at the Deutsche Sporthochschule Köln.

Kultusministerium des Landes Nordrhein-Westfalen. (1948). *Richtlinien und Stoffpläne für die Leibeserziehung der Knaben in NRW* [General directions and subject schemes of the physical education of boys in NRW]. Köln: Author.

Kultusministerium des Landes Nordrhein-Westfalen. (1949). *Richtlinien und Stoffplan für die Leibeserziehung der Mädchen an Volks-, Mittel-, Berufs-, Fachund höheren Schulen in Nordrhein-Westfalen* [General directions and subject scheme of the physical education of girls in elementary, high, vocational, technical and secondary schools in NRW]. Köln: Author.

Kultusministerium des Landes Nordrhein-Westfalen. (1960). *Richtlinien und Stoffplan für die Leibeserziehung der Mädchen an Volks-, Mittel-, Berufs-, Fachund höheren Schulen in Nordrhein-Westfalen* [General directions and subject scheme of the physical education of girls in elementary, high, vocational, technical and secondary schools in NRW]. Frankfurt/Main: Author.

Kultusministerium des Landes Nordrhein-Westfalen. (1963). *Die Schule in Nordrhein-Westfalen—Richtlinien für den Unterricht in der höheren Schule Leibeserziehung* [School in NordrheinWestfalen—General directions of instruction in secondary school physical education]. Ratingen: Author.

Kultusministerium des Landes Nordrhein-Westfalen. (1969). *Richtlinien und Lehrpläne für die Grundschule/Schulversuche in Nordrhein-Westfalen* [General directions and school curriculum of elementary school/school attempts in Nordrhein-Westfalen]. Ratingen: Author.

Kultusministerium des Landes Nordrhein-Westfalen. (1972). *Reform der Gymnasialen Oberstufe Fach Sport* [Reform of the last three classes of grammar school—subject physical education]. Krefeld: Author.

Kultusministerium des Landes Nordrhein-Westfalen. (1973). *Richtlinien und Lehrpläne für die Grundschule in Nordrhein-Westfalen* [General directions and school curricula of the elementary school in NRW]. Ratingen: Author.

Kultusministerium des Landes Nordrhein-Westfalen. (1974a). *Curriculum Gymn. Oberstufe—Fach Sport* [Curriculum of the last three classes of grammar school—subject physical education]. Ratingen: Author.

Kultusministerium des Landes Nordrhein-Westfalen. (1974b). *Sek. II-Gymnasium-Empfehlungen für den Kursunterricht des Faches Sport* [Sect. II-grammar school. Recommendations for the course instruction of the subject physical education]. Ratingen: Author.

Kultusministerium des Landes Nordrhein-Westfalen. (1975). *Sek. I-Gymnasium Sport um Terrichtsempfehlungen* [Sect. I-grammar school. Physical education instruction recommendations]. Ratingen: Author.

Kultusministerium des Landes Nordrhein-Westfalen. (1980). *Richtlinien für den Sport in den Schulen im Lande Nordrhein-Westfalen* [General directions for physical education in schools in NRW]. Bd. 1-5. Köln: Author.

Kultusministerium des Landes Nordrhein-Westfalen. (n.d.). *Richlinien und Lehrpläne fur die Grundschule in Nordrhein-Westfalen—Sport* [General Directions and school curriculums of elementary school in NRW—physical education]. Ratingen: Author.

Kultusministerium des Landes Schleswig-Holstein. (1949). *Richtlinien für die Lehrpläne der 6-jährigen Grundschule in Schleswig-Holstein* [General directions for the curricula of the sexennial primary school in Schleswig-Holstein]. Kiel: Author.

Kultusministerium des Landes Schleswig-Holstein. (1950). *Lehrplan für die sechs-jährigen Grundschulen der Stadt Kiel* [School curriculum for the sexennial primary schools of the city Kiel]. Kiel: Author.

Kultusministerium des Landes Schleswig-Holstein. (1955). *Lehrplanricht-linien für die Gymnasien* [General curriculum directions for grammar schools]. Lübeck: Author.

Kultusministerium des Landes Schleswig-Holstein. (1961). *Richtlinien für die Lehrpläne der Grundschulen in Schleswig-Holstein* [General directions for the school curricula of elementary schools in Schleswig-Holstein]. Kiel: Author.

Kultusministerium des Landes Schleswig-Holstein. (1972a). *Vorläufige Rah-menrichtlinien für Sport in der Studienstufe (Grundkurs)* [Provisional general directions for physical education in the last three years of grammar school (fundamental course)]. Kiel: Author.

Kultusministerium des Landes Schleswig-Holstein. (1972b). *Ergänzungen zu den vorläufigen Richtlinien* [Supplement to the provisional general directions]. Kiel: Author.

Kultusministerium des Landes Schleswig-Holstein. (1974). *Vorläufige Richt-linien für das Leistungsfach Sport* [Provisional general directions for achievement subject physical education]. Kiel: Author.

Kultusministerium des Landes Schleswig-Holstein. (1975). *Lehrplan Sport Grundschule in Schleswig-Holstein* [School curriculum physical education elementary school in Schleswig-Holstein]. (n.p.).

Kultusministerium des Landes Schleswig-Holstein. (1978a). *Lehrplan Grundschule und Vorklasse* [School curriculum elementary school and pre-school]. (n.p.).

Kultusministerium des Landes Schleswig-Holstein. (1978b). *Leistungsan-forderungen im Fach Sport in der gymnasialen Oberstufe* [Performance norms in the subject physical education in the last three years of grammar school]. Kiel: Author.

Kultusministerium des Landes Schleswig-Holstein. (1978c). *Lehrplan Gym-nasium—Sport Orientierungsstufe* [Curriculum grammar school—physical education orientation classes]. Kronshagen: Author.

Lubowicz, A. (1976). Cele. In Z. Jaworski (Ed.), *Szkolne Wychowanie Fizyczne w Polsce Ludowej*. Warsaw: Akademia Wychowania Fizycznego.

Schulabteilung der Regierung Zu Schleswig. (1946). *Lehrplan für die Grund-schulen Schleswig-Holstein* [Curriculum for the elementary schools of Schleswig-Holstein]. Schleswig: Author.

CHAPTER 16

An East-West Comparative Study of Physical Education and Sport

March L. Krotee,

James E. Larson, and

Peter Rattigan

Any comparative study of physical education and sport has as its primary objectives: the presentation, the description, the interpretation and evaluation, the juxtaposition or preliminary comparison, and ultimately the simultaneous comparison of the central issues at hand (Jones, 1971). It is with this intention that an East-West comparison of selected physical education and sport data gathered in the Republic of China, the United Kingdom, and the United States is offered. The data for the investigation were compiled by employing a myriad of research techniques including observations, surveys, primary and secondary literature reviews, and personal interviews with representatives from each country's physical education and sport domains. The data have been tempered and shaped in part by the international education comparison model that was developed by Hanafy and Krotee in 1986 to assess Middle East perspectives (Hanafy & Krotee, 1986).

Like any comparative study of physical education and sport, no country's or nation's physical education and sport can be fully represented or understood. How physical activity and sport is engaged in, under what circumstances, who performs it, at what level of intensity, as well as who observes it, are all of prime importance in understanding the meaning of physical activity and sport. Bearing this in mind, the authors have attempted to present just a small segment of the salient physical education and sport processes (e.g., historical background, underlying aims and objectives, various delivery systems and administrative structures, and curriculum) and also a view into the future of physical education and sport in the sociocultural process of each country. The study as presented is not meant to be comprehensive in nature, but rather to offer to the reader a glimpse of the physical education and sporting processes (characteristics and developments) in relation to East-West variation, similarity, and uniqueness. The significance of such an investigation is to educate serious students about various educational systems, styles, issues, and problems so that we, as professionals, can realize more fully the global educational awareness that is needed so that we may develop to our fullest potential (Krotee, 1981 and 1986; Mallinson, 1957).

Historical Background

The roots of ancient physical education and sport in East Asia may be traced to Huang Ti, the first Emperor of China (2697-2596 B.C.), who is credited with the invention of the bow and arrow and with an ancient version of football. The infusion of physical education in the ancient school systems of China did not evolve until approximately 1122 B.C. when the ''Six Arts'' (a form of dance) and such physical activities as various dance forms, football, juggling, dragon boat racing, boxing, and wrestling permeated the Chou Dynasty. Toward the decline of the Ching Dynasty (1644-1911), various Western physical education programs and sports, as well as philosophies, began to influence the Republic (established in 1912). Early influences such as formalized calisthenics, athletics, and basketball took firm hold. The importance of physical education and sport was nurtured and grew within China, and in 1929 the National Physical Education Act was consummated. The following presents an idea of its sociocultural significance:

National Physical Education Act

Article 1: The main purpose of physical education programs of the Republic of China is the development of a sound body and a sense of justice and fair play with a view to training the people to be able to defend themselves and the nation.

Article 2: All Chinese, regardless of sex and age, shall be given proper physical training, which shall be carried out in families, schools, and public organizations under the supervision of parents, teachers and officials so as to achieve a balanced and rapid development of physical education.

(Ministry of Education, 1982)

England's physical education and sport roots may also be traced into antiquity. Similar to China, England's roots stemmed from the need for national defense and self-protection and were founded on the medieval chivalric educational goals of war, religion, and gallantry (1150-1350). Sports were popular during this period and included such activities as dancing, swimming, horseback riding, playing quoits, bowling, playing handball, playing bandy-ball, stone throwing, playing bat and ball games, wrestling, and playing football. It was recorded that, on more than one occasion, merchants petitioned the government to forbid sports that lead to riots and destruction of property. In 1314, Edward II proclaimed football illegal and Edward III (1312-1377) decreed all sports except those with military usefulness (i.e., archery) illegal. These actions, however, did little to dampen the English passion for physical activity and sport. Physical activity has stood the test of time; the 1800s found physical education and sport firmly entrenched in the renowned English public schools (fee-paying schools) where games such as football, cricket, and rowing were practiced to instill discipline and "character" in the students. In 1870, the Foster Education Act empowered the local authorities to organize elementary schools (physical education was not included in these schools as of 1870). A year later, however, an amendment to the bill permitted drill to count for attendance purposes. Therein lay the foundation for the inclusion of physical training within the elementary schools. The early 1900s yielded further government support and aid in the form of "free places," as well as an extension of mandatory schooling and age requirements; physical education and sport continued within the English curricular structure.

In the late 19th century several colleges for the physical training of women were founded (i.e., Dartford, 1885); but no such luxury prevailed for the men until the 1930s (Carnegie, 1933; Loughborough, 1935). This somewhat accounted for the men's rigid military drill and posture inoculation, while the women received somewhat more systematic training based on the Swedish gymnastics system; each gender's activities were included under the auspices of the Medical Department of the Board of Education. England is famous, of course, for its sport organizations; soccer (1863), swimming (1869), rowing (1870), cycling (1878), skating (1879), athletics (1880), and tennis (1886) lead the way in this regard. Further evidence of the English passion for physical activity and the outdoors include scouting (1907), the development of the National Playing Fields Association (1926), the hostel movement (1930s), and the founding of the Central Council for Recreative Physical Training (1935), now the Central Council for Physical Recreation. England today continues its physical education and sport tradition and leadership and its bond of association; cooperation between physical education, amateur sport, and public recreation continues to be a model for everyone.

The history and roots of physical education and sport in the United States are not as difficult to grasp as those of China and the United Kingdom. The USA was established as an English colony in 1607 (in Virginia); its colonists had little time for play and physical activity. Any physical activities that were displayed were settled around military emphases, the three Rs, and the statement "the devil finds plenty of work for idle hands to do." In 1774, the First Continental Congress called upon the Colonies to discourage extravagance—especially horse-racing, gaming, cockfighting, and participating in other forms of entertainment. Physical training in the form of military drills pervaded the schools of this era, and the Morrill Act of 1862 required physical training in all state colleges. Until this act, gymnastics, manual training, and calisthenics, along with such extracurricular sporting movements as the Turnverein (1848), Caledonian Games (1853), and the beginning of baseball (1850s), sporadically represented the interest in physical education and sport within the American schools of the 1850s. Popular activities of the time included horse-racing, boxing, and pedestrianism; education continued to mature and develop to the point where free schooling became an established principle supported by public taxation (Kalamazoo case of 1872). The American Association for the Advancement of Physical Education was founded in 1885; 200,000 spectators witnessed the Cincinnati Red Stockings play baseball (1869); the inaugural America's Cup (1870) and the first running of the Kentucky Derby (1875) highlighted this era. The development of YMCAs as professional training schools (1890s), and the growth of intercollegiate sport in the form of football (1869), rowing, baseball, and athletics spread and popularized physical activity and sport throughout the nation.

Faculties of physical education were established at Amherst, Harvard, Yale, Oberlin, California, Stanford, and Nebraska, and a master's degree program was offered by Columbia in the early 1900s. Recreational sports in the form of intramurals surfaced in 1913 at the University of Michigan and Ohio State University. World War I brought physical education to the high schools as conflict had done with China and England throughout history; the awareness of requisite military fitness continued to influence public education. Physical education and sport continued to spread through the nation and became one of the primary processes of Americanization. Today physical education and sport permeates nearly every segment of America. From kindergarten to the golden master, from recreational to professional, and from community endeavor to educational outreach programs, physical education and sport has become a dominant social force in the lives of many Americans.

Aims and Objectives

To assist in the understanding of any nation's physical education and sporting process, it is requisite that some of the basic foundations of these processes be identified.

For example, in China, according to the National Physical Education Act of 1929, the fundamental goal of physical education and sport is to educate the people so as to assure balanced development in the qualities of virtue, wisdom, and physical fitness and to promote a sense of togetherness. Further objectives of each school level where physical education is mandatory include the following:

Objectives of Physical Education in Primary Schools
- To promote the physical and mental well-being of the child and thus assure his balanced development
- To guide the child in the learning of basic skills and thus develop his athletic abilities
- To cultivate such virtues as fairness, obedience, responsibility, honesty, friendliness, cooperativeness, courage, and decisiveness, etc. as a firm basis for his later participation in community life
- To teach the child the ways of health and sanitation and develop his good habits

- To encourage an interest in sports in the child and thus enrich his recreational life

Objectives of Physical Education in Junior High Schools
- To train the body, to enhance vitality, and to promote the full development of the physique
- To cultivate a spirit of public virtue and mutual cooperation through athletic competition
- To develop a love for physical activity, to promote mental and physical health, and to establish a firm basis for recreational life
- To train in athletic skills, to increase the efficiency of the use of body energy, and to strengthen capacity to adapt in security and self-defense situations

Objectives of Physical Education in Senior High Schools and Colleges
- To guide students in training their bodies, to enhance their vitality, to promote a balanced development of their bodies
- To cultivate a spirit of sportsmanship in students as a basis for their good moral conduct
- To develop in students love for physical activity, to establish a firm basis for recreational life
- To enhance the athletic skills of the student and his capacity to adapt in security and self-defense situations
- To enrich the athletic knowledge and ability of normal school students and prepare them for work as physical education instructors

(Ministry of Education, 1982)

In 1934, the British Medical Association Physical Education Committee reported that schools contributed little to the physical education and leisure-time activity process. From that point, a national effort culminating in the Education Act of 1944 was instituted to provide programs, facilities, and training on the local level to remedy the situation and meet the nation's needs.

The following are some of the major physical education objectives of the highly decentralized educational system in the United Kingdom:

- Development of coordination and movement skills, ball skills
- Fostering of enjoyment and cooperation through non-competitive games (elementary)
- Development of social skills (teamwork, cooperation, competition)
- Physical development and enjoyment of active/passive participation
- Lifetime participation
- Development of a knowledge of sports
- Development of a knowledge of bodily functions and health
- Aesthetic development

(Data from survey conducted by authors in schools of
Bedfordshire and Kent, England, 1984)

Aims and/or purposes of physical education and sport are dynamic in nature. Sargent, a pioneer physical educator, introduced some of his innovative ideas concerning physical education when he came to Harvard in 1879. He suggested the aims of physical education to be fourfold:

1. Hygienic: the consideration of the normal proportions of the individual, the anatomy and the physiological functions of various organs, and a study of the ordinary agents of health such as exercise, diet, sleep, air, bathing, and clothing.
2. Educative: the cultivation of special powers of mind and body used in the acquisition of some skillful trade of physical accomplishment, such as golf, swimming, or skating.
3. Recreative: the renovation of vital energies to enable the individual to return to his daily work with vigor and accomplish his tasks with ease.
4. Remedial: the restoration of disturbed functions and the correction of physical defects and deformities.

(Sargent, 1906, p. 66-71)

He further stated in an article in 1883 that the purpose of muscular exercise was not to attain bodily health and beauty alone, "but to break up morbid mental tendencies, to dispel the gloomy shadows of despondency, and to ensure serenity of spirit" (Sargent, 1883, p. 177).

In 1918 in the United States, the Seven Cardinal Principles of Secondary Education were established. They included the following:

1. Health
2. Command of fundamental processes
3. Worthy home membership
4. Vacation competence
5. Citizenship
6. Worthy use of leisure time
7. Ethical character

(Voltmer & Esslinger, 1949)

A restructuring of these principles by the Educational Policies Commission in 1938 found the following four objectives and subobjectives in its *Purposes of Education in American Democracy:*

1. The objectives of self-realization
2. The objectives of human relationship
3. The objectives of economic efficiency
4. The objectives of civic responsibility

(Educational Policies Commission, 1938)

In 1961, the Educational Policies Commission redesigned the purpose of American education. The following quotation contains the Commission's concluding statement:

Individual freedom and effectiveness and the progress of the society require the development of every citizen's rational powers. Among the many important purposes of American schools, the fostering of that development must be central.

Man has already transformed his world by using his mind. As he expands the application of rationale methods to problems old and new, and as people in growing numbers are enabled to contribute to such endeavors, man will increase his ability to understand, to act, and to alter his environment. Where these developments will lead cannot be foretold.

Man has before him the possibility of a new level of greatness, a new realization of human dignity and effectiveness. The instrument which will realize this possibility is that kind of education which frees the mind and enables it to contribute to a full and worthy life. To achieve this goal is the high hope of the nation and the central challenge to its schools.

(Educational Policies Commission, 1961, p. 21)

To place these purposes in focus in the United States physical education and sport context, the following program philosophy and set of goals from a typical public school setting are offered.

Physical education is an essential and basic part of the total educational program, K-12. It is a process that contributes to the total development of every student through the natural medium of physical activity—HUMAN MOVEMENT—and recognizes the unique characteristics of students—physical, mental, emotional and social.

Physical education is helpful immediately to the individual and also prepares students for a productive life. Their bodies are important to the way they think, feel and act, thereby establishing pathways to success. Learning how to function well physically provides one of the best life assurances students can develop in preparation for survival in today's society.

The physical education program in Minnesota is designed to provide a variety of motor experiences to help all students, K-12, develop skills, knowledge and attitudes necessary to maintain health and to function effectively in society. The program goals are as follows:

- Fosters vigorous physical activity and the improvement of physical fitness
- Develops motor skills
- Cultivates opportunities for creativity
- Emphasizes health and safety
- Motivates expression and communication
- Promotes self-understanding and acceptance of self and others
- Stimulates social development
- Encourages worthy use of leisure time
- Provides stimulation for perceptual motor competencies

(Survey conducted by authors of St. Paul, Minnesota School District, 1984)

Delivery Systems and School Systems

The three countries included in this investigation offer both similarities and differences in the delivery of physical education and sport within their respective school system structures. The delivery systems, including some data concerning number of pupils, age, and divisional structure, of China, the United Kingdom, and the United States, are offered in Tables 1, 2, and 3. Some fundamental similarities are the inclusion of preschool and kindergarten and free education until high school

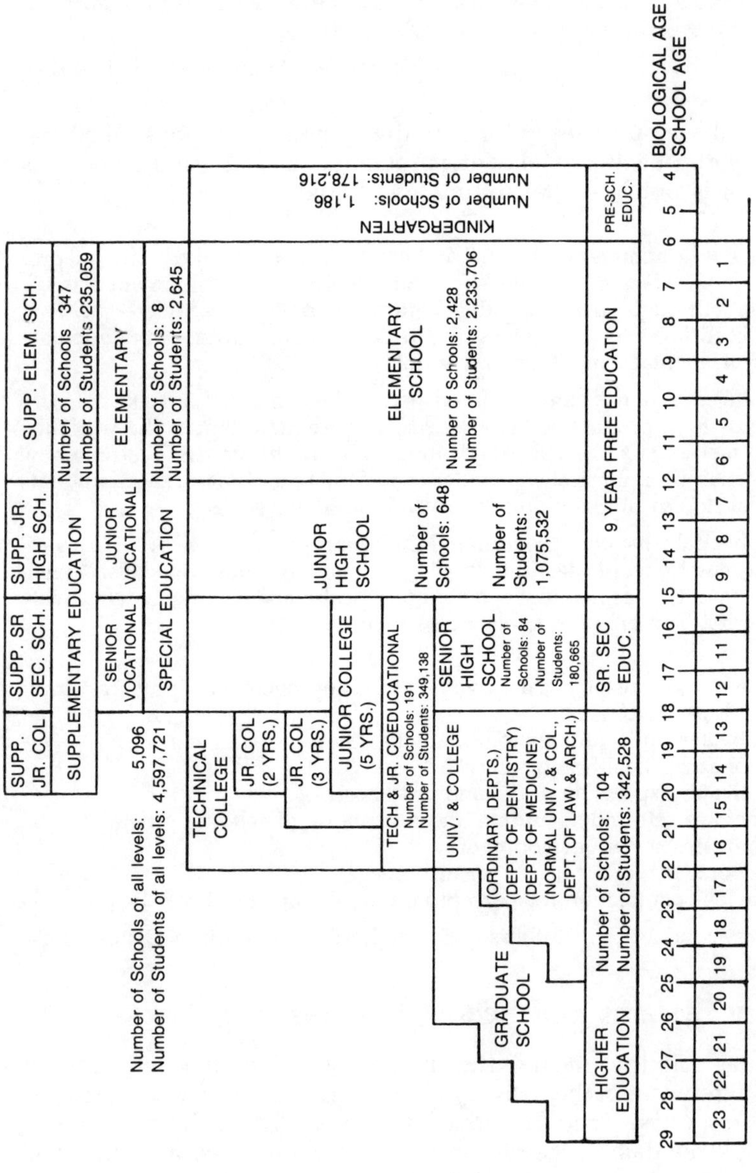

BIOLOGICAL AGE

SCHOOL AGE

SUPP. ELEM. SCH.
Number of Schools 347
Number of Students 235,059

SUPP. JR. HIGH SCH.

SUPP. SR SEC. SCH.

SUPP. JR. COL.

SUPPLEMENTARY EDUCATION

Number of Schools of all levels: 5,096
Number of Students of all levels: 4,597,721

KINDERGARTEN
Number of Schools: 1,186
Number of Students: 178,216

PRE-SCH. EDUC.

ELEMENTARY

Number of Schools: 8
Number of Students: 2,645

SPECIAL EDUCATION

ELEMENTARY SCHOOL
Number of Schools: 2,428
Number of Students: 2,233,706

9 YEAR FREE EDUCATION

JUNIOR VOCATIONAL

JUNIOR HIGH SCHOOL
Number of Schools: 648
Number of Students: 1,075,532

SENIOR VOCATIONAL

SENIOR HIGH SCHOOL
Number of Schools: 84
Number of Students: 180,665

SR. SEC EDUC.

TECHNICAL COLLEGE

JR. COL (2 YRS.)

JR. COL (3 YRS.)

JUNIOR COLLEGE (5 YRS.)

TECH & JR. COEDUCATIONAL
Number of Schools: 191
Number of Students: 349,138

UNIV. & COLLEGE
(ORDINARY DEPTS.)
(DEPT. OF DENTISTRY)
(DEPT. OF MEDICINE)
(NORMAL UNIV. & COL.,
DEPT. OF LAW & ARCH.)

GRADUATE SCHOOL
Number of Schools: 104
Number of Students: 342,528

HIGHER EDUCATION

4 5 6 7 8 9 10 11 12 13 14 15 16 17 18 19 20 21 22 23 24 25 26 27 28 29

1 2 3 4 5 6 7 8 9 10 11 12 13 14 15 16 17 18 19 20 21 22 23

Figure 1. The Chinese school system.

Note. Adapted from data supplied by the Ministry of Education, Department of Physical Education and Sports, with the courtesy of Dr. Min-Chung Tsai, former Director.

age. Differences include delivery system structures, entrance and exit requirements, course requirement variations, provisions for the handicapped, costs, and staffing and training of educators.

The English system seems more complex and fragmented by including three systems within one—the traditional state system, the comprehensive system, and the private school system. After completing "A"-level exams, students can continue on to higher education (university, polytechnic, or teacher-training college) while students who do not obtain "A" levels may progress to further education (vocational and technical colleges).

In China the entrance requirements to their limited university system require academic competition, and the opportunity for higher education seems more limited. In both cases, education is heavily subsidized by the federal government (unlike most United States colleges and universities). The contrasts of the countries' delivery systems are varied, as shown in Figures 1, 2, and 3; in each instance a study of the nature and components of each substance of the system is worthy of in-depth and systematic study.

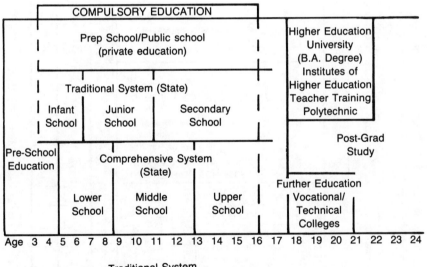

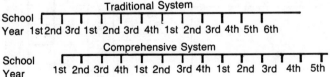

Figure 2. The English school system.

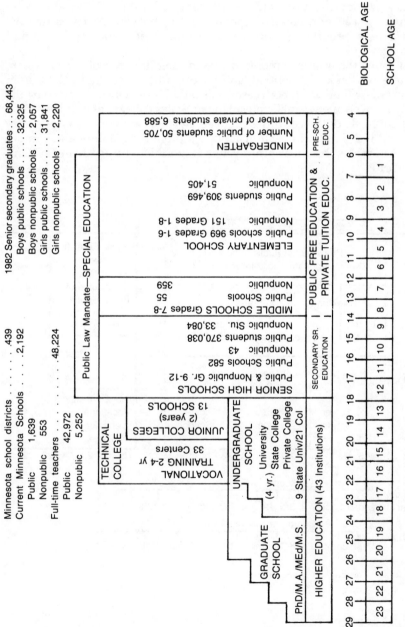

Figure 3. The current school system for the state of Minnesota, USA

Administrative Structures

Each of the three countries possesses contrasting administrative structures and functions. The Chinese system seems to differ in that each school operates somewhat independently under the authority of the principle and various committees staffed with licensed physical education teachers. Both England and the United States have varied administrative structures, and their programs, especially at the elementary level, are not always staffed with trained physical education personnel.

In England, the Department of Education and Science (DES) is the central governing body and each city/county also has a Local Education Authority (LEA). There is usually an area inspector for the schools and also a headmaster/mistress or chief administrative officer of the school.

The United States is even less centralized in nature and scope concerning administrative structuring; for the most part, it functions within separate and independent school districts. In each case, responsibility for most physical education planning is in the hands of the individual physical education departments. The models of various systems shown in Figures 4, 5, and 6 present an idea of the prevalent administrative structure of each respective country.

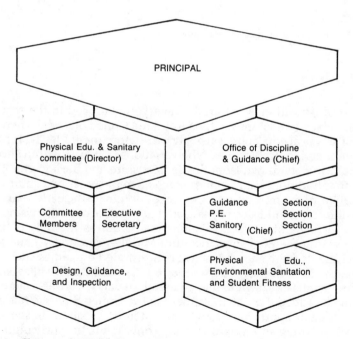

Figure 4. Chinese administrative structure.

Note. Adapted from data supplied by the Ministry of Education, Department of Physical Education and Sports, with the courtesy of Dr. Min-Chung Tsai, former Director.

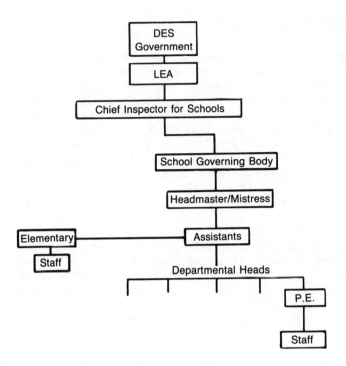

Figure 5. English administrative structure.

Curriculum

Physical education is required of everyone enrolled in the schools of China. Tables 1 and 2 show China's and the United States's (where some form of physical education is usually mandatory for grades 1-11) curricula content and indicate some of the variations that exist within curricula. The English data drawn from the Bedfordshire and Bexley schools indicated that traditional mini-games, such as mini-soccer and short tennis, and Laban-based movement experiences dominate the early years of the curriculum. It should also be realized that physical education is not mandatory in England; in fact, religious instruction is the only obligatory course within the English curriculum. Middle-, secondary-, and upper-level students were shown to have concentrated on games such as soccer, rugby, field hockey, badminton, tennis, basketball, volleyball, and squash. Gymnastics, swimming, and modern dance were also mentioned.

It may be added that the movement in the United States to teach carry over or lifetime sports has brought more tennis, racquetball, swimming, golf, conditioning and weight-training content into the curriculum. A focus toward the individual rather than the cooperative and competitive team sport seems to be the dominate theme now.

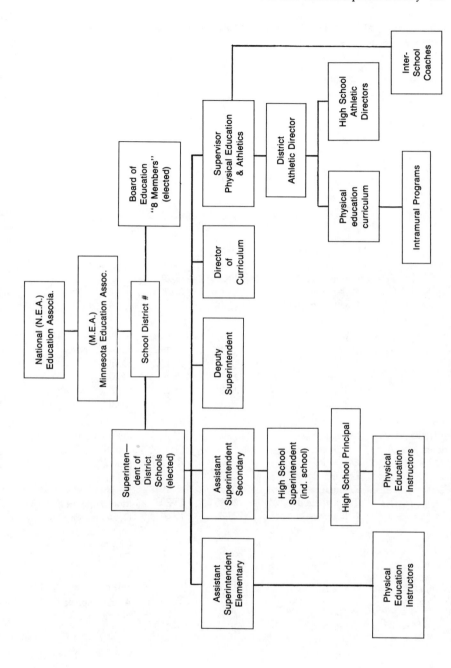

Figure 6. School district structure for the State of Minnesota, USA.

Table 1 Physical Education Curriculum in Chinese Schools

Grades	Required Courses	% of Program Male	% of Program Female	Electives
1-2	Track & field	10	10	
	Ball games	10	10	
	Listening ability	5	5	
	Voice training	5	5	
	Performance &	20	20	
	rhythmic activities	10	10	
	Appreciation	5	5	
	Games	20	20	
	Singing	15	15	
	Gymnastics	10	10	
3-6	Track & field	20-25	10-25	Self-defense
	Dance	5-10	20-25	Aquatic sports
	Gymnastics	20-25	15-20	
	Ball games	30	20-25	
	Martial arts &	5-10	5	
	Chinese boxing			
7-9	Games	10	10	Self-defense
	Dance	5-10	20-25	Aquatic sports
	Gymnastics	10-15	10-15	Skiing
	Ball games	25-30	15-20	Skating
	Track & field	20-25	15-20	Ice polo
	Martial arts &	10	10	Cycling
	Chinese boxing			
10-12 & voca-tional school	Martial arts & Chinese boxing	10	10	Self-defense Aquatic sports
	Dance	5	20-25	Skiing
	Gymnastics	15-20	15	Skating
	Games	5-10	5-10	Ice polo
	Track & field	20-25	15-20	Mountaineering
	Ball games	25-30	15-30	Horsemanship
				Archery
				Gliding
				Cycling
College & university	Martial arts & Chinese boxing	5-10 / 5-10	5-10 / 25-30	Self-defense
	Dance	25-30	15-20	Aquatic sports
	Track & field	25-30	15-20	Skiing
	Ball games	30-35	25-30	Skating
	Gymnastics	10-15	5-10	Ice Polo
				Recreational activities

Note. Physical education is not required in graduate school. Table is adapted from data supplied by the Ministry of Education, Department of Physical Education and Sports, with the courtesy of Dr. Min-chung Tsai, former Director.

Table 2 Physical Education Curriculum in United States Schools

Grades	Required Courses	% of Program Male	Female
1-2	Gymnastics & tumbling	5	5
	Dance & rhythm	35	35
	Structured games	20	20
	Ball games	20	20
	Fine motor skills	10	10
	Gross motor skills	10	10
3-6	Gymnastics & tumbling	5	5
	Track & field	5	5
	Team sports	20	20
	Dance & rhythm	20	20
	Music appreciation to dance	5	5
	Structured games	20	20
	Ball games	25	25
7-9	Team sports	40	40
	Rhythm & dance	25	25
	Gymnastics	5	5
	Health appreciation	5	5
	Track & field	5	5
	Ball games	10	10
	Structured games	10	10
10	Gymnastics	0	10
	Wrestling	10	0
	Team sports	10	10
	Football	10	10
	Tennis	10	10
	Volleyball	10	10
	Basketball	10	10
	Softball	10	10
	Track & field	10	10
	Swimming & aquatics	10	10
	Rhythm & dance	10	10
11-12			

Note. Table was constructed by authors in cooperation with various school systems in the state of Minnesota.

Future Direction

The future of physical education and sport in each country faces a myriad of tremendous challenges as each attempts to interweave physical education and sport into its sociocultural process. One way to plan for a positive future is to review the past, view the present, and discuss, examine, and analyze their merits and distractions; but we must also pragmatically push on to address the future. In fact the profession has dwelled too much and must begin to formulate a positive strategy for the future. Today's challenges are complex and multidimensional in scope and form. As the world grows smaller, comparative communication and sharing of physical education and sporting practices should enable us to prepare for more productive and healthy futures. Thinking divergently and convergently on shared issues, concerns, and problems is one way to ensure a more informed future. Whether the challenge is funding, employment, transfer of credit, government involvement, facility design and management, teacher training, sport dysfunction, professional specialization, physical education for the handicapped, shared space, pragmatic research, curriculum content, teaching methodology, or maintaining a delicate balance beween physical education, amateur sport, and community sport factions, the challenges must be met not in isolation but in a global sphere of interest, concern, and transnational knowledge. This paper was constructed to bring about a partial understanding of the past and present concerning some common areas of concern within our profession. The profession must continue to grow, share, develop, mature, reach out, and, through cooperative and transnational effort, contribute to the full potential of humankind through the medium of movement and physical activity. It is through shared forums and interactions that East-West perspectives are able to be offered and discussed. Scholars interested in assisting future East-West endeavors are invited to contact us.[1]

Note

1. Correspondence concerning future East-West research endeavors may be forwarded to Professor March L. Krotee, 218 Cooke Hall, University of Minnesota, Minneapolis, Minnesota 55455 U.S.A.

References

Educational Policies Commission. (1938). *Purposes of education in American democracy.* Washington, DC: National Education Association.

Educational Policies Commission. (1961). *The central purpose of American education.* Washington, DC: National Education Association.

Hanafy, E.H., & Krotee, M.L. (1986). A model for international education comparison: Middle East perspective. In M.L. Krotee & E.M. Jaeger (Eds.), *Comparative physical education and sport* (pp. 253–266). Champaign, IL: Human Kinetics.

Jones, P. (1971). *Comparative education: Purposes and method.* St. Lucia: University of Queensland Press.

Krotee, M.L. (1981). The saliency of the study of international and comparative physical education and sport. *Comparative Physical Education and Sport, 8*, 23-27.

Krotee, M.L. (1986). The role of comparative and international physical education and sport in modern society. In M.L. Krotee & E.M. Jaeger (Eds.), *Comparative physical education and sport* (pp. 7–12). Champaign, IL: Human Kinetics.

Krotee, M.L., & Jaeger, E.M. (Eds.). (1986). *Comparative physical education and sport*. Champaign, IL: Human Kinetics.

Mallinson, V. (1957). *An introduction to the study of comparative education and sport*. London, England: Heinemann Educational Books.

Ministry of Education. (1982). *Physical education and sports*. Republic of China: Author.

Sargent, D.A. (1883, February). Physical education in colleges. *North American Review*, CXXXVI, 166-180.

Sargent, D.A. (1906). *Physical education*. Boston: Ginn and Co.

Voltmer, E.F., & Esslinger, A.A. (1949). *The organization and administration of physical education*. New York: Appleton-Century Crofts.

PART III

Comparative Research: Physical Activity Outside of Schools

Sport and Physical Activity in Out-of-School Settings: A Review of Comparative Research

Eric F. Broom

The material for this state of the art report on comparative research on sport and physical activity in out-of-school settings was obtained from bibliographic searches, primarily through the Sport Information Resource Centre (SIRC) in Ottawa and the Sport for All Information Centre in Brussels, and obtained by soliciting information by mail from members of the International Society on Comparative Physical Education and Sport (ISCPES). Two factors emerged in the process. First, there is a dearth of completed empirical comparative research in this area, and second, the term *comparative research* is widely misunderstood, particularly, but by no means exclusively, in nonEnglish-speaking countries. The basis of all research is to compare, and thus, in both bibliographic printout and material received from colleagues, there was much that would not be considered comparative research by members of this society. We should address ourselves to this problem.

Despite the dearth of empirical comparative research, it was readily apparent that there exists a very great interest in things comparative. In the out-of-school field, this interest manifests itself in books, reports, and accounts of sport systems, the majority of which would best be categorized as case studies of a single country.

It should come as no surprise that information on sport systems, with primarily implied differences from other systems, should command such interest. A major reason for this widespread interest is that one of the products of sport delivery systems, namely competitive athletes and their achievements, is constantly paraded before us by the sport media. A measure of media sport coverage is provided by the recent Winter Olympic Games in Sarajevo, where 1,437 athletes were pursued by 4,491 journalists and television personnel. Like much else in the Olympic Games and international sport in general, one is tempted to question who the competition is for.

This review groups the comparative work done on sport and physical activity in out-of-school settings in 12 categories: sport systems; government involvement in sport; funding of sport; sport policies; "sport-for-all" programs; youth sport; university sport; professional preparation; high-performance sport; geography of sport; provision, management, and use of facilities; and cultural studies.

Sport Systems

Comparisons of the structure and functions of sport systems of two or more countries or regions, or an examination of the organizational model of sport in one country has received considerable attention. Studies of this nature have compared the systems in Canada and England (Broom, 1971), in the USA and Nigeria (Eleyae, 1974), and in Canada and the USSR (Cantelon, 1980). A further study has also compared the development and operation of the Provincial Sport Federations in the provinces of British Columbia, Alberta, Saskatchewan, and Manitoba in Canada (Nicholls, 1982).

Further studies include an examination of the development and structure of sport in Great Britain and West Germany (Collins, 1979); a comparison of the development of physical education in African countries (Nkongo, 1979); a study of the role of sport in capitalist and socialist development as seen in Great Britain and the USSR (Riordan, 1980a); and two comparisons of women in sport in England and Mexico (Hankins, 1972) and in Great Britain and the USSR (Shenton, 1979). Other scholars have compared sport systems in the Federal and Democratic Republics of Germany (Hardman, 1981) and have compared sport and physical education in the People's Republic of China and the USSR (Cribb, 1978).

One of the few comparative studies of the United States sport system focused on certain aspects of the Socialist model of international sport, as practiced in the German Democratic Republic and the People's Republic of China, and of the American approach to international sport (Clumpner, 1980). A second comparative study examined the development of social behavior in sport within the context of the American and the USSR systems (Pavek, 1983).

Case studies of sport and physical education systems in a single country include Estonia (Nuremberg, 1972) and USSR (Bradock, 1973; Riordan, 1977), France (Brockpool, 1977; Marshall, 1976), West Germany (Hardman, 1979), New South Wales (Seddon, 1979), Cuba (Slack, 1980), Hungary (Varpalotai, 1983a), and the People's Republic of China (Pendleton, 1984).

Two reports containing a series of case studies are worthy of mention because they reveal the interest that governments have in learning about foreign sport systems and practices. The first report, prepared by the Department of National Health and Welfare of the Canadian government, at the request of the National Council on Physical Fitness, contains information on the organization and administration of sport in the United

Kingdom, Australia, New Zealand, South Africa, Sweden, and Switzerland (Canada, 1949). The second report, published by the Fitness and Amateur Sport Directorate of the same government department, discusses the philosophy behind sport in six European countries—England, West Germany, Denmark, Sweden, Yugoslavia, and the USSR—and lists practices and policies that could benefit Canadians (Howell & Van Vliet, 1965). This second report was based on a study tour of the six European countries by the authors.

A series of 51 case studies of national systems of sport and physical education are provided in seven volumes in the Physical Education Around the World monograph series (Johnson, 1967-1976). A collection of case studies, including selections from the monographs and new articles, has also been published (Johnson, 1980).

During the past 20 years, analytical accounts of the sport systems of Eastern Bloc countries, particularly those that have dominated international sport, have been published in book form. The sport system in the USSR has been most popular (Louis & Louis, 1964; Morton, 1963; Riordan, 1977, 1980b; Schneidman, 1978; Speak & Ambler, 1976). In addition, the systems of several socialist countries have been described within the covers of one book (Riordan, 1978), and there is also a comprehensive account of the sport system in the German Democratic Republic (Gilbert, 1980).

A segment of a sport system with an importance that has long been recognized but which has only recently attracted serious research is the voluntary, or nonmarket, sector. One study, which made comparisons of the voluntary sector in sport and artistic associations in France, the United States, and Canada, was reported at our Halifax Seminar (Dauriac, 1980).

Government Involvement in Sport

One of the most significant developments in sport in the second half of the 20th century has been the increase in government involvement in sport. It is widely recognized that government and sport are inextricably linked in Eastern Bloc countries. What is less understood is the increased involvement in sport of governments in many Western countries. It should come as no surprise that this area of research has proven to be attractive to Canadian scholars because Canada, among English-speaking countries at least, probably has the highest level of government involvement.

Empirical studies of government involvement in sport include comparisons of Canada and England (Broom, 1971), of Canada and the United States (Corran, 1979), and of Canada and Australia (Baka, 1983) and include an examination of modern sport as an instrument of national policy with reference to Canada and selected countries (Bedecki, 1971). In addition, the roles of four western Canadian provincial governments in sport—British Columbia, Alberta, Saskatchewan, and Manitoba—have been subjected to comparative analysis (Baka, 1978).

Two further studies examine models of national government involvement in sport. The first draws comparisons among Western countries (Howell, 1978), while the second has a more global perspective (Bedecki, 1979).

Case studies of government involvement in sport in a single country include examinations of the United States (Clumpner, 1976), Canada (Hallet, 1981), and Australia (Semotiuk, 1982).

A review of the various ways that governments in western and socialist states developed and that Third World countries use sport examines the relationship of sport and politics (Pooley & Webster, 1972). In a similar vein, a major contribution to this area is a paper presented by a former British Minister for Sport under the title "Sport and Politics—An International Perspective" (Howell, 1984). The paper deals at length with government involvement in sport—more specifically, governmental abuse of sport.

Funding of Sport

The massive increase in national and international sport activities and the development of comprehensive support services for sport teams since the midpoint of this century have dramatically increased funding requirements. The source and extent of funds for sport in other countries is therefore of considerable interest.

An early study examined central government aid to sport in 13 West European countries (Molyneux, 1962). The findings, which emphasized the utilization of football pools to generate revenue for sport, were published as a contribution to the debate following the publication of the Wolfenden Report, "Sport and the Community" in England. A more recent study has looked at sources of financing competitive sport in Israel and several European countries (Simri, 1973). Further, reports on the financing of sport by gambling in 10 countries in Western Europe have been compiled and published for the Council of Europe (Clearing House, 1978).

Sport Policies

The rationalization of sport policies, or more accurately, "Sport for All" policies, has been the object of much attention among the member countries of the Council of Europe for a number of years. This interest has resulted in a major comparative study in an attempt to determine the extent of participation and nonparticipation in physical activity and to identify the individual and social mechanisms that influence participation, dropout, and nonparticipation. The overall purpose of the enquiries was to give policy makers and administrators an opportunity to see their own problems, and possible solutions, in a broader international perspective and to reexamine national policies in the wider framework of international experience. In a nutshell, the purpose was for the policy makers and administrators to learn from each other. It is hoped that this will lead to guidelines for more rational sport policies.

To date, two major investigations have been completed (Claeys, 1982; Rodgers, 1977, 1978). The project group has also published the results of an evaluation meeting (Van Lierde & DeClercq, 1983), and another major evaluation of "Sport for All" policies in member states is scheduled for completion in the summer of 1984.

The Council of Europe has also carried out two preliminary surveys: one concerned with accident insurance for athletes (Clearing House, 1977) and the other on policies and practices for the prevention of drug use by athletes (Clearing House, 1978). It was intended that both should form the basis for comparative studies, but to date disappointing responses have forced delays.

Three published papers have made brief comparative explorations of policies in other spheres of sport. Two papers examine aspects of United States university sport, a comparative analysis of the NCAA's athletic conferences (Steger, 1979), and a comparison of selected NCAA and AIAW regulations (NCAA, 1981). The third paper compares Canadian and American sport policy and law (Moriarty, 1979).

Sport-for-All Programs

The idea of "Sport for All" was adopted in 1966 by the Council for Cultural Cooperation within the Council of Europe to describe one of its long-term aims. Since that time, there has been a remarkable growth of "Sport for All," or national physical activity programs, around the world. The large number of similar programs with generally common aims has been the object of widespread comparative interest.

A report presenting the "Sport for All" experience of five European countries—the Federal Republic of Germany, the Netherlands, Norway, Sweden, and the United Kingdom (Council for Cultural Cooperation, 1970)—has been followed by a UNESCO-sponsored report. The UNESCO report charts and analyzes the progress of governments in the "Sport for All" movement around the world (McIntosh, 1980). There also has been a regional survey on the status of physical education and "Sport for All" in Asia and the Pacific (Jobling & Saunders, 1982).

A paper presented at the ISCPES Seminar in Halifax compared the Canadian and Australian models of national physical fitness programs (Howell & Howell, 1980), and the results of a comparative study of the "Sport for All" programs in the Federal Republic of Germany, Norway, Great Britain, and the Canadian Participation Program were presented at this conference (Schams, 1982).

Youth Sport

In a large number of societies there is a great deal of sport for youth in out-of-school settings. Three empirical studies in this area are a comparison of the organization and development of ice hockey during childhood in the Soviet Union, Czechoslovakia, Sweden, and Canada (Kingston, 1977) and two comparisons of sport involvement among 11-18-year-olds in three Scandinavian countries (Stensaasen, 1980, 1982).

In addition, the UNESCO survey of National Policies and Practices Concerning the Role of Physical Education and Sport in the Education of Youth, which includes responses from 56 countries, contains information on sport out of school (UNESCO, 1980).

Finally, the contribution of youth sport programs to the quality of life is assessed through an examination of current practices in a cross-national perspective (Pooley, 1982).

University Sport

Among the early examinations of university sport are two excellent comparative studies. The first study looked at physical education programs open to the general student population in 87 universities in 21 European countries (Pelton, 1968), and the second study was equally comprehensive (Reitmayer, 1972). Two more recent studies in the area of service programs are one study that compared nonprofessional programs of physical education in 4-year colleges in Brazil and the United States (Piccoli & Beran, 1983) and a second study that compared the opinions of international physical educators, United States leaders in physical education, and college students on the value of physical education for students not studying to be teachers or coaches (Pelton, 1982).

A historical comparative analysis of the development of football at Yale and Harvard in the latter 19th century reveals the influence of industrialization (Sack, 1974). By way of contrast, two case studies of university sport in the Philippines and Nigeria (Beran, 1980) provide insights of Third World, nonindustrialized countries.

Other studies throw light on problem areas in university sport. The relative opportunities for women—as athletes, coaches, and administrators—as compared to men are examined in Canadian universities (Vickers, 1982). A second study examines the implications of government funding for university sport through two case studies of Canada and Hungary (Varpalotai, 1983b). Finally, the major differences in philosophy and provision of university sport in North America, other developed countries, and Third World nations are reviewed (McIntosh, 1983).

Professional Preparation

Comparisons of professional preparation programs for physical education teachers and coaches have generated considerable interest, particularly since the middle of this century, since which time the various systems have experienced major changes.

In 1963, a series of three studies were completed by the International Council on Health, Physical Education and Recreation (ICHPER) in cooperation with UNESCO, two of which focused on the preparation and employment of physical education teachers. The surveys elicited responses from 51 countries; Part I deals with teacher training practices, and Part II deals with the status of physical education teachers (ICHPER, 1963).

Under the rubric of comparative studies in physical education, two Anglo-French symposia have compared aspects of professional preparation in the two countries. The first symposium compares the place of sport in education, and within that it compares the place of sport in the training of physical education teachers; the second deals specifically with the training of physical education teachers for secondary schools (Physical Education Association of Great Britain and Northern Ireland, 1976, 1977).

Three studies examine aspects of the professional preparation of physical education teachers. In the first study, comparisons are made between the preparation programs of teachers in Norway, Sweden, and Denmark (Polidoro, 1977). The second study compares the responses of Italian and American female physical education majors to a coaching code of ethics (Bazzano, 1981). A third study examines the practical aspects, or required physical activities, of prospective physical education teachers in six West European countries (Moolenizer & Clark, 1981).

Finally, several studies make comparisons of professional preparation among Eastern Block countries. One study compares the university physical education curriculum in socialist countries (Jaworski, 1979). In addition, a collection of eight studies on the same topic has been published by the Central Committee of the Czechoslovak Union of Physical Education in conjunction with Charles University, Prague (Svoboda, 1980).

High-Performance Sport

The extraordinary increase in amount and standard of high-performance sport has generated a widespread universal interest, not only in sporting achievement but also in the systems and support systems that nurture athletic talent.

A study of national models for meeting the educational and sporting needs of highly talented young athletes compared schools for sport in the USSR, the German Democratic Republic, the German Federal Republic, France, the United Kingdom, and Canada (Broom, 1981). In a similar vein, a second study made comparisons of the hours of training of high-level young athletes in the USSR, West Germany, and Canada (Cantelon, 1981). Also on this topic is an excellent case study of youth sports, particularly of sport schools in the Soviet Union (Jefferies, 1983).

Support systems are vitally important to athletes striving for excellence; one investigation compared the programs of financial assistance available to individual high-level athletes in the United States, Canada, Great Britain, France, and West Germany (Broom, 1982).

Finally, two studies examined different aspects of international competition. The first looked at the nature and scope of international competition and at the implications for international relations and made comparisons across 12 countries (Chu, 1976). A second study made a comparative analysis of pretournament preparation of the 10 top teams in a women's field hockey world championship (Broom, 1980). An opportunity will occur in 1986 to replicate the study and to compare changes in preparation training over the 7-year period.

Geography of Sport

The identification and comparison of regional differences in participation, provision, interest, and level of excellence is an emerging area of comparative research. A geography of sport initially focuses on the single question "Where are people involved in sport?" Further analysis seeks to explain spacial variations in participation and levels of achievement.

Early work in this area was done by Landry et al. in their study of French Canadian participation in major international sport festivals—the Olympic, Pan-American, and Commonwealth Games—in comparison to athletes from other areas of Canada. The early studies were carried out in the mid1960s and achieved prominence in the Quebec preparations for the 1976 Summer Olympic Games (Boileau, Landry, & Trempe, 1976).

The first major work in this area led to the publication of a geography of American sport, which focused primarily on the "national" games of football, basketball, and baseball (Rooney, 1974). A brief review of less popular sports was also included.

This early work has been followed by a number of studies by an English scholar. A geography of European track and field (Bale, 1978) was followed by a geography of world track and field (Bale, 1979). Subsequent studies include an examination of the distribution of women's football in England and Wales (Bale, 1980), and a major work on the mosaic of cultural, historic, economic, and spacial elements that produce the geography of sport in England, Scotland, and Wales (Bale, 1982).

Finally, a Canadian study found that, in proportion to the population of Canada, Saskatchewan, Manitoba, and Ontario produced the most players for the National Hockey League; and factors were analyzed relating to this variability (Lea, 1974).

Provision, Management and Use of Facilities

A program of provision of community sport and leisure facilities has made a major contribution to the sport delivery systems in developed countries in the past 2 decades. The extent of provision, design specifications, innovative developments, and management practices have attracted cross-national comparisons. An example of such interest is the report of a study tour of sport and recreation facilities in three European countries—England, Holland, and West Germany—with applications to the province of British Columbia in Canada (Broom & Olenick, 1974).

Comparative user studies are of great value to planners and managers. One long-range study examined the influence of a sport center on the sporting life of a town by conducting surveys of residents' leisure patterns before the sport center was opened, 4 months after it opened, and several years after it opened (Knapp, Jenkins, & Bonsor, 1976). Another user study compared the results of surveys of participation in squash, badminton, and indoor soccer at three sports centers (Gregory, 1979; Peacock, 1979a; Rookwood & Gregory, 1979). A further study compared user surveys at seven squash centers, representing three different market sectors, to search for evidence of demand saturation (Peacock, 1979b).

In the management sector, a recent publication is based on a series of case studies of sport and leisure centers in several countries (Jackson, 1984).

In developing the case for a National Sport Institute—a combined sport training and sport research center—comparative studies of such centers in other countries have been utilized. The first such use was in the proposal for the Australian Sport Institute (Coles et al., 1975). A similar approach was followed in developing a case for a network of sport institutes in Canada (Broom, 1979).

Cultural Studies

Work in the field of cultural studies has developed rapidly in Britain during the last few years, and a number of Canadian scholars are now involved in a team approach. Comparative studies of leisure and sport patterns are receiving some attention, and three papers on working-class sport in England, Canada, and the USSR in the 1930s were presented by two Englishmen and a Canadian at the British Sociological Association Conference in April 1984. The three papers will be integrated into a comparative paper for publication by one member of the team. Other areas of comparative interest to this group of scholars include sport and the media.

Summary and Conclusions

It is clear from the review of the 12 areas of comparative research that a widespread interest exists in comparative knowledge in all aspects of the sport delivery system—using the term *sport* in the widest possible sense. Comparative findings are in demand not only by scholars but also by politicians, planners, policy makers, and administrators at all levels from national to local. Knowledge of other systems acts as a sounding board for one's own system and encourages reexamination and redevelopment, if desired, to produce increased effectiveness. In a nutshell, comparative knowledge enables one to learn from the experience of others.

A large majority of the work in the area of sport delivery systems and subsystems is in the form of case studies (i.e., studies of a single country), so the reader is left to make his or her own analyses, comparisons, and conclusions.

The review suggests that much of the full comparative study being done is undertaken by graduate students, more particularly by those working toward their doctorates. Full comparative research requires description, explanation, juxtaposition, and comparison, creating a very time-consuming process. It would appear that graduate students, more than other scholars, have the time and motivation for such work.

The team approach to comparative surveys, or to more accurately collected case surveys, is best exemplified by the work of the Clearing House in Brussels for the member countries of the Council of Europe. Much of the work is based on "Sport for All" programs, and the common purpose of all member countries with these programs make knowledge of other programs, and the comparisons that may be drawn, of great interest to all countries. The large number of respondents adds to the difficulties of ensuring comparability, and information is presented in descriptive form with little or no analysis offered.

Individual researchers can do full comparative studies, particularly of subsystems and separate programs. However, perhaps the most promising avenue for full comparative research for the future is the team approach. Teams composed of several researchers could, each in their own country, examine a common problem. Close coordination of team members would ensure tight control over the development and use of the instrument and of the analysis of the data.

The membership of the International Society for Comparative Physical Education and Sport is ideally placed to initiate such team research projects. An opportunity to present the findings of team research projects would be at our next international seminar.

References

Baka, R.S. (1978). *A history of provincial government involvement in sport in Western Canada*. Unpublished doctoral dissertation, University of Alberta, Edmonton.

Baka, R.S. (1983). *Similarities between Australian and Canadian government involvement in sport*. Victoria, Canada: Department of Physical Education and Recreation, Footscray Institute of Technology.

Bale, J. (1978, Winter). The geography of European athletes. *Sports Exchange World*, pp. 12-13.

Bale, J. (1979, Winter). A geography of world-class track and field athletes. *Sports Exchange World*, pp. 26-31.

Bale, J. (1980, Autumn). Women's football in England and Wales: A social-geographic perspective. *Physical Education Review*, 111, 137-145.

Bale, J. (1982). *Sport and place: A geography of sport in England, Scotland, and Wales.* London: C. Hurst & Co.

Bazzano, C. (1981). A comparison of responses to a code of ethics for coaches by Italian and American female physical education majors. *Comparative Physical Education and Sport,* 8(3/81), 14-20.

Bedecki, T. (1979). Models for national government involvement in sport. In D. Howell (Eds.), *Methodology in comparative physical education and sport* (pp. 136-146). Champaign, IL: Stipes.

Beran, J. (1980). University sport, two case studies: Philippines and Nigeria. In *Proceedings ISCPES Seminar* (pp. 78-87). Halifax: Dalhousie University.

Boileau, R., Landry, F., & Trempe, Y. (1976). French Canadians and the major national games (1908-1974). In R.S. Gruneau & J.G. Albinson (Eds.), *Canadian sport: Sociological perspectives* (pp. 141-169). Don Mills, Ontario, Canada: Addison Wesley (Canada) Ltd.

Bradock, J.F. (1973). *Fifty years of physical culture and sport in the Soviet Union, 1917-1967.* Unpublished master's thesis, University of Manchester.

Brockpool, G. (1977). *The development of p.e. and sport in France.* Unpublished master's thesis, Liverpool University.

Broom, E.F. (1971). *Comparative analysis of the central administrative agencies of amateur sport and physical recreation in England and Canada.* Unpublished doctoral dissertation, University of Illinois, Urbana.

Broom, E.F. (1979). The case for sports institutes. *Coaching Review, 2,* 51-63.

Broom, E.F. (1980). The changing face of amateur international sport: An analysis of pretournament preparation and team characteristics of ten top teams in the 1979 women's world hockey championship. *International Council of Sport and Physical Education Review.*

Broom, E.F. (1981). Meeting the educational and sporting needs of the elite young athlete: A comparison of national organizational models. *Comparative Physical Education and Sport,* 8(3/81), 3-13.

Broom, E.F. (1982). Elite amateur athlete dependency on financial assistance programmes. In *Proceedings of the International Committee for the Sociology of Sport Regional Symposium* (pp. 522-536). Vancouver: University of British Columbia.

Broom, E.F., & Olenick, N.F. (1974). *Study tour of sports and recreation facilities in Europe.* Victoria, British Columbia: Queen's Printing.

Canada. (1949). *Sports and athletics in other countries.* Prepared by Physical fitness division in the Department of National Health and Welfare.

Cantelon, H. (1980). Ideal-typical models of sport: The USSR and the Canadian adaptation. In *Proceedings NAPEHE* (pp. 262-281). Champaign, IL: Human Kinetics.

Cantelon, H. (1982). High performance sport and the child athlete: Learning to labour. In *Proceedings of the International Committee for the Sociology of Sport Regional Symposium* (pp. 258-286). Vancouver: University of British Columbia.

Chu, E.J. (1976). *Nature and scope of international amateur sports participation by selected countries and the implications for international relations.* Unpublished doctoral dissertation, New York University.

Claeys, U. (1982). *Sport in European society: A transnational survey into participation and motivation. Rationalising sports policies. Parts I and II.* Belgium: Catholic University of Louvain.

Clearing House (1977). *Accident insurance for athletes.* Brussels: Council of Europe.

Clearing House (1978). *Financing of sport by gambling.* Brussels: Council of Europe.

Clumpner, R.A. (1976). *American federal government involvement in sport, 1888-1973.* Unpublished doctoral dissertation, University of Alberta, Edmonton.

Clumpner, R.A. (1980). Socialist offshoots and the American model: Concerns, implications, and possible directions. In *Proceedings NAPEHE* (pp. 282-291). Champaign, IL: Human Kinetics.

Coles, A. et al. (1975). *Report of the Australian sports institute study group. Australian Government.* Canberra: Publishing Service.

Collins, L. (1979). A comparative study of the development and structure of sport in Great Britain and West Germany. *Physical Education Review, 2,* 101-114.

Corran, R. (1979). *A comparison of the involvement of the federal governments of Canada and United States in sport and physical education since 1960.* Unpublished doctoral dissertation, Ohio State University, Columbus.

Council for Cultural Cooperation, Council of Europe. (1970). *Sport for all: Five countries report.* Strasbourg: Author.

Cribb, R.J.P. (1978). *Sport and p.e. in the People's Republic of China and some comparisons with Soviet Russia.* Unpublished master's thesis, Liverpool University.

Dauriac, C.M. (1980). Sport and the voluntary nonprofit sector of the economy: A Franco-American comparison. In *Proceedings ISCPES Seminar* (pp. 57-77). Halifax: Dalhousie University.

Eleyae, A. (1974). *A comparative assessment of the central organizations for amateur sports in the U.S.A. and Nigeria.* Unpublished doctoral dissertation, University of Illinois, Urbana.

Gilbert, D. (1980). *The miracle machine.* New York: Coward, McCann & Geoghegan.

Gregory, S. (1979). *Badminton at three sports centres.* (Sports Council Research Working Paper, No. 11). London: Sports Council Publications.

Hallet, W. (1981). *A history of federal government involvement in sport in Canada.* Unpublished doctoral dissertation, University of Alberta, Edmonton.

Hankins, D.D. (1972). *A comparative study of the role of women and sport in England and Mexico.* Master of science thesis, Eastern Illinois University, Charleston.

Hardman, K. (1979). *The development of physical education and sport in the Federal Republic of Germany.* Master's dissertation, University of Liverpool.

Hardman, K. (1981). *Sport systems in the Federal and Democratic Republics of Germany.*

Howell, D. (1984). Sport and politics—An international perspective. *Comparative Physical Education and Sport,* **6**(1), pp. 4-16.

Howell, M., & Howell, R. (1980). A model for national fitness programmes. In *Proceedings ISCPES Seminar* (pp. 333-344). Halifax: Dalhousie University.

Howell, M.L., & Van Vliet, M.L. (1965). *Physical education and recreation in Europe.* Information Services, Department of National Health and Welfare. Canada.

Howell, R. (1978). The Western world and sport: National government programs. *Proceedings of Comparative P.E./Sport Seminar.* San Diego State University.

ICHPER (1963). *Questionnaire report, Part II. Teacher training for physical education and Part III, Status of teachers of physical education.* Washington, DC: ICHPER.

Jackson, J.J. (1984). *Leisure and sports center management.* Springfield, IL: Charles C. Thomas.

Jaworski, Z. (1979). Study curriculum for physical education of the universities of the socialistic countries. *International Journal of Physical Education,* **16**, 37-39.

Jefferies, S. (1982). *Youth sports in the Soviet Union.* Unpublished doctoral dissertation, University of Oregon, Eugene.

Jobling, I., & Saunders, J. (1982). *The current status of physical education and 'sport for all' in the region of Asia and the Pacific.* Regional Survey for UNESCO.

Johnson, W. (1967-1976). Physical education around the world. *Phi Epsilon Kappa,* **1-7**, Indianapolis.

Johnson, W. (Ed.). (1980). *Sport and physical education around the world.* Champaign, IL: Stipes.

Kingston, G.E. (1977). *The organization and development of ice hockey during childhood in the Soviet Union, Czechoslovakia, Sweden and Canada.* Unpublished doctoral thesis, University of Alberta, Edmonton.

Knapp, B., Jenkins, C., & Bonsor, K. (1976). *A long-term study of the influence of Rugby Sports Centre on the supporting life of the town* (Research Memorandum No. 51). Birmingham: University of Birmingham, Department of Physical Education.

Lea, S. (1974). *Factors related to the regional variability in the development of professional hockey talent in Canada.* Unpublished bachelor's of science thesis, University of Waterloo.

Louis, V., & Louis, J. (1964). *Sport in the Soviet Union.* Great Britain: MacMillan.

Marshall, B.W.S. (1976). *The development of physical education and sport in France since 1945.* Unpublished master's dissertation, University of Manchester.

McIntosh, P.C. (1980). *'Sport for all' programmes throughout the world.* ICSEP submission to UNESCO, Contract No. 207604.

McIntosh, P.C. (1983). Universities and sport. In *Proceedings FISU/CESU Conference Universiade* (pp. 1-12). Edmonton.

Molyneux, D.D. (1962). *Central government aid to sport and physical education in countries in Western Europe.* Birmingham: University of Birmingham.

Moolenizer, N.J. & Clark, E. (1982). Sport international: A preliminary investigation of practical aspects of professional preparation requirements for secondary school physical education teachers in selected European institutions. *Comparative Physical Education and Sport, 1*(9), 22-26.

Moriarty, D. (1979). Comparing Canadian-American sport/athletic policy and law. *CAHPER Journal, 45*(3), 39-42, 44.

Morton, H. (1963). *Soviet sport.* New York: Collier Books.

NCAA (1981). Comparison of selected NCAA and AIAW regulations. *NCAA News,* 6-8.

Nicholls, E.A. (1982). *An analysis of the structure and function of three provincial sports collectives in Western Canada 1977-78.* Unpublished doctoral thesis, University of Alberta, Edmonton.

Nkongo, J. (1979). *Factors influencing the development of P.E. in Tanzania as compared with other African countries.* Unpublished master's thesis, University of Manchester.

Nurmberg, R. (1972). *Sport and physical education in Estonia.* Unpublished doctoral dissertation, University of California, Berkeley.

Pavek, B. (1983). Sociological observations of sport in the U.S.S.R. and the United States: A comparison of the development of social behavior through sport. *Comparative Physical Education and Sport, 5*(2), 6-27.

Peacock, S. (1979a). *Squash at three sports centres.* (Sports Council Research Working Paper, No. 10). London: Sports Council Publications.

Peacock, S. (1979b). *Gloucestershire squash study: To examine any evidence of demand saturation in a relatively well-provided area to examine differences between three market sectors of provision.* Polytechnic University of Central London.

Pelton, B. (1968, Spring). International programs of physical education for college age youth. *Gymnasion,* pp. 11-13.

Pelton, B.C. (in press). A comparison of personal beliefs held by international physical educators, United States leaders in physical education, and college students concerning physical education for college and university students who are not studying to be teachers/coaches. In M.L. Krotee & E.M. Jaeger (Eds.), *Comparative physical education* (Vol. 3, pp. 287-300). Champaign, IL: Human Kinetics.

Pendleton, B.B. (in press). Development patterns in the Chinese sport delivery system. In H. Haag, D. Kayser, and B. Bennett, *Comparative physical education* (Vol. 4). Champaign, IL: Human Kinetics.

Physical Education Association of Great Britain and Northern Ireland (1976, 1977). *Comparative studies in physical education: France, the place of sport in education.* Report of Symposium held at the Crystal Palace National Sports Center.

Piccoli, J.C.J., & Beran, J.A. (1983). Physical education basic instruction programs in selected four-year colleges in Brazil and the United States. *Comparative Physical Education and Sport,* 5(1), 6-20.

Polidoro, J.R. (1977). Professional programs of physical education teachers in Norway, Sweden and Denmark. *Research Quarterly,* 48, 640-646.

Pooley, J.C. & Webster, A.V. (1972). *Sport and politics: Power play.* Presented at Symposium on Sport, Man, and Contemporary Society. New York: Queens College.

Pooley, J.C. (1982). The contribution of youth sport programs to the quality of life: Current practices in cross-national perspective. *Arena Review,* 6(1), 31-39.

Reitmayer, L. (1972, January-March). An endeavor to amass information and experience gained from physical education taught at universities throughout the world. *Bulletin of the Federation Internationale d'Education Physique,* 42, 73-82.

Riordan, J. (1977). *Sport in Soviet society.* Cambridge: Cambridge University Press.

Riordan, J. (1978). *Sport under communism.* London: C. Hurst & Company.

Riordan, J. (1980a). Sport and physical education in West and East: A comparative study of approaches to sport and physical education in

Britain and the U.S.S.R. In *Proceedings ISCPES Seminar* (pp. 1-37). Halifax: Dalhousie University.

Riordan, J. (1980b). *Soviet sport*. England: Basil Blackwell.

Rodgers, B. (1977). Sport in its social context: International comparisons. Rationalising sports policies. University of Manchester.

Rodgers, B. (1978). Sport in its social context: Technical supplement. Rationalising sports policies. University of Manchester.

Rookwood, A., & Gregory, S. (1979). Indoor soccer at three sports centres. (Sports Council Research Working Paper, No. 12). London: Sports Council Publications.

Rooney, J.F. (1974). *A geography of American sport*. Reading, MA: Addison-Wesley.

Sack, A.L. (1974). *The commercialization and rationalization of intercollegiate football: A comparative analysis of the development of football at Yale and Harvard in the latter nineteenth-century*. Unpublished doctoral dissertation, Pennsylvania State University, University Park.

Schams, R. (1984). The international trim movement-origin, development, successes. *Comparative Physical Education and Sport*, 1(15), 17-23.

Seddon, M.A. (1979). *The development of physical education, sport, and physical recreation in New South Wales*. Unpublished master's thesis, University of Liverpool.

Semotiuk, D.M. (1982). National government involvement in amateur sport in Australia 1972-1981. In M.L. Krotee & E.M. Jaeger (Eds.), *Comparative physical education* (Vol. 3) (pp. 159-172). Champaign, IL: Human Kinetics.

Shenton, P.A. (1979). Women in sport: A comparative study of Britain and the U.S.S.R. Master's thesis, Liverpool University.

Shneidman, N. (1978). *The Soviet road to Olympus*. Toronto: The Ontario Institute for Studies in Education.

Simri, U. (1973). *The sources of financing of competitive sports in Israel and in various European countries*. Tel-Aviv: Beth-Berl.

Slack, T. (1980). *Sport and physical education in Cuba*. Term Paper, Department of Physical Education, University of Alberta, Edmonton.

Speak, M.A., & Ambler, V. H. (1976). *Physical education, recreation and sport in the U.S.S.R.* University of Lancaster.

Steger, J.M. (1979). Comparative analysis of the NCAA's athletic conferences. *Athletic Administration*, 13(3), 17-26.

Stensaasen, S. (1980). Sport involvement among Finnish, Norwegian and Swedish youngsters. In *Proceedings ISCPES Seminar* (pp. 395-436). Halifax: Dalhousie University.

Stensaasen, S. (1982). Coordinated, comparative study of sports involvement among Scandinavian youngsters. *Scandinavian Journal of Sports Sciences*, 2, 17-25.

Svoboda, B. (1980). *Coaches and physical education teachers training in socialist countries*. Prague: Olympia.

UNESCO (1980). *National policies and practices concerning the role of physical education and sport in the education of youth*. International Council of Sport and Physical Education.

Van Lierde, A. & DeClercq, L. (1983). *Evaluation of the impact of sport for all policies and programmes*. Brussels: Council of Europe, CDDS Research Committee.

Varpalotai, A. (1983a). *Physical culture in Hungary: A case study utilizing cultural studies theory*. Master's thesis, Queen's University, Kingston, Ontario.

Varpalotai, A. (1983b). The implications of government funding for university sport: A comparative study of Hungary and Canada. In *Proceedings FISU Conference Universiade '83* (pp. 562-576). Edmonton: University of Alberta.

Vickers, J. (1982). Comparative study: Relative opportunities for women. In *Canadian Intercollegiate Athletic Union Update 1981-82*, p. 38.

CHAPTER 18

To Moscow and Back: International Status of Comparative Research in Regard to Physical Activity Outside of Schools

Arnd Krüger

From their beginnings, modern elite sports have lived on international comparisons. Results of the Olympic Games have been compared by countries from the 1896 Games onward. With the rivalry of Germany and France prior to World War I, the nation-state got involved and put the financial and organizational resources of the state at the disposal of the sport organizations (Krüger, 1982). Carl Diem made the first fact-finding tour for the benefit of international comparison and practical improvement of elite sport as early as 1913 by going from Germany to the United States to improve the level of performances of the German national teams particularly in track and field and swimming (Diem, 1914). Over the past 70 years of comparative research in physical education and sport outside the schools, not much has changed since Diem concluded that it was not worthwhile to describe accurately the actual situation that is found, but to draw from the situation proper conclusions which suited the needs at home. So in elite sports it was not comparison for comparison's sake, but for its practical utility that the sponsor of such a trip wanted (i.e., improvement of performance of the elite athlete). It was always the dominant aim to learn from the leading sporting nation.

In the years after, Nazi Germany's attempt to demonstrate Aryan superiority and later the struggle between the two blocks of the communist and the free enterprise system helped to create a climate in which each faction attempted to copy everything that seemed to explain the success of the other system.

It is therefore understandable that hundreds of studies compare factors (Krüger, 1980) that influence the elite sport system; some studies compare the superb performance of top athletes in records, medals and points, yet few studies focus on general sports for all, rehabilitation programs, therapy sports, or sport leadership (Le Pogam, 1979). Although it would be fascinating to compare the various socioeconomic and athletic systems, the club structures, the connections between school physical education and club sports at all levels of performance, and the means of movement therapy and adapted physical education in their social and psychological contexts, this paper is limited to elite sports. It is not expected, as in Seppänen (1972) or Novikov and Maksimenko (1972), that from this any conclusions about the relative value and socioeconomic strength of a particular country or system can be drawn. Instead, it tries to show cross-influences and explain some of the particularities of elite sport outside the actual training regimen, although it would be interesting to show how certain techniques or forms of training have spread.

Looking at the state of the art of this type of comparison, it becomes obvious—just as Eric Broom shows in this volume elsewhere for the English language area—that very few real comparisons have been done. At the most, some precomparative collections of material under the same systematization have been assembled (Krüger, 1985; Krüger & Riordan, 1985). Of those few proper comparisons, most have been done on various aspects of the different developments in East and West Germany (Burger & Voigt, 1980; Pfetsch, 1977; Pfister & Voigt, 1982; Voigt & Messing, 1977; Weisspfennig, 1983). Authors from Eastern European countries have shown the differences between their systems (Jaworski, 1981; Melchert, 1973, 1977; Simon, 1970) or between their systems and the West (Oehmigen, 1982; Rudolph, 1981). The Scandinavian countries have been compared (Stensaasen, 1982), and cross influences have been shown (Gronen & Lemke, 1978; Hancock & Higashi, 1910; Heinilä, 1982; Kugel, 1981; Watanabe, 1978). Few works have attempted to complete a systematic analysis (Krüger, 1980; Meynaud, 1966). The same sort of questionnaire has been used occasionally to compare people from different countries (Krüger, 1978; Krüger & Casselman, 1982; Stensaasen, 1982) or institutions (Cantelon & Riordan, 1982; Olafson & Coughlan, 1982; Remans, 1982).

Works in which an author from one country works explicitly and exclusively on problems of another country are excluded here. Although a certain merit exists in studying a different country than one's own and using criteria different from those an author of that country would apply, it is not self-evident that such a work is any more useful than what an author from his or her own country would produce. It can therefore not be accepted that language barriers comprise the actual problem of comparisons. The different language, with a different systematization of meaning, does open new paths for analysis. Finding a meta-language that fits for the sport systems of more than one language area may be somewhat difficult. The elite sport system of a particular sport can be regarded around the world as one unified system which would then only need one system of symbolic meanings.

The approach used here is to some extent diffusionistic because the international sport scene has had a close and fast network of communication. This network has helped to influence the less-successful countries quite rapidly, for instance when new features are presented at international sporting competitions.

Looking at the dominant countries in the Olympic Games in the past World War II era, the rise of the Soviet sport system is very visible. In regular coordination conferences the other Eastern European countries went to Moscow to adopt major features into their own traditional sport systems. "To learn from the Soviet Union" has become a standard phrase in the past 30 years even though the German Democratic Republic has outdone its teachers by far on a per capita basis. It has been often overlooked, however, that the USSR itself has always been willing to learn from others (Lathe, 1979, p. 259); in fact, several of the early features of the Soviet sport, such as youth sport schools (Riordan, 1977, p. 146), can be traced back through Nazi Germany (Krüger, 1972) and into fascist Italy (Isidora Frasca, 1983).

Therefore this paper is called "To Moscow and Back" because the mode of analysis is the same as has been practiced there and because the degree of international competition which has risen far above the struggle of individuals or teams or nations has become a struggle of socioeconomic systems, which in elite sports have monitored each other so closely that very few hidden features are left. Only the enormous amount of material makes a comparison so difficult (Svoboda, 1980).

Factors That Influence Athletic Success

When West German sport was outdone by the German Democratic Republic for the first time in 1968 in Mexico, considerable effort was put into regaining a decent position in the international sport world (Krüger, 1975). One of the key organizers of the Polish elite sport system who had "learned" from the Soviet Union for over 10 years was hired to analyze and reorganize the West German elite sport set-up. He discarded the theory of the superiority of the socioeconomic system of the Communist block and looked one level below at the various factors that influenced the elite sport system in detail (Lempart, 1969, 1973; Lempart & Spitz, 1977, 1979). After gathering all of the recommendations spread over various publications, 17 different factors can be isolated that provide the framework for success in elite sports.

What are the main features of the Moscow system? Just as was done in the economic sphere, a central organ of planning for elite sport was installed that was made responsible for the centrally distributed means. In this respect, none of the systems in the West that were modeled according to Eastern examples differed. The differences that were introduced had to do with the amount of state involvement, which ranged from direct formal control in France to only nominal control in Italy and West Germany. Yet a comparison of the formal structure does not suffice. The amount of government leverage exhibited by the attempted boycott of the Moscow Olympics shows that the countries with the strongest formal government influence are not always the ones that give in to government requests the easiest (Killanin, 1983).

In the following, the factors that Lempart isolated and that are the same as those at the root of all comparisons of elite sport as done in communist countries for the sake of analysis and improvement of their own performance (Wonneberger, 1982) are discussed.

Social and political conditions. These are the given constraints that cannot be altered by the sport system if a reorganization and gearing toward success is intended. It is because of these constraints that comparisons on anything but a formal level are so difficult between one country and another. It would be quite useless to compare psychological data on athletes and coaches at face value between different countries because the value systems and the social conditions are very different. Therefore international comparisons are difficult and can only be handled if the test inventory is not only translated but adapted to the different system. At times this makes all comparisons futile because the social and political conditions are incomparable.

The economic conditions. This is the factor that Novikov and Maksimenko (1972) stress in particular. They do point out, however, that it is not the maximal availability of economic possibilities that assures sporting success; rather, a minimal standard is required that allows a certain amount of resources to be put into elite sport as a national prestige venture.

Comparing the gross national product or the amount of money spent on sport as parameters for economic conditions as they relate to sport is only a very crude comparison: In the 60,000 West German sport clubs, so many hours are put in by volunteer, unpaid coaches, that their effort, valued at $4 per hour, has been estimated at $800 million per year—more than the total amount that federal, state, and local governments put into all sectors of sport annually (Weyer, 1981). Thus covering all hidden economic factors is very difficult.

The geophysical conditions. Comparing the athletic success of countries with different climatic and geographic conditions also is very difficult. Measuring only medals won, a medal in ice hockey has the same value as one in sprinting. Yet the African countries will never have a chance to win a hockey medal but practically all countries can produce and have produced sprinters.

Small countries are generally easier to organize than large countries. Countries that stretch out, that are very long and slim, have different organizational problems than countries that are more compact. Yet the geography of sport is emerging only now as a new subdiscipline (Bale, 1982).

The traditions of sports. New sports are difficult to introduce, even with expansive media input, as can be seen in the case of soccer in the United States. It may take another generation before the young can bring soccer to a status that makes it reasonably strong internationally. The current sport tradition—to be Western and dominated by a tendency toward standardization, measurement, and records—(Guttmann, 1979) makes it difficult for African and Asian states to compete and keep their indigenous identities.

Local traditions also help to explain why athletes of certain sports always come from a particular area. Tradition is the only reason why more Olympic fencers come from tiny Tauberbischofsheim than from any other German town. Fencing is a first-priority sport for children in this town, whereas soccer interests come first in the rest of West Germany. Therefore the tradition steers the most talented children into the most popular local sport. The German Democratic Republic successfully overcame the power of tradition by diminishing its influence. Talent tests and statewide distribution of talented youth into the respective centers took the place of self-recruiting according to local preference by tradition.

The training systems and methods.   A rich exchange has been going on in this field in training-related literature from the Renaissance onward (Krüger & McClelland, 1984). The same holds true today: Many training concepts have come from the Soviet Union via East and West Germany into the Western world. For example, Matwejew (1972) formulated his statistical approach of "periodization" to make an athlete reach a peak performance at the proper moment as the result of an analysis of the data of several hundred athletes between 1956 and 1960. His system was employed in all of the Eastern European countries without anybody in the West copying it from 1962 to 1969. West Germany used its new system to adopt Matwejew's approach by 1972. Only from 1973 on was the concept introduced to the English-speaking world (Krüger, 1973), yet not even today has the United Olympic Committee drawn any practical consequences from the approach.

On the other hand, many training regimens were copied very quickly, such as interval training or a Lydiard-type of endurance training. Fact-finding tour groups and "spies" reported on the training of top international athletes and teams. A special kind of sport literature has developed that explains how "so and so" is training, assuming that another athlete can copy the training system and become as good as the first athlete but neglecting the individuality of the athlete. For all practical purposes, training systems and methods are unified around the world, new systems are copied within 4 years, and the results of new approaches are published in a limited number of journals. One only needs to cover these to see what is going on in the world of coaching.

The level and number of experts available.   The curricula of the education of coaches has been a major topic for international comparison and cross-influence (Krüger, 1980). Whenever a fact-finding tour group has been sent to learn about top-level sports, the formal analysis of curricula for coaches has been a must. Yet when a new course that is supposed to lead to higher qualifications and better results is installed, it takes a while until the new curriculum can be evaluated by coaching effectiveness. Active coaches bring far more experience to their jobs than newly graduated "experts" (Florl & Peters, 1983; Scheiding, 1983).

The possibility of crossing over from teacher to coach and back is differently organized in most countries. Its likelihood depends primarily on the integration of the elite sport system in a society. In this respect, the West German club system, admired for its ability to mobilize the youth of the country and to provide for free and self-regulated sport, does have its disadvantages. It is so separate from the school system that switching teachers and coaches is practically impossible under the current economic conditions.

Coaching certification schemes have been developed in the Soviet Union and have been copied all over the world to increase the number of sport experts. Meanwhile, such a degree of international cooperation exists that a considerable number of sport coaching certificates acquired in one country are also acceptable in another. This has led to a sort of "brain drain" in the coaching field. In particular, the German Democratic Republic has always claimed that West Germany was recruiting coaches from the other side of the Iron Curtain.

The material basis. The material basis for a particular sport may differ considerably from a country's general economic conditions; a country may be so large that certain sports may be available only in a particular area although the economical basis and the tradition may support practicing it elsewhere too. In this case, a comparison on the basis of tracks or swimming pools per head or their distribution may be feasible.

A comparison is not that easy, however, as obtaining accurate data for Western countries is difficult because ownership of sport installations may differ considerably; and although a sport installation may exist on a material basis, the access may be very limited. The same is the case in the Eastern bloc: If an installation is for an elite sport club, then it cannot be used by a "normal" athlete.

The level and the amount of sport-related research. As could be seen in the section on training systems and methods, it is one matter to have a certain number of research institutes available—they can be counted for the sake of comparison, their financial resources can be compared, and their outputs can be measured in terms of papers, books, and doctorates. Yet all of this does not help to explain the degree of ready application of research results to the sporting practice and the closeness of the researcher to the actual problems of elite sport. The differentiation between the different loci of control for such projects does not even help. An independent research team may have good ideas and apply them to a small group of athletes nearby, and a research team on behalf of a national organization may have no ideas or may not be able to get its results across to the athletes and coaches. Thus comparisons at face value are difficult to draw. It can be shown, however, that, in general, totalitarian states have and use the power to bring results across to the coaches and athletes, while in democratic countries it is up to the individuals to accept or not to accept the research findings.

In this respect the use of different means of communication between the researchers, the sport-governing bodies, and the coaches and athletes should be closely watched. In general, pertinent results are only openly published 4 years after their actual uses so that during one Olympic cycle the country with the results has the benefit of the research advantage. The results generally are published beforehand with a limited edition, mimeographed, numbered, and given to a select few who can apply these results.

Although the U.S. has a vast amount of sport-related research, very little is done in the actual field of improving performance because the groups that can be analyzed very often are too small because the college system has small units in each sport. Because athletes are in concentrated groups in other countries, it is easier to come up with larger samples which make for statistically better results. If the researcher is then employed by the sport-governing body and is made responsible for the athletic success and even is permitted to share some of the rewards, then he or she will be interested even more in improving the performance of the athlete and not just in turning out good research papers.

The social position of sport outside the schools.   A comparison here is equally difficult. West Germany has the highest percentage of people organized in voluntary sport organizations (i.e., 18.3 million members in 60,000 sport clubs). This means that 29.78% of the population are members of a sport club. Yet the whole system is geared so much toward clubs that practicing a sport outside the clubs is next to impossible or extremely expensive. While such a high percentage of membership should be able to move something politically, the money allocated for sport has been cut considerably at all levels recently. Although the amount of money spent by the local, state, or federal government and industrial sponsors varies from country to country, a comparison of allocated money is next to impossible because it would have to take into account tax benefits and mixed financing for school sport and sport outside the school system. The attempt to compare the amount of money allocated by Germany and France failed even though both countries keep their budgets open (Krüger, 1980, p. 22; Pfetsch, 1975) because the whole sport structure and the financial structures are quite different.

Finances are generally the easiest indicators for the social positioning of a field and its acceptance. The sport system outside the schools is, however, also influenced by the media and public discussion about the value of certain behaviors. If the discussion is about the relative value of children's elite sport in a context of manipulation of the free will (Howald & Hahn, 1982) or of the technological side of improving performance (Sass & Vogt, 1980), then it does make quite a difference in the climate provided by the social acceptance in a society.

Of course covering the press in relation to certain phenomena (Digel, 1983; Hackforth, 1975; Hackforth & Weischenberg, 1978; Quanz, 1974) and making conclusions about the social position of the athlete or certain features is possible. This does require, however, that the press give a fair picture about the social situation in a particular country, which is unlikely even in uncensored media. On a different level, the function of media in positioning sport can be analyzed (e.g., Digel, 1980, for the German Democratic Republic). But even this is quite difficult because the author's bias about a certain social system may become apparent.

The personal conditions of the athletes.   The personal conditions of athletes could be compared down at the grassroots level. This could be done for the amount of money earned in elite sport, for the favors granted, and for the feeling of security or insecurity if large amounts of time are invested in sport. Here the Communist countries with their long-range planning of athletic and personal goals and positions do have a certain advantage for the average athlete. On the other hand, the greater personal risk in the West is generally better rewarded. Social deprivation of the individual gives a different meaning to sport, and for many in the East, it offers one of the few legal possibilities to travel and to acquire social prestige. Comparing data on this basis requires that the social and economic conditions as discussed in the social and political conditions section be analyzed for the athlete. This is difficult at times because sociological methods are interpreted differently in the East (Voigt, 1975), and the situations are so individually diversified in the West that they are even difficult to group for the sake of comparison. Ulrich (1977) and Lehnertz (1979) have provided data for the situation of elite athletes in West Germany, and Holz (1981) has done the same for high school athletes, which clearly indicates how difficult it is to work on an individual basis. Hammerich's (1972) model of career patterns of athletes is the best available approach for an international comparison.

The spreading and development of sport around the world. If a comparison of countries is made strictly on a medal and point basis, then the question of how many countries have to be competed against is of considerable importance. Field hockey is one of the examples of sports in which few countries participate and in which relatively little training suffices to achieve international success, while in swimming, track and field, and weight lifting the international standard is by now so high that it is extremely difficult to compete with the best. Keep in mind that in sports like swimming or gymnastics far more medals can be won than in team sports in which 11 or more competitors are needed for just one medal. Additionally, teams cannot win more than one medal in the same sport whereas individual superiority in another sport may lead to a clean sweep of three medals.

Comparisons have to take these differences into account because they help to explain why the Communist countries have concentrated on so-called "medal intensive" sports (i.e., sports in which a maximum number of medals can be obtained with minimum investment). As soon as you change the mode of comparison the criteria for the preference of a less practiced sport with more medals over a more practiced sport with only one is automatically changed.

The development of sport organizations. Lüschen (1981) attempted to classify the national Olympic committees according to their effectiveness, their efficiency, their relation to social values, and their dependence on social groups. Although he had to depend on the willingness of respondents to answer his questions truthfully, he indicated on which level a comparison is possible. On the other hand, it can also be shown how and when a larger degree of professionalization in the sport-governing bodies took place in recent years. Just as the Coaching Association of Canada was the result of a major reorganization, the breakup of the AAU in the United States by the Amateur Sports Act of 1978 was a significant action. Elite sport in many other western countries also has gone through a change in recent years to keep up with a development which started in its current phase with the entry of the USSR in international competition.

Rational systems of long-term planning in sports. Because the development of athletes from the start of regular training to top performance takes many years, continuity is needed to assure that the talents are not wasted and that the individuals are steered in the right direction. In this respect it is interesting to compare the means of finding and developing athletic talent. This involves identifying the best athletes at a given moment, who, by competitions among the young, will win or whom a scout may or may not identify to hire for a better team. It also involves spotting the athlete who progresses the fastest in a standardized training program. Although in practical sports the same anthropometric measurements and tests are applied for a particular event, these systems are constantly refined, and the most sophisticated international comparisons are done on these grounds. What the standardization of physical fitness tests (Schönhölzer, 1974) did openly for the "sports for all" programs was done by the various sports organization for the benefit of long-term planning.

The application of optimal training loads. Judging what is and what is not an optimal training load is very difficult. The discussion about the anaerobic threshold is but one example of the difficulty of properly defining a training load. International comparisons of the form and amount of training are done by most coaches to judge what the developmental possibilities of their own athletes are. Obviously, sport becomes for many a full-time occupation which leads to a greater degree of professionalization (Fischer, 1986) because more emphasis is placed on everything relating to training and competing. So the number of full-time staff people for sport outside the school system who have greater degrees of responsibility plays as much a role here as the application of research results does.

In general, the training loads tend to be larger and the training hours tend to be longer in the Eastern countries than in most Western countries. This has brought more success to the East, particularly in events of strength and endurance such as rowing, canoeing, boxing, and so forth in which the largest amounts of training are necessary.

The development of techniques in particular sports. International sporting events are covered very closely by an ever-increasing amount of observers who help to standardize athletic techniques all over the world. Although considerable variations exist according to national tradition or the acute situation, particularly in team sports (Winkler, 1984), the level of uniformity reached has constantly grown. As far as development of techniques is concerned, it is an open question whether a systematic search as done in the Eastern bloc—which produced among others, the Baryshnikov technique in shot-putting—or a more spontaneous development in the West—which produced Dick Fosbury with his flop—is more successful.

The perfection of sporting gear and installations. A general standardization can be observed in this area, too. Although Olympic games always show some new developments, such as supposedly super-fast skis or bobsleighs, in general the number of inventions is decreasing. After counting the expensive arenas and comparing them on a per capita basis, it is obvious that the rich industrialized countries have an advantage over the poorer countries. Yet top installations do not guarantee success and/or happiness.

The optimal relationship between these factors. Under the conditions of state planning, it is easier to influence all of these factors; on the other hand, an increasing number of Western states have attempted to improve their performances by optimizing at least some of the factors. The problem remains, however, that a country that is run along the lines of a free enterprise system cannot use a system of state planning in sport to improve performance. All attempts to copy the efforts of the USSR or the German Democratic Republic to improve performance are therefore bound to fail unless their socioeconomic systems are copied with those efforts, as has been the case in Cuba.

The Internationality of Elite Sport

After looking at these 17 factors, there are more possibilities to compare than can be handled reasonably in the time given. If a world report of sport in all countries must be written, then language is of minor concern, because a computerized system could be devised to handle the quantitative, qualitative, and nominative data available in data banks such as at the Bundesinstitut für Sportwissenschaft or the Sport Information Resource Centre. These factors also show that the internationality of sport and the increasing denseness of international communication has produced a considerable amount of uniformity at the top level of sport outside the school system. This fact makes it often easier for a top-level athlete or coach to communicate about his or her sport with someone of comparable caliber from a foreign country than with someone of a lower rank in his or her own country. The athletic "circus" that travels the globe in skiing or track and field, and the international transfers of soccer stars are just some examples of this.

After looking at elite sport as a multinational trust of the entertainment industry, it becomes obvious that local peculiarities exist; but the law of rational improvement in sport and the rules of telecommunication bring various sports closer together and thus make us aware of the distinguishing features of particular countries.

The International Olympic Committee, with the help of international sport federations, is increasing this uniformity with the so-called "Olympic Solidarity Program," which brings modern techniques to the developing countries and thus decreases the amount of differences that are left. National sport programs that aid developing countries have the same tendency.

The reader may wonder why a complete comparison was not made since we are dealing with comparative physical education and sport here. Many comparisons are available. In West Germany a special research branch has occupied itself with comparing East and West Germany; the author has personally joined in these comparisons (Krüger, 1980). But after looking at most of these comparative analyses very closely, it is obvious that, just like Diem (1914), the major aim is generally not to compare but to draw conclusions for the benefit of a person's own country from experience elsewhere. This is a legitimate policy and of good practical but very often doubtful theoretical value. To improve on this, a person would have to keep in mind Lempart's 17 factors and the social determination of the person's own position (Brohm, 1976; Forchel & Heise, 1984). Thus many comparisons are available, but they have to be questioned very carefully to see if they actually live up to the standard of decent scholarship or whether they are of practical and political use.

In conclusion, a paradox becomes obvious: No other sport field has experienced so many comparisons done on results, national rankings, and point scores. Yet no other sport field has experienced so many fact-finding tours, observer groups, and international clinics organized to closely monitor the developments in the leading countries and thus to cope with the international competition on fairly equal footing. Because of all of these comparisons and competitions, no other sport field has achieved a greater amount of uniformity for the better or for the worse (Quirion & Guay, 1982), and therefore has lent itself less and less for comparison. By now, few distinguishing features are left in many sports, and it is as if you are looking at the local branches of one single international system.

References

Bale, J.R. (1982). *Sport and place—A geography of sport in England and Wales*. London: Hurst.

Brohm, J.M. (1976). *Sociologie politique du sport*. Paris: Jean Pierre Delarge.

Burger, H.G., & Voigt, D. (1980). "Sportunterricht" und "Körpererziehung." Inhaltsanalytischer Vergleich zweier Sportlehrerzeitschriften der Bundesrepublik und der DDR. In M. Quell (Ed.), *Sport, soziologie und erziehung* (pp. 164-182). Berlin: Bartels & Wernitz.

Cantelon, H., & Riordan, J. (1982). Great Britain and Canada in the Olympic Games: Politics and policies. In M. Jlmarinen (Ed.), *Sport and International Understanding* (pp. 138-151). Berlin: Springer.

Diem, C. (1914). *Sport und Körperschulung in Amerika. Bericht über die Sportstudienreise nach den Vereinigten Staaten im August-September 1913*. Berlin: Selbstverlag des Deutschen Reichsausschusses.

Digel, H. (1980). Sportberichterstattung in der DDR—Ein Modell? *Leistungssport*, **10**, 510-521.

Digel, H. (Ed.). (1983). *Sport und Berichterstattung*. Reinbek: Rowohlt.

Fischer, H. (1986). *Professionalisierung im Sport*. Berlin: Bartels & Wernitz.

Florl, R., & Peters, H. (1983). Absolventenbild, Anforderungscharakteristik und Studienziele—Orientierungsgrundlage für die Gestaltung des Hochschulstudiums von Sportlehrern und Trainern. *Theorie und Praxis der Körperkultur, 32*, 182-188.

Forchel, H., & Heise, N. (1984). Ökonomische und politische Determiniertheit der Kommerzialisierung des bürgerlichen Sports. *Theorie und Praxis der Körperkultur, 33*, 63-68.

Gronen, W., & Lemke, W. (1978). *Geschichte des Radsports. Von den Anfängen bis 1939*. Eupen: Edition Doepgen.

Guttmann, A. (1979). *Vom Ritual zum Rekord. Das Wesen des modernen Sports*. Schorndorf: Hofmann.

Hackforth, J. (1975). *Sport im Fernsehen*. Münster: Regensberg.

Hackforth, J., & Weischenberg, S. (Eds.). (1978). *Sport und Massenmedien*. Bad Homburg: Limpert.

Hammerich, K. (1972). Berufs Karrieren von Spitzensportlern. *Sportwissenschaft, 2*, 168-181.

Hancock, H.I., & Higashi, K. (1910). *Das Kano Jiu-Jitsu (Jiudo)*. Stuttgart: Julius Hoffmann.

Heinilä, K. (1982). The totalization process in international sport. Toward a theory of the totalization of competition in top-level sport. *Sportwissenschaft, 12*, 235-254.

Holz, P. (1981). Nachwuchsathleten im Spannungsfeld sozialer Wirklichkeit. *Leistungssport, 11*, 5-19.

Howald, H., & Hahn, H. (Eds.). (1982). *Kinder im Leistungssport*. Basel: Birkhäuser.

Isidora Frasca, R. (1983). *E il duce le volle sportive*. Bologna: Patron.

Jaworski, Z. (1981). *Wyzsze Studia Wychowania Fizycznego*. Warsaw: Akademii Wychowania Fizycznego w Warszawie.

Killanin, L. (1983). *My Olympic years*. London: Secker & Warburg.

Krüger, A. (1972). *Die Olympischen Spiele 1936 und die Weltmeinung*. Berlin: Bartels & Wernitz.

Krüger, A. (1973). Periodization—Or peaking at the right time. *Track Technique, 14*(54), 1720-1724.

Krüger, A. (1975). Sport und Politik. In *Vom Turnvater Jahn zum Staatsamateur*. Hannover: Fackelträger.

Krüger, A. (1978). Vergleich zwischen deutschen und schweizer Diplomtrainer-Studenten. Eine empirische Untersuchung zur Selbsteinschätzung von Arbeitsbedingungen von Trainern. *Trainer-Information-Entraîneur* (vol. 5). Magglingen: Eidgenössische Turn- und Sportschule.

Krüger, A. (1980). *Das Berufsfeld des Trainers im Sport.* Schorndorf: Hofmann.

Krüger, A. (1982, August 26-29). Sport, state, and the Olympic Games. The origin of the notion of sport as a medium of political representation. *Proceedings. 5th Canadian Symposium on the History of Sport and Physical Education* (pp. 369-379). University of Toronto.

Krüger, A. (Ed.). (1985). *Leibesübungen in Europa: I. Die Europäische gemeinschaft.* London: Arena.

Krüger, A., & Casselman, J. (1982). A comparative analysis of top level track and field coaches in the USA and West Germany. *Comparative, Physical Education and Sport,* 3(11), 20-29.

Krüger, A., & McClelland, J. (Eds.). (1984) *Die Anfänge des modernen Sports in der Renaissance.* London: Arena.

Krüger, A., & Riordan, J. (Eds.). (1985). *Der internationale Arbeíter Sport. Der Schlüssel zum Arbeíter Sport in lo Landern.* Köln: Pahl-Rugenstein.

Kugel, J. (1981). *Geschiedenis van de Gymnastiek.* Haarlem: De Vriesborch.

Lathe, H. (1979). *Geheimnisse des Sowjetsports. Hintergründe internationaler erfolge.* Düsseldorf: Econ.

Lehnertz, K. (1979). *Berufliche Entwicklung der Amateurspitzensportler in der Bundesrepublik Deutschland.* Schorndorf: Hofmann.

Lempart, T. (1969). *Die Ergebnisse der deutschen Olympiamannschaft bei den XIX. Olympischen Spielen in Mexico. Ursache und Wirkung.* Frankfurt: Selbstverlag des DSB.

Lempart, T. (1973). *Die Olympischen Spiele in München 1972. Probleme des Hochleistungssports.* Berlin: Bartels & Wernitz.

Lempart, T., & Spitz, L. (1977). West German Preparations for the Olympic Games. In Coaching Association of Canada (Ed.), *1976 Post Olympic Symposium* (pp. 40-70). Ottawa: Coaching Association of Canada.

Lempart, T., & Spitz, L. (1979). *Probleme des Hochleistungssports. Olympische Analyse. Montreal 1976.* Berlin: Bartels & Wernitz.

Le Pogam, Y. (1979). *Démocratisation du sport: Mythe ou réalité.* Paris: Jean-Pierre Delarge.

Lüschen, G. (1981). Die Verbandspolitik Nationaler Olympischer Komitees. Ergebnisse und methodische Probleme aus einer Leitstudie. *Sportwissenschaft,* 11, 183-197.

Matwejew, L.P. (1972). *Periodisierung des sportlichen Trainings.* Berlin: Bartels & Wernitz.

Melchert, S. (1973). Zu gesellschaftswissenschaftlichen Bestandteilen des Sportlehrerstudiums in einigen sozialistischen Ländern. *Theorie und Praxis der Körperkultur*, **22**, 838-842.

Melchert, S. (1977). Zur Sportlehrerausbildung in sozialistischen Ländern Europas. *Körpererziehung*, **27**, 334-342.

Meynaud, J. (1966). *Sport et politique*. Paris: Payot.

Novikov, A.D., & Maksimenko, M. (1972). Soziale und ökonomische Faktoren und das Niveau sportlicher Leistungen verschiedener Länder. *Sportwissenschaft*, **2**, 156-167.

Oehmigen, G. (1982). Die Rolle der internationalen Sportbeziehungen für die Verständigung der Völker. *Theorie und Praxis der Körperkultur*, **31**, 830-835.

Olafson, G.A., & Coughlan, J. (1982, July 7-10). Structural variations and sport policy: A comparison of Canadian and British sport systems. In M. Jimarinen (Ed.), *Sport and international understanding* (pp. 346-351). Berlin: Springer.

Pfetsch, F. (1975). *Leistungssport und Gesellschaftssystem. Sozio-politische Faktoren im Leistungssport*. Schorndorf: Hofmann.

Pfetsch, F. (1977). Zur sozialwissenschaftlichen Analyse des Sports. Methodische Anmerkungen zum Systemvergleich Bundesrepublik Deutschland—DDR. *Handlungsmuster Leistungssport. Karl Adam zum Gedenken* (pp. 132-137). Schorndorf: Hofmann.

Pfister, G., & Voigt, D. (1982). Geschlechterstereotype im Systemvergleich. Eine Analyse von Heiratsanzeigen. In D. Voigt & M. Messing (Eds.), *Beiträge zur Deutschlandforschung* (Vol. 1; pp. 238-285). Bochum: Norbert Brockmeyer.

Quanz, L. (1974). *Der Sportler als Idol. Sportberichterstattung: Inhaltsanalyse und Ideologiekritik am Beispiel der Bild-Zeitung*. Gießen: Focus.

Quirion, A., & Guay, B. (1982, July 7-10). Sport: A universal culture. *Proceedings of the Congress on Sport and International Understanding*. Helsinki.

Remans, A. (1982, July 7-10). Clearing House. European co-operation through exchange of sports information. *Proceedings of the Congress on Sport and International Understanding*. Helsinki.

Riordan, Y. (1977). *Sport in soviet society*. Cambridge: Cambridge University Press.

Rudolph, E. (1981). Die Aggressionstheorie und ihre Beziehungen zur zunehmenden Brutalisierung im imperialistischen Sport. *Theorie und Praxis der Körperkultur*, **30**, 371-378.

Sass, H., & Vogt, M. (Eds.). (1980). *Gestaltung und Leitung des außerunterrichtlichen Kinder—und Jugendsports*. Berlin: Sportverlag.

Scheiding, G. (1983). *Analyse der Sportlehrer—und Trainerausbildung in der UdSSR*. Ahrensburg: Czwalina.

Schönhölzer, G. (1974). *Standardization of physical fitness tests*. Basel: Birkhäuser.

Seppänen, P. (1972). Die Rolle des Leistungssports in den Gesellschaften der Welt. *Sportwissenschaft*, **2**, 133-155.

Simon, H. (1970). Die Bedeutung der deutsch-sowjetischen Freundschaft für die Entwicklung der DHfK. *Theorie und Praxis der Körperkultur*, **19**, 861-869.

Stensaasen, S. (1982). A coordinated, comparative study of sports involvement among Scandinavian youngsters. *Scandinavian Journal of Sport Sciences*, **4**, 17-25.

Svoboda, B. (1980). *Coaches and physical education teachers training in socialist countries. A collection of studies in the international scientific cooperation*. Prague: Olympia.

Ulrich, H.E. (1977). *Leistungssport zwischen Idealisierung und Professionalisierung*. Köln: Selbstverlag.

Voigt, D. (1975). *Soziologie in der DDR*. Köln: Wissenschaft & Politik.

Voigt, D., & Messing, M. (1977). Sozialstruktur im deutschen Sport. Ein Beitrag zum Systemvergleich. *Deutschland-Archiv*, **10**, 709-724.

Watanabe, T. (1978). The introduction and transplant of Western sports in Japan. *History of School Physical Education and Sports Promotion Movement* (pp. 541-547). Tokio: ICOSH.

Weisspfennig, G. (1983). *Die sportwissenschaftliche Elite in beiden Teilen Deutschlands*. Berlin: Bartels & Wernitz.

Weyer, W. (1981). Die freiwillige Leistung der Vereine. In Deutscher Sportbund (Ed.), *Jahrbuch des Sports 1981* (pp. 35-48). Niedernhausen: Schors.

Winkler, W. (1984). Zur Taktik im Fußballspiel. *Leistungssport*, **14**, 5-13.

Wonneberger, G. (Ed.). (1982). *Körperkultur und Sport in der DDR. Gesellschaftswissenschaftliches Lehrmaterial*. Berlin: Sportverlag.

CHAPTER 19

Methodological Problems in Comparative Educational Research: The Case of Youth Participation in the United States and Latin America

Darío Menanteau-Horta

Comparative methodology and crossnational research have long been considered necessary allies in the persistent quest for universality of science (Marsh, 1967; Narroll, 1970). Over the years, comparative research has aimed to enhance the formulation of generalizable propositions about social behavior and to become a fundamental methodological tool for analysis and verification. According to Ritzer (1975), the only effective methods to study social and cultural phenomena are those utilized by historical and comparative research.

Crosscultural comparisons are particularly useful in sociology and education because they help the researcher gain a better understanding about the factors and conditions related to human behavior in various groups or societies. A major challenge of the comparative method is determining the extent to which differences found in behavior and social processes are a consequence of differences in institutional structures and larger cultural units.

This report focuses on some issues concerning youth participation from a comparative, crossnational perspective. It aims to assess patterns of social participation of young individuals in three countries that are at different stages of economic development: the United States, Chile, and Bolivia.

The central hypothesis of this study is that the structural conditions and the institutional arrangements of a social system determine not only the feasibility but also the form of participation.

Within this context the analysis addresses the following points:

- The extent to which social participation of youth varies among social systems that differ in levels of industrialization.
- The institutional mechanisms that foster participant behavior and factors associated with youth participation.
- An assessment of the consequences of participation not only from the standpoint of expected results but also from those unexpected consequences relevant to youth and society.

Youth Participation and the Socialization Process

Every society provides guidelines and procedures for socialization of its youth. Mayer (1970, p. xiii) refers to socialization as the process by which society transmits and inculcates in the individual "the skills and attitudes necessary for playing given social roles." Thus youth participation, including sport and physical activities, can be defined as a complex set of practices, techniques, and actions which, through the mechanisms of formal or informal structures, fulfills general socialization functions.

Extracurricular activities have been seen as a microcosm of life and social reality (Sawyer, 1977). Sutton-Smith (1977) suggests that they have been supported and justified "by the contribution they are supposed to make to the individual's or group's socialization into the larger society"(p. 4).

According to Karlin and Berger (1971), youth activities (particularly those provided by educational institutions) help to fulfill (a) the psychological needs of the individual including peer acceptance, security, and the acquisition of knowledge and skills; (b) the fostering of friendship; (c) the more effective use of leisure time; and (d) the expansion and development of leadership qualities.

Other studies have also found a relationship between participation in extracurricular activities and student educational and occupational expectations (Otto & Alwin, 1977; Spreitzer & Pugh, 1973).

Rehberg and Schafer (1968) found a positive association between educational expectations and participation in sport activities. Findings reported by Bend (1968) and Snyder (1969) support the thesis suggesting positive relationships between sport participation and educational pursuits. Comparing student athletes with nonathletes, Rehberg & Cohen (1975) found that participants in interscholastic sports were more likely to (a) have higher educational aspirations and expectations, (b) spend more time on homework, (c) value academic competence, (d) receive more advice from teachers and guidance counselors to enroll in a 4-year college, and (e) accept and conform to norms and rulings of the school.

Sexton (1969) asserts that sports that emphasize individual performance but involve reduced aggression and physical violence are associated more with higher achievement motivation than sports requiring team activities and physical strength.

Participation, however, is heavily influenced by socioeconomic characteristics and other structural conditions in a society (Coleman, 1961; Hyman & Wright, 1971; Stewart, 1967). Havighurst, Bowman, Liddle, Mathews, & Pierce (1962) remark that the adolescent society in the United States is run primarily by middle- and upper-class individuals. Rice (1978) indicates that youngsters from extremely poor families are usually nonjoiners in school activities, seldom elected to positions of prestige, and often have to find status through antisocial behavior.

Guttmann (1978) summarizes the findings and views of other researchers in the area of leisure activities, games, and sports, indicating that "structured games mirror structured society"(p. 47).

Crosscultural comparisons on many of these complex dimensions of youth participation, however, are still rather limited. Moreover, much needs to be learned about the roles of extracurricular activities, sports, and leisure in the socialization of children and adolescents in the world.

Method and Procedures

The Samples

Data reported here are drawn from a crosscultural study on youth and society conducted by the author in the United States (Minnesota) and Latin America (Bolivia and Chile). The analysis is based on responses from a state-wide sample of 4,012 seniors attending about 30 Minnesota high schools and members of two national random samples of high school seniors from Bolivia (1,110) and Chile (2,460).

Participating schools were randomly selected, and questionnaires were administered during a regular school hour with the cooperation of teachers, counselors, and administrators. Students' responses were obtained on an individual and voluntary basis in each country. A standard questionnaire, varying only in local language, was used in all three settings to measure participation of students in extracurricular activities and other aspects of youth life. Because respondents were attending their last year of secondary education and some of the major functions and procedures of formal schooling are quite similar in the three countries, individual student characteristics such as age, sex, and educational attainment are equivalent in the three samples.

The dependent variable was measured by responses to a series of questions about participation in extracurricular activities in school and youth organizations. Students were asked to indicate the type and number of organizations they belonged to and their levels of commitment to these memberships.

In addition to student participation, the survey also included data concerning social and economic characteristics of respondents, family- and school-related variables, youth attitudes and social problems, student educational expectations, and future plans.

The Research Settings

From a perspective of industrial and economic development, the three research settings offer substantial variability in their organizational structures. They range from a more industrialized society (U.S.) to a less-developed economy (Bolivia); Chile is in a transitional stage of industrial growth.

Minnesota has a total population of over 4 million inhabitants, and about one third of them live in rural areas. Although farming continues to be important to Minnesota's economic development, the state's economy is highly diversified with about 6,000 industries. By 1978, manufacturing accounted for 24.1 percent of all personal income. Minnesota Gross State Product of approximately U.S. $30 billion is almost double the GNP of Chile (U.S. $16.5 billion) and is nearly 10 times larger than the Bolivian GNP (U.S. $3.1 billion).

Chile, with a total population of 11.3 million, was one of the first countries of Latin America to shift from a rural to an urban society. Today, over 83% of the Chilean population is urban, compared with 66% in Minnesota and 33% in Bolivia.

Bolivia has a total area of 537,792 square miles. More than half of its 5.9 million population is full-blooded Indian, compared with about eight percent for the rest of Latin America. About a fourth of Bolivians are mestizos, people of mixed Indian and white blood. A rapid rate of demographic growth of 2.7% per year (Chile: 1.6%; Minnesota: 0.6%), high infant mortality (157 per 1,000 live births compared with 40 per 1,000 in Chile and 14 per 1,000 in the U.S.), high illiteracy (36%), and a life expectancy still under 50 years of age (Chile: 66; U.S.: 73) make Bolivia one of the least developed countries of Latin America.

Findings

The Participation Structure in Three Societies

Overall participation differed substantially among members of the three samples. Membership in various types of youth programs is higher among Minnesota students than among Bolivians and Chileans. Participation in sports, cocurricular programs, voluntary associations, clubs, political and religious groups, and academic and leisure activities was reported by 59% of Minnesota respondents, 50% of Bolivians, and 38% of Chilean students.

The most striking differences, however, are in type and location of activity. Over one half of Minnesotans participate in extracurricular functions within their schools and in youth programs sponsored by the school and community combined. About one fourth of Minnesota students belong to school-related organizations and programs. Such activities were reported by 14% of Chileans and by only 2% of Bolivians. A vast majority of the Bolivian respondents who participated (90%) and about half of the participants in Chile belong to organizations operating at the local or national level of their societies. Minnesota participants involved only in community organizations were limited to 12% of the sample.

These differences in forms of affiliation and participation among Minnesotans, Chileans, and Bolivians may be considered consequences of opportunity structures for student participation in each country. Moreover, these comparisons may certainly reflect some fundamental differences in the educational systems of those societies.

Table 1 Percentage of Students Involved in Social Participation

Membership in youth programs	Minnesota (n = 4012)	Chile (n = 2460)	Bolivia (n = 1110)
General participation	59	38	50
School organizations only	26	14	2
School & comm./educ. programs	26	5	3
Community activities only	7	19	45

In the U.S. after World War II, government-funded programs and local support to school systems were decisive in bringing extracurricular activities under the institutional umbrella of education. The school became increasingly involved in the total socialization of the young.

Education in Chile and Bolivia, on the other hand, is hampered by problems of social inequality, lack of economic resources, and severe restrictions in political democracy. Both countries have made substantial gains in expanding educational opportunities at the elementary level. However, secondary schooling and higher education remain limited to a considerably small proportion of young people. In Minnesota about 94% of school-age adolescents (13–19 years of age) are enrolled in high school. The proportion of individuals within the same age category attending secondary schools is 47% in Chile and 18% in Bolivia (UNICEF, 1979).

Under these circumstances, in Chile, and more severely in Bolivia, extracurricular activities constitute at best a marginal priority for most schools which have neither the necessary facilities nor the teaching staff to serve students. Having little opportunity to participate within the schools, Chilean and Bolivian youths who wish to become involved in extracurricular activities must seek opportunities outside the boundaries of the school system. About one half of the participants in Chile and most of the Bolivian students are involved in such organizations. From this viewpoint, the lack of institutionalized mechanisms for student participation as part of the educational system may place Chilean and Bolivian students at a clear disadvantage when compared with their Minnesotan counterparts.

Factors Related to Participation

Although the last 2 decades have seen a substantial increase in studies analyzing structural elements related to social participation, they largely reflect conditions found in the U.S., Canada, and Western Europe (Babchuck & Booth, 1969; Coleman, 1961; Coleman et al., 1966; Cutler, 1973; Hausknecht, 1962; Loy, McPherson, & Kenyon, 1978; Smith, 1975; Smith & Freedman, 1972; Tomeh, 1973). Comparative research, therefore, in which social participation is viewed within the context of cross-cultural variations is still needed.

The findings in Table 2 show a higher intrasocietal variation in most of the characteristics among Minnesota participants than among the Chileans and Bolivians when each group is compared to nonparticipants. This might suggest that factors which may help to explain social participation in one country (i.e., the U.S.) differ from those factors necessary to explain similar behavior in another culture (i.e., Latin America). The lack of internal variability in some of the independent variables for the Chilean and Bolivian data may also be a consequence of a relatively high level of sample homogeneity because of the process of student elimination throughout the 12 years of formal schooling.

Table 2 Characteristics of Students Who Participate in Social Organizations and Extracurricular Activities

Student characteristics	Minnesota		Chile		Bolivia	
	(n)	%	(n)	%	(n)	%
Sociodemographic characteristics						
Sex						
Males	(1,895)	51	(1,277)	50	(648)	70
Females	(2,113)	66	(1,176)	26	(428)	30
Size of community						
Small	(1,010)	70	(1,674)	40	(104)	63
Medium	(1,734)	59	(432)	42	(402)	45
Large	(1,265)	49	(354)	29	(581)	51
Family background characteristics						
Family SES						
High	(567)	62	(674)	39	(143)	50
Middle	(2,523)	60	(1,412)	38	(502)	53
Low	(768)	61	(345)	40	(426)	48
Father's education						
College	(1,291)	69	(731)	40	(317)	54
High School	(1,485)	59	(891)	38	(281)	47
Elementary	(947)	56	(714)	40	(393)	50

Table 2 (cont.)

Table 2 (cont.)

Father's occupation						
Professionals and managers	(1,133)	68	(936)	40	(289)	54
Farmers	(383)	71	(190)	33	(47)	51
Clerical workers	(437)	60	(753)	39	(238)	51
Laborers	(1,675)	55	(322)	39	(323)	50

School-related characteristics						
Size						
Small/medium	(2,586)	54	(1,220)	36	(502)	46
Large	(1,425)	67	(1,189)	40	(569)	54
Student's grade average						
A	(373)	82	(109)	39	(79)	48
B	(1,799)	68	(1,101)	40	(424)	51
C or less	(1,768)	46	(856)	39	(540)	50
Educational aspirations						
College	(2,147)	71	(2,135)	40	(854)	51
Vocational	(959)	38	(204)	34	(193)	49
Get a job	(788)	53	(108)	25	(24)	50
Self-concept						
High	(1,622)	73	(764)	44	(363)	51
Low/average	(2,373)	49	(1,668)	36	(703)	49

Comparisons between participants and nonparticipants among Minnesota students show a higher proportion of females (66%) than males (51%) enrolled in extracurricular activities. In Bolivia and Chile, however, the reverse is found (Bolivia: 70% of the males versus 30% of the females; Chile: 50% versus 26%).

In Minnesota a relatively higher percentage of rural residents (63%) than urban residents (57%) are participants, while the opposite seems to be the case in Chile and Bolivia. Findings also show higher participation in smaller and medium-sized places than in large cities. This is particularly true in Minnesota and Chile.

Higher levels of socioeconomic status lead to greater participation among Minnesota respondents. In Chile and Bolivia, however, socioeconomic position does not appear to be consistently associated with participation.

Student grades, educational aspirations, and occupational choices show a positive association with participation in Minnesota. In Chile and Bolivia the findings are different: Student involvment in extracurricular functions does not appear to be associated with grades, and only a moderately higher proportion of Chilean college-oriented students are participants than those having other plans for after high school.

This difference between the Minnesota and the two Latin American samples may be traced back to the role played by schools in sports and extracurricular activities. In Minnesota, where participation is largely structured within the school, student organizations and programs are likely to function as mechanisms reinforcing schoolwork and academic achievement. Within this organizational context, class schedules are accommodated, programs are supervised, and participants' behaviors tend to be more readily accepted by their peers, supported by their parents, and encouraged by their teachers. This social approval contributes to the positive relationship between participants and scholastic progress. It may also explain why participation in Minnesota is more strongly related to student self-concept than in the Latin American samples.

In Bolivia and Chile, where youth participation occurs mostly outside the educational system, extracurricular activities tend to compete and conflict with academic requirements and other school tasks. Community events and programs organized by structures outside the school may well be directed toward ends quite different from those established within the educational system. Under these conditions, youth in Latin America may find it more difficult and frustrating to blend their objectives and role expectations as students with their commitments and as active participants in the larger society.

Participation, Values, and Social Alienation

An assessment of the consequences of youth participation includes two dimensions: (a) the type of values most likely held by participants in sport activities and other extracurricular programs and (b) the differences in attitudes of social distress and alienation between participants and nonparticipants.

Values are defined as shared conceptions of what is good and desirable (Williams, 1965). They represent standards which guide relationships and influence the functioning of social institutions. From the individual standpoint, value orientations imply the direction in which behavior may be guided and also involve varying degrees of individual decision and choice.

Value orientation discussed here corresponds to students' preferences in (a) the selection of a future career, (b) the choice of going to college, (c) job selection, and (d) the choice of where to live.

Respondents were asked to indicate the most important quality desired in each of these four areas. The desire to serve and help others, to be creative and humanitarian, and to be willing to assume responsibilities more than personal rewards were considered to represent *intrinsic values*. Other orientations, including a strong desire to achieve status and social recognition, economic rewards, and material gains were conceived as examples of *instrumental values*.

In relation to these two sets of value orientations, it was hypothesized that social participation of the young would be associated with intrinsic values rather than with instrumental orientations. This is based on the assumption that involvement and commitment to extracurricular activities are largely voluntary and focus on the noninstrumental aspects of social interaction.

Minnesota participants consistently stressed intrinsic values over instrumental concerns in each of the four choice areas. In Chile and Bolivia, however, participation appeared unrelated to these value orientations. Although Chilean participants tended to favor intrinsic over instrumental values, percentage differences between these two categories were small. Among Bolivian participants, the pattern of response is less consistent: students were more likely to choose instrumental over intrinsic values only in decisions concerning future career and college attendance. Yet these differences are too small to be conclusive.

Personal development and social adjustment of youth may also be affected by levels of distress and alienation felt by individuals. Social alienation was measured by a scale of six items assessing students' views about quality of life, uncertainty about the future, trust in others, and perception of fairness in their society. Responses could range from total agreement to complete disagreement with each item, including two intermediate categories. The results appear in Table 3.

Findings show that a higher proportion of Bolivian students than Minnesotans and Chileans expressed agreement with these indicators of social distress. At least 80% of Bolivians agreed with the statement that "a young person doesn't know with whom he counts . . . ," compared with 65% in Chile and 52% in Minnesota. Also, a certain degree of pessimism (Item 1) and uncertainty about the future (Item 2) is revealed by the majority of respondents from the three samples.

Among Minnesotans, differences between participants and nonparticipants are significant for each item. Although in Chile and Bolivia these differences are more moderate, the general pattern of students' responses indicate that participation in extracurricular activities may contribute to lower levels of social alienation.

Conclusions

Data show that organizational and institutional conditions largely determine opportunities for youth participation. They constitute the mechanisms that facilitate, shape, or limit extracurricular activities. From a cross-cultural perspective it appears that certain factors usually considered to be associated with participation in one society are not necessarily the best predictors of involvement in another cultural context.

In settings where participation is highly structured within school functions, youngsters are more likely to find activities helpful to their role as students. In developing societies, however, the fragile institutionalization

Table 3　Percentage of Students in Agreement With Scale Items Indicating "Social Distress"

Items	Minnesota		Chile		Bolivia	
	Partic. (n = 2,353)	Nonpart. (n = 1,659)	Partic. (n = 1,515)	Nonpart. (n = 945)	Partic. (n = 560)	Nonpart. (n = 550)
1. In spite of what is said, the general situation is worsening.	59	63**	62	64	76	75
2. Because of a highly uncertain future, it's better to live in the present.	57	67**	57	63*	64	71**
3. Nowadays a young person doesn't know with whom he counts or whom he can trust.	46	60**	62	68*	77	82
4. As things are going today, it's unjust to bring more children into this world.	30	39**	45	48	50	59**
5. Today adults do not care to help young people with their problems.	19	26**	23	23	43	42
6. Good luck and "influence" give you more than skill and hard work.	16	22**	47	50	41	40

Note. Percentages marked at p < .05 significance level are for chi-squared values.

*p < .05. **p < .01.

of extracurricular activities within schools seems to have negative effects upon students' academic performances.

Findings underline the theoretical and practical importance of comparative research for both the replication and verification of theory and the solving of educational and social problems.

References

Babchuck, N., & Booth, A. (1969). Voluntary association membership: A longitudinal analysis. *American Sociological Review, 34*, 31-45.

Bend, E. (1968). *The impact of athletic participation on academic and career aspiration and achievement.* New Brunswick, NJ: National Football Foundation and Hall of Fame.

Coleman, J.S. (1961). *The adolescent society.* Glencoe, IL: The Free Press.

Coleman, J.S., Campbell, E.Q., Hobson, C.J., McPartland, J., Mood, A.M., Weinfeld, F.D., & York, R.L. (1966). *Quality of educational opportunity.* Washington, DC: Government Printing Office.

Cutler, S. (1973). Voluntary association membership and the theory of mass society. In E. Laumann (Ed.), *Bonds of pluralism: The form and substance of urban social networks* (pp. 133-159). New York: John Wiley.

Guttmann, A. (1978) *From ritual to record, the nature of modern sports.* New York: Columbia University Press.

Hausknecht, M. (1962). *The joiner: A sociological description of voluntary association membership in the United States.* New York: Bedminster Press.

Havighurst, R.J., Bowman, P.H., Liddle, G.P., Matthews, Ch. V., & Pierce, J.V. (1962). *Growing up in river city.* New York: John Wiley.

Hyman, H.H., & Wright, C.R. (1971). Trends in voluntary association memberships of American adults. *American Sociological Review, 36*, 191-206.

Karlin, M.S., & Berger, R. (1971). *The effective student activities program.* New York: Parker.

Loy, J.W., McPherson, B.D., & Kenyon, G. (1978). *Sport and social systems* (pp. 236-237). Boston: Addison-Wesley.

Marsh, R. (1967). *Comparative sociology.* New York: Harcourt, Brace, Jovanovich.

Mayer, P. (Ed.). (1970). *Socialization: The approach from social anthropology* (Introduction, pp. xiii-xxx). London: Tavistock.

Narroll, R. (1970). What have we learned from cross-cultural surveys? *American Anthropologist, 72*, 1227-1288.

Otto, L.B., & Alwin, D. (1977). Athletics, aspirations and attainments. *Sociology of Education, 42*, 102-103.

Rehberg, R.A., & Cohen, M. (1975). Athletes and scholars: An analysis of the compositional characteristics and damage of these two youth culture categories. *International Review of Sport Sociology, 10*, 91-107.

Rehberg, R.A., & Schafer, W.E. (1968). Participation in interscholastic athletics and college expectations. *The American Journal of Sociology, 73*, 732-740.

Rice, F.P. (1978). *The adolescent: Development, relationships and culture*. New York: Allyn and Bacon.

Ritzer, G. (1975). *Sociology: A multiple paradigm science*. Boston: Allyn and Bacon.

Sawyer, K.C. (1977). Ultimate goalpost: The human spirit. In T. Craig (Ed.), *The humanistic and mental health aspects of sports, exercise and recreation* (p. VI). Chicago: American Medical Association.

Sexton, P.C. (1969). *The feminized male*. New York: Vintage Books.

Smith, C., & Freedman, A. (1972). *Voluntary associations: Perspectives on the literature*. Cambridge, MA: Harvard University Press.

Smith, D.H. (1975). Voluntary action and voluntary groups. In A. Jukeles (Ed.), *Annual review of sociology* (Vol. 1, pp. 247-270). Palo Alto, CA: Annual Reviews.

Snyder, E.E. (1969). A longitudinal analysis of the relationship between high school student values, social participation, and educational-occupational achievement. *Sociology of Education, 42*, 261-270.

Spreitzer, E., & Pugh, M. (1973). Interscholastic athletics and educational expectations. *Sociology of Education, 46*, 171-182.

Stewart, C.W. (1967). *Adolescent religion*. New York: Abingdon.

Sutton-Smith, B. (1977). Current research and theory on play, games and sports. In T. Craig (Ed.), *The humanistic and mental aspects of sports, exercise and recreation* (pp. 1-5). Chicago: American Medical Association.

Tomeh, A. (1973). Formal voluntary organizations: Participation, correlates and interrelationships. *Sociological Inquiry, 43*, 89-122.

UNICEF, Oficina Regional para las Americas. (1979). *Situación de la infancia en America Latina y el Caribe* [The Situation of Children in Latin America and the Caribbean]. Chile: Editorial Universitaria.

Williams, R.M. (1965). *American society* (wnd ed., rev.). New York: Alfred A. Knopf.

CHAPTER 20

Sport and National Character: Opening the Door to International Understanding

Ralph C. Wilcox

> The Sports of the people afford an index to the character of the nation. They show how the people have met the stress and the exigencies of life by varying their pursuits during those hours of leisure stolen from the more serious efforts of bread-winning; how they have taken advantage of the climatic and other physical environment for the purposes of recreation; what progress they have made along the paths of civilisation towards culture and moral refinement; and, generally, it may be accepted that the temperamental qualities of a people not infrequently manifest themselves in the outlets they seek for their superabundant energies. (Hackwood, 1907, p. 1)

In a world increasingly threatened by a breakdown of communication and the subsequent attrition of understanding between nations, a need exists to reassess the role of international studies within the walls of academe. While curiosity, self-evaluation, and reform continue to represent valuable goals in themselves, scholars must begin to show a deeper commitment toward more fully understanding and appreciating those qualities that make national, cultural, and social groups so unique.

Throughout recent years, the study of national character has fallen out of academic favor as scholars continue to underscore the perceived naivete inherent within national generalizations. Indeed, the lowly status afforded such study by contemporary social scientists was summarized by Max Weber, who felt that addressing the question of national character was merely a confession of ignorance (Wood, 1974). Yet without questioning the very existence of such a notion, the centrality of resultant social constructs provides justification enough for an examination of its nature and role; for even though many people take a dim view of painting a nation's citizenry with one brush, most people continue to do so. This paper does not seek to describe those frequently antiquated yet commonly held beliefs pertaining to the sociopsychological traits of nationalities but rather it examines the utility of this notion in the quest for rapprochement.

Although the study of national, cultural, and social institutions can contribute much toward improved understanding, this essay proposes that the identification and assessment of the underlying motives for action will prove to be more fruitful. An area of study once reserved for the psychologist or anthropologist now attracts the historian, sociologist, economist, and political scientist as scholars strive to better understand and more fully explain the collective behavior of national groups. It would seem reasonable to expect individuals to reflect the most common personality and shared values of the group through their behavior in a given political, familial, or perhaps sporting situation. So what is this concept of national character? Is it something more than abstraction? How can it be measured? and of central importance to this paper, What is its relationship to sport?

Since Juvenal's cynical perception of the "little Greeks" and Tacitus's painstaking description of the attitudes, customs, and morals of *Germania* (circa 98 A.D.), national character and its subsequent stereotypes have interested mankind. Reinforced by Shakespeare's collection of national portraits (see Clark, 1972), it would seem that the power of association brought by individuals has been significant in the creation of stereotypical images. Still others contend that national character represents the world view of a nation as seen from the outside. Whichever may be the case, and while the reality of social change prohibits the enduring quality of national character, stereotypes clearly tend toward perpetuation. Indeed, seldom does one associate such tropes as Sybarite, Lesbian, and Hun with civilizations of yesteryear when describing the constitution of contemporary mankind. Further, our image of Germans today is not unlike that picture painted by Tacitus nearly 2,000 years ago wherein Germans were colored as disciplined, industrious, war-like beer drinkers (for additional reading see Foot, 1973; Forgas, 1976; Fyfe, 1940; Kracauer, 1949, and McDonald, 1978). Similarly, one might speak of the brash, crude, and noisy American or perhaps the arrogant English gentleman. Of course the latter "breed" is well-known for "blowing his own trumpet," a trait not uncommon among other races and early recognized by Jean Jacques Rousseau who wrote:

> I am aware that the English make a boast of their humanity and of the kindly disposition of their race which they call "good natured people" but in vain do they proclaim this fact; no one else says it of them. (Rousseau, 1974, p. 118)

The United States represents a more complex case. It is a culturally pluralistic nation within which assimilation and acculturation, products of the "melting pot" phenomenon, have drawn citizens out of their ethnic enclaves toward the focal value system of a white Anglo-Saxon Protestant hegemony, creator of the American national character.

While contemporary international commentators speak freely about Swedish films, Japanese industry, and British humor, this paper seeks to identify the existence and relevance of national patterns of sport and the behavioral connotations that may accompany them. Clearly, some observable national differences can be recorded in the sport arena, as one will likely be able to identify the African competitor in a race run between two Norwegians and a Nigerian. However, with the substitution of a Kenyan and an American for the Norwegians, identification of the Nigerian runner becomes more difficult, as greater emphasis must be placed upon assumed behavioral traits characteristic of the West African nation. In a search for improved understanding between nations it is imperative that mankind's current strategy to jealously guard personal preferences by attacking those beliefs of others as something less than moral be discontinued. Only when we view others as different rather than echo the bigotry of ego supremacy (by insisting that others internalize the beliefs of ourselves) can there be hope for peace as Washington Platt, a retired American Brigadier, clearly realized:

> A study of national character starts with a realization that the character of other people is usually very different from our own. It is useless to *pretend* they are like ourselves, and it is foolish to try to change them to conform to our patterns. (Platt, 1961, p. 5)

The very nature of national character has led to considerable debate over the years. In essence, two contrasting pictures have been painted by early social scientists: the first is colored by the collective traits of the citizens of a country, and the second is seen as the distinctive features of government (sometimes viewed as the "national mind").

National character is but one of many types of characters dependent upon demographic variables that include maternal (hereditary) factors such as gender, race, and perhaps ascribed socioeconomic status and spiritual (environmental) factors which include political and religious preferences (see Barker, 1927). Collectively described as "social character," national character was seen by Riesman as being "the patterned uniformities of learned response that distinguish men of different regions, eras and groups" (Riesman, 1950, p. v.). Once perceived as the psychological peculiarities characteristic of the people of a given nation, the expansion of social science has precipitated a more refined interpretation of this complex phenomenon which can be considered closely analogous to personal character. Alexander Shand reflected this early view of character through his lengthy examination of human emotions and sentiments that included love, hate, fear, anger, and curiosity (Shand, 1914). More recently, that personality structure claimed by the largest number of a group's members has led to an alternative explanation, one in which "National character refers to relatively enduring personality characteristics and patterns that are modal among adult members of a society" (Duijker, 1960; Inkeles & Levinson, 1954, p. 983; Smith, 1966).

Perhaps the most readily accepted interpretation today is one represented by a shared system of beliefs, attitudes, values and norms. Held in common by the members of an identifiable group, these underlying motives for action lend themselves more favorably to the emergence of a cultural (or subcultural) character learned and reinforced through the group's literary, artistic and sporting institutions (see Gorer, 1953; Shepherd, 1981; Terhune, 1970).

A clear and deliberate omission at this juncture is the idea of "nation," which may be defined as a group possessing a sovereign government and inhabiting a circumscribed geographical area. This visible absence implies a potential for shared value systems straddling national boundaries and resulting in the appearance of, by way of example, a "North American character" or "Scandinavian character." Moreover, it is important to note that national character is not merely the product of citizens' personalities, emotions, and values but should rather be viewed in combination with the influence of government. Perhaps this is best demonstrated by the Western World's perception of the Soviet citizen who is frequently characterized as overbearing, truculent, and aggressively communistic. To the contrary, visitors to the USSR repeatedly describe the nation's citizens as friendly, peace-loving, and seldom active in the Communist party. In light of this example, people would do well to heed the words of Platt, who explained:

> The national character is not the arithmetic mean of the character of the individuals in the nation, any more than the football-playing ability of a football team could be computed by considering the average weight, running ability, passing ability, kicking ability of the team members. (Platt, 1961, p. 74)

Furthermore, past studies of national character typically made the assumption that all people belonging to a select nation are alike in some respect and, more particularly, are different from the people of other nations. The peculiarities ascribed to these unique traits are assumed to be related to membership of a given national group. It comes as little surprise that contemporary social scientists encounter great difficulty in accepting such premises and have furnished ample evidence in criticism of this notion.

The prescientific label of national character is in itself rather unfortunate and has been the catalyst toward rendering such studies nearly obsolete. Having emerged during an era of relative geographic stability, few award such study any relevance in a world where cultural diversity and pluralism, wrought of improved transportation, media, and communication, have torn down the psychological barriers that once followed national boundaries. Moreover, if a collection of national characters can be verified in today's world, then the question of how they might be measured only leads to ongoing controversy. While some sceptics consider that the patterning of human behavior has been overdone, others question the value of such study in predicting national behavior on the basis that the character of a nation's citizens does not necessarily impinge upon political decisions. Indeed, even if a nation's leaders do share a common value system with their constituents, all too frequently they are influenced more strongly by the concrete knowledge of power, geography, economy, and history. This represents the very foundation of Platt's simplified predictive model wherein national action is seen as the product of hard facts times national character times the situation (Platt, 1961, p. 83). The difficulties inherent in objectively evaluating national character remain the primary reason for the absence of current related research within the social sciences. As early studies fell short because of subjective impressionism, so parallel inquiries into the character of a nation seldom showed any resemblance in terms of outcome. However, despite these shortcomings, mankind apparently continues to find little hardship in stereotyping the character of nations, which creates generalizations that dictate the degree of international communication and understanding prevalent in the world today.

The relevance of national character to sport is examined in the shadow of this collective criticism. While character development has long represented the foremost justification for participating in sport across most nations, little, if any, evidence exists to support this belief. Nevertheless, because athletes are as much products of their cultures as teachers, housewives, and politicians it seems to follow that those sociopsychological traits learned through sport would be characteristic of the parent culture. As such, sport can be viewed as a social mirror—an image shared by Joseph Strutt who wrote: "In order to form a just estimation of the character of any particular people, it is absolutely necessary to investigate the Sports and Pastimes most generally prevalent among them" (Strutt, 1855, p. xvii). Despite such early realizations, sport, particularly in its international context, has not traditionally enjoyed a pleasing status throughout the world of academe.

Sadly neglected by students of international sport to date, relatively enduring stereotypical images of national sporting behavior persist. From the calm and poised perception of the Soviet ice hockey team to the razzmatazz of the American professional and collegiate athletic arena, contrasts are all too obvious. It is interesting to consider what sporting ideologies can reveal about the character of a nation, such as the English worship of fair-play promulgated through the middle class, amateur gospel of "muscular Christianity,"; the belief of "Friendship first, competition second" pursued by athletes of the People's Republic of China; the dictum "Winning isn't everything, it's the only thing," so frequently attributed to sport in America; and the Soviet fitness program "Gotov Trudu Oberonie" ("Ready for Labour and Defense")(see Bennett, Howell, & Simri, 1983; Harf, Coate, & Marsh, 1974; Lowe, Kanin, & Strenk, 1978; Wilcox, 1984). Further, many observers have maintained that European soccer players display a different style of play and temperament than South American players—a behavior apparently reflective of their national character.

Of central concern must be the outcome of a situation in which two or more contrasting value systems confront one another. At stake is the feasibility of international competition in sport. Is it possible that, in a world where incongruencies between the value systems of national groups are commonplace, two or more parties might compete according to shared instrumental rules in an attempt to reach a common goal? The Olympic Games, paramount of international sporting events, were resurrected by Pierre de Coubertin at a time relatively stable in terms of geographic mobility and during a period dominated by the value orientations of a Western European bourgeois elite. Indeed, it would appear that recent attempts to rekindle the now-antiquated flame of Olympic idealism are futile and unrealistic in a world characterized by a plurality of value systems. An alternative view is the possibility of identifying a common system of values shared by sportsmen and sportswomen across all nations. However, the idea of an international sporting character is somewhat negated by the influence of deep-rooted ultimate values, considered the primary motivating force in all human action. Today the greatest philosophical gulf appears to be between those countries that look upon sport as an end in itself and those countries that see sport as instrumental toward reaching a higher-order goal.

While the diversity of approaches utilized in past research of national character represents a cause for criticism, this paper proposes that, to ensure greater validity and reliability, a broad and multifaceted definition of national character should be accepted. Also, future studies should try to combine methodologies that would include observation, interviews and questionnaires, sociopsychological tests of selected measures, and a systematic analysis of relevant cultural institutions. By way of conclusion, the study of sport and national character must be recognized as crucial to the fostering of worldwide relations in the sport arena and thus enhance international understanding at the global level. Underlining a pressing need to study the fundamental and distinctive features of nations, this paper cautions the student of international sport against judging another nation in light of his or her own value system; instead, the student should seek to appreciate the complexity of motives behind the characteristic national behavior of others.

References

Barker, E. (1927). *National character and the factors in its formation*. London: Harper and Brothers.

Bennett, B.L., Howell, M.L., & Simri, U. (Eds.). (1983). *Comparative physical education and sport* (2nd ed.). Philadelphia: Lea & Febiger.

Clark, C. (1972). *Shakespeare and national character: A study of Shakespeare's knowledge and dramatic and literary use of the distinctive racial characteristics of the different peoples of the world*. New York: Haskell House.

Duijker, H.C.J. & Frijda, N.H. (1960). *National character and national stereotypes*. Amsterdam: North-Holland.

Foot, M.R.D. (1973, July 27). The nature of character: At national level. *Times Literary Supplement*, 877.

Forgas, J.P. (1976). An unobtrusive study of reactions to national stereotypes in four European countries. *The Journal of Social Psychology*, **99**, 37-42.

Fyfe, H. (1940). *The illusion of national character*. London: C.A. Watts and Co.

Gorer, G. (1953). National character: Theory and practice. In C. Kluckhohn, H.A. Murray, & D.M. Schneider (Eds.), *Personality in nature, society and culture* (rev. ed., pp. 246-259). New York: Alfred A. Knopf.

Hackwood, F.W. (1907). *Old English sports*. London: T. Fisher Unwin.

Harf, J.E., Coate, R.A., & Marsh, H.S. (1974). Trans-societal sport associations: A descriptive analysis of structures and linkages. *Quest*, **22**, 56-62.

Inkeles, A., & Levinson, D.J. (1954). National character: The study of modal personality and sociocultural systems. In G. Lindzey (Ed.), *Handbook of social psychology: Vol. II* (pp. 977-1020). Cambridge, MA: Addison-Wesley.

Kracauer, S. (1949). National images; national types as Hollywood presents them. *Public Opinion Quarterly*, **13**, 53-72.

Lowe, B., Kanin, D.B., & Strenk, A. (Eds.). (1978). *Sport and international relations*. Champaign, IL: Stipes.

McDonald, P.I. (1978, February). National stereotypes. *Geographical Magazine*, **50**, 301-302.

Platt, W. (1961). *National character in action—Intelligence factors in foreign relations*. Brunswick, NJ: Rutgers University Press.

Riesman, D. (1950). *The lonely crowd. A study of the changing American character*. New Haven, CT: Yale University Press.

Rousseau, J.J. (1974). *Emile*. London: Everyman. (Original work published 1762)

Shand, A.F. (1914). *The foundations of character: Being a study of the tendencies of the emotions and sentiments*. London: Macmillan.

Shepherd, D.H. (1981). Perception of nations: Government vs. citizenry. *Perceptual and Motor Skills*, **52**, 271-276.

Smith, D.D. (1966). Modal attitude clusters: A supplement for the study of national character. *Social Forces*, **44**, 526-533.

Strutt, J. (1855). *The sports and pastimes of the people of England*. London: W. Hone.

Terhune, K.W. (1970, June). From national character to national behavior: A reformulation. *Journal of Conflict Resolution*, **14**, 203-263.

Wilcox, R.C. (1984, April 14). *Muscular Christianity: Synthesis of the Victorian body and mind*. Paper presented at "Framing the Victorians," a conference of the Northeast Victorian Studies Association, Hempstead, NY.

Wood, M. (1974, January 31). Film images of nations. *New Society*, pp. 266-267.

CHAPTER 21

"Sport for All" and "Trim"— An Idea and Its Realization

Rainer Schams

The idea of "Sport for All" was initiated in 1966 by the Council for Cultural Cooperation of the Council of Europe. Though it was still a long way to the resolution of the "European Sport for All Charter" in 1975, the overall aim of "Sport for All" was already clear, namely "to enable everyone—of both sexes and in all age groups—to preserve the physical and mental powers necessary for survival and to protect the human species from deterioration" (Council of Europe, 1980, p. 3). The humanitarian approach to the European initiative is obvious—but have the national "Trim" campaigns that emerged from it retained this honorable objective? In which ways does the "Trim" idea differ from the notions of the Council of Europe?

These are the key questions of the following investigation. Thus the investigation begins by reviewing the considerations and actions that led to the "Sport for All" initiative of the Council of Europe, and then it sketches its realization by the international "Trim" movement.

This paper will not concentrate on the institutional framework or the internal development of the "Sport for All" program or of certain "Trim" programs of certain countries.[1] Though we are aware of the methodical shortcomings of such a procedure, we shall take the initiative of the Council of Europe as a whole and concentrate on its motives and objectives. Similarly, we will not give an account of the execution of certain national "Trim" programs, but will try to show common and distinctive features of "Trim" in general compared with "Sport for All."

"Sport for All"

What was it that caused the Council for Cultural Cooperation to adopt the slogan "Sport for All" as the major long-term objective for the sport program of the Council of Europe? To answer this question, let us start with the term *sport* itself.

The Council of Europe defines *sport* as "free, spontaneous activity engaged in during leisure time" (Council of Europe, 1980, p. 3). Such a broad concept of sport covers a great range and variety of activities: competitive games and sports as well as outdoor pursuits, aesthetic movement, and conditioning activity (Council of Europe, 1980, p. 3). Moreover, for the Council of Europe, sport is to be "an important means of attaining peaceful aims" (Rat für Kulturelle Zusammenarbeit, 1972, p. 40).

Proceeding from these definitions, three main functions of sport which all bear a close relationship to social phenomena of modern industrial societies were named: biological, sociocultural, and personal-emotional.[2]

The *biological function* of sport was seen in its compensational role for the predominance of a sedentary lifestyle and the degenerative diseases that it triggers. The lack of physical activity in modern occupations, and often in leisure time, was seen as highly unnatural and as responsible for "more illnesses and deaths than infections and cancer." (Council of Europe, 1970, p. 226). Cardiovascular diseases alone often accounted for more deaths than all other causes put together, and "there can be no doubt that a satisfactory level of regular physical activity can play an important role as a prophylactic and therapeutic agent" in this illness (Council of Europe, 1980, p. 4). What is more, economies could then save substantial sums of money invested in public health.

The *sociocultural function* of sport was especially emphasized by the Council of Europe: "Sport for All is concerned with the role of sport in society" (Council of Europe, 1980, p. 3). The inhibition of social contact and interpersonal relationships in highly urbanized societies was deplored as was the social isolation and alienation of man from himself and from his environment.

Therefore the Council of Europe maintained that "it was not the question of adopting man to environment but of creating an environment which is suited to man and worthy of man" (CCC, 1972, p. 9). Sport was apt to be an answer to these challenges of modern society by helping to preserve the human element in a mechanized civilization. Not only does sport increase social contact, but its function of emotional release is an important social factor, considering the increase of leisure time and the rise in the standard of living.

This argumentation leads to the *personal-emotional function* of sport and to its positive influence on the physical, psychic, and mental balance of man (Rat für Kulturelle Zusammenarbeit, 1972). Sport provides opportunities for self-realization and creativity and for relaxation and satisfaction. Here the element of "play" and the notion of the "homo ludens" were especially stressed by the Council of Europe (CCC, 1972).

The Objectives of "Sport for All"

However, as long as sport remained "a pastime of a privileged minority or a favoured class" (Rat für Kulturelle Zusammenarbeit, 1972, p. 39), the multifarious functions of sport could not become really efficient—this is the actual reason for the concept of "Sport for All."

In the 1960s, mainly young people engaged in physical activities, although people of all ages were interested in them (Council of Europe,

1970). Thus the slogan "Sport for All" means exactly what it says: As many people as possible are to have a share of the advantages of sport.

"All citizens irrespective of age, sex, occupation or means shall be helped to understand the value of sport and engage in it throughout their lives" (Council of Europe, 1980, p. 9). This statement is more than just "the right of the individual to participate" (Article 1 of the European Sport for All Charter). It is the claim for an active sport policy that sets out to stimulate participation at all levels of performance (Council of Europe, 1980)—(elite competition as well as mass sport; with the postwar increase of leisure, however, the emphasis should be on the latter).

Sport itself did not have to change, but its social setting did—it was to be "for all." That was the novelty and the actual discovery of "Sport for All" that also made sport "a factor capable of changing society; in other words . . . a *political* instrument" (Jackson, 1978, p. 491). From this line of reasoning, the Council of Europe, as a political organization, derived its mission and its competence for "Sport for All."

Recommendations for National Campaigns

Of course the initiative of the Council of Europe only made sense when it resulted in concrete actions by the national governments and sport organizations. The Council therefore encouraged member countries to develop sport policies as integral parts of their sociocultural policies (Jackson, 1978).

And because sport was to be propagated "as an important factor in human development" and because "appropriate support out of public funds" was to be made available (Article 2 of the European Sport for All Charter; Council of Europe, 1980, p. 2), it had to be promoted effectively. The Council of Europe proposed the "use of the mass media at local and national levels, campaigning literature and rigorous publicity services" (Council of Europe, 1980, p. 7) to persuade people to take part.

But while doing so, the Council of Europe also saw the dangers that might emerge from such a media-oriented approach and that could jeopardize the humanitarian content of "Sport for All." Namely the Council warned of commercialization, regimentation, and productivism which could arise because of the political and sociocultural relevance of such national sport campaigns.

According to the Council of Europe, while *commercialization* could be either beneficial or harmful (to the benefit or to the exploitation of individuals), *regimentation* (compulsory physical education and exercise) and *productivism* (the mobilization of sport to increase productivity) were to be avoided at all costs (Jackson, 1978).

These warnings were also documented in Article 5 of the Sport for All Charter, which maintained that "methods shall be sought to safeguard sport and sportsmen from exploitation for political, commercial or financial gain, and from practices that are abusive and debasing . . ." (Council of Europe, 1980, p. 2). This charter, which also made recommendations for organizational details like facilities, management, and personnel, passed the Parliamentary Assembly, the Conference of Minister for Sport, and finally the Committee of Ministers; thus the principles recorded in the European Sport for All Charter became part of the official policy of the member states. Now how have they realized this policy?

"Trim"—The Realization of "Sport for All"

The successful transformation of the European initiative "Sport for All" into national "Trim" programs is already history. By 1970, six countries (Norway, Sweden, Holland, Iceland, the Federal Republic of Germany, and Denmark) had started campaigns; the further expansion of the movement is documented by the representation of 19 countries at the "Trim" conference in Frankfurt in 1973. From then on, it spread even beyond the European borders (Jackson, 1978).

It is not possible to give details of the institutions and contacts that rendered this rapid expansion. Let it suffice to say that this expansion has been mainly because of personal contacts between representatives of national sport organizations, because of leisure and sport conferences like "Trim and Fitness International," and because of activities of the Council of Europe itself (see Bellmer, 1980).

Likewise, the immense universal increase of active participation in sport and physical activity during the 1970s is almost common knowledge today and has been substantiated a number of times (e.g., in CDDS, 1982a). The "Trim" campaigns, though certainly not the sole cause for this encouraging development, have helped to create an awareness and to change behavior in physical activity and lifestyle in general. Obviously the "Trim" movement awoke a strong dormant desire, namely the growing awareness of the preservation of life in an environment worthy of living (Palm, 1978).

Common and Distinctive Features of "Trim" and "Sport for All"

But what does "Trim" really mean? Is it just a synonym for the notion of "Sport for All"?

Though some authors do not differentiate these terms (e.g., Hauge-Moe, 1970; Palm, 1978), we would like to maintain that "Sport for All" is the broader and the more general notion. Not only does the word *trim* have a meaning of its own that mainly tends to evoke the idea of fitness (Jackson, 1978) ("to keep oneself in good condition through physical activities," Landry, 1979, p. 24), but "Trim" also connotes a plan of action, which, first and foremost, relates to the advertising campaign developed to propagate the new program. Indeed, the application of modern mass communication and propaganda systems is *the* characteristic element of the "Trim" movement (Landry, 1979), but is not necessarily the prime element of "Sport for All."

Nonetheless, many elements clearly show the close relationship of both concepts. Above all, the overall objective of "Trim" is the same as the one of the European initiative: namely "Sport for *All*." The affirmation that the number of participants was to be increased and that particular efforts for the underprivileged and the minorities were to be undertaken is a universal characteristic of all "Trim" campaigns.

Closely connected to this common premise is the rise of the sociocultural motive for sport—the "fun, fitness, recreational and social experiences" (Landry, 1979, p. 24)—as reasons for physical activities. This is another important similarity of "Trim" and "Sport for All." The traditional emphases on competition and achievement, pyramidal organization, and a system of incitements via badges and certificates have clearly proven to obstruct rather than encourage active participation (CDDS, 1982a).

Though a permanent argument rages whether to favor the health and fitness aspect or the aspect of fun and relaxation, this discussion seems to be a rather theoretical one—both aspects have clearly been of considerable importance and can also be subsumed under the general considerations of the Council of Europe.

Some Critical Remarks on the Development of "Trim"

But what about the warnings that the Council of Europe had expressed about the adoption of "Sport for All" as an official national policy?

There can be hardly any doubt that regimentation has been almost entirely avoided. "A fundamental characteristic of the informal TRIMM approach is the entirely elective choice of fitness, sports, and recreational goals and levels of achievement" (Landry, 1979, p. 24). Although the governments soon played an active part in the development of the "Trim" programs, they have resisted the temptation to use this policy as a means of tutelage (Jackson, 1978).

However, what this involvement of governments in the world of sport has triggered is a subtle ideological and economic dependency. Though the independence and exclusive competence of the organizations responsible for "Trim" were often officially sanctioned, political activities of local governments, of the parties, and of pressure groups within the sport organizations have had an impact on the development of the campaigns (Jackson, 1978). In this respect, the Council of Europe was right in warning about political exploitation and claiming to protect sport against any encroachments by powers and influences . . . seeking to subordinate it to aims that negate the intrinsic value of sport" (Council of Europe, 1980, p. 11).

Commercialization, considered another threat by the Council, has evidently become a universal characteristic of "Trim" programs. It can probably not be entirely avoided once the decision to start an advertising campaign is made. Any modern marketing techniques include production and distribution of pamphlets, posters, stickers, and "Trim" equipment and kits, and therefore employ the usual salesmanship techniques. And, to a certain extent, such techniques are a priori contradictory to a humanitarian concept because they are "closer to the totalitarian concept that the masses cannot be educated but they can be bamboozled" (Levy, 1976, p. 47).[3]

What is more, the enormous costs of the campaigns overstrained the "Trim" organizers and the governments, although the governments were willing to help within limitations. (The economic crisis of the late 1970s, to be sure, also had a negative influence on public funding.) Thus the "Trim" organizations had to look for sponsors from industry, from the mass media, from the pools, and so forth, which often yielded a second dependency and, again, fostered commercialization and the entanglement of humanitarian and economic interests. Who should blame the companies for using the fashionable name of "Trim" to increase their own prestige and profit? (Jackson, 1978).

Close contacts between sport organizations and industry have also caused occasional productivist tendencies—another "prophetic" warning of the Council of Europe. The audacious promotion of "employee fitness" (Canada), and the more subtle cooperation of health insurance and sport organizations (West Germany) indicate such tendencies.[4]

Why "Trim" Fell Short of Its Objectives

Notwithstanding the huge increase in participation in the 1970s, the gravest shortcoming of the "Trim" programs relates to those who have stayed outside. The target groups of "Sport for All" and of "Trim"—older people, less-educated people, people with lower income, and so forth—have remained underprivileged. Young males with better schooling and occupations still comprise the most active group; but the gaps, especially the one between men and women, have been narrowing (Council of Europe, 1980).

Like the political and commercial influences mentioned earlier, this limited efficacy of "Trim" on certain social groups and classes of society shows its subjection to the general sociocultural pattern. Programs like "Trim" only can be as successful as the social and political situation permits. They are, at best, both elements and reflections of sociocultural development because "the concepts that the masses have of sports are for their part markedly influenced by the prevailing social philosophies, by the economic climate, and, as such, by the manner in which work, leisure, happiness and existence are experienced" (Landry, 1979, p. 15).

Summary

In June 1966 the Council of Europe started the program "Sport for All" with a Declaration of Principle. The motives for this initiative were multifarious:

- On the one hand, modern civilization was suffering from ever-increasing social, emotional and physical defects;

- on the other hand, sport and physical activity were considered helpful to ease these problems; by then, however, it was open only to a privileged minority;
- consequently sport was to be propagated as a beneficial means to trigger personal, sociocultural, and biological advantages.

The humanitarian approach of the Council of Europe was underlined by its warning of "commercialization," "regimentation," and "productivism," which might result from the realization of the idea.

The national "Trim" campaigns that emerged from this European initiative proved how well-founded these warnings were. With their decision to start intensive advertising campaigns for the propagation of the "Sport for All" idea, the "Trim" organizations were forced to look for partners who could help organize and fund the "Trim" programs. They found them either on the side of government or on the side of industry. The humanitarian motives of "Sport for All," however, were now at stake: The commercial partners of the "Trim" organizations fostered commercialization and exploitation; the political partners of the "Trim" organizations influenced the propagandistic and executive measures of the campaigns; and consequently the success of the "Trim" campaigns fell short of the objectives, notwithstanding the indisputable improvements of the 1970s. The overall objective, "Sport for All," is still just a vision, not reality.

Notes

1. For these aspects, the interested reader is referred to investigations by Agten, 1978; CDDS, 1978, 1982a, 1982b; Jackson, 1978; Landry, 1979; Palm, 1977; and Rat für Kulturelle Zusammenarbeit, 1972.
2. Compare Jackson's terminology: "a biological function, a social communication function, a self-expression function" (Jackson, 1978, p. 500).
3. Levy's remark refers to "Participaction," the Canadian campaign, but it holds true for the majority of cases.
4. The Eastern mass sport programs, which we do not regard as "Trim" campaigns, have always openly utilized sport "to increase productivism and to improve defense capability" (Jackson, 1978, p. 501).

References

Agten, J.M. (1978). The Clearing House—A "Sport for All" information centre under the auspices of the Council of Europe. In W. Kloock (Ed.), *Sportinformation in Theorie und Praxis—VI. Internationaler Kongreß für Sportdokumentation* (pp. 18-23). Schorndorf: Hoffmann.

Bellmer, K. (1980). *10 Jahre Trimm-Aktion* [Ten years of Trim]. Frankfurt: DSB.

Council for Cultural Co-Operation (CCC). (1972). *Sport for all—Low cost sports halls*. Strasbourg: Author, Council of Europe.

Committee for the Development of Sport (CDDS). (1982a). *Rationalising sports policies—Sport in European society: A transnational survey into participation and motivation* (Part I). Strasbourg: Author, Council of Europe.

Commitee for the Development of Sport (CDDS). (1982b). *Rationalising sports policies—Sport in European society: A transnational survey into participation and motivation* (Part II, tech. Suppl.). Strasbourg: Author, Council of Europe.

Council of Europe. (1970). *Manual of the Council of Europe.* London: Author.

Council of Europe. (1980). *Principles for a policy for sport for all—European Sport for All charter.* (Resolution (76)41 of the Committee of Ministers, Text and Background, CDDS (79)28-E (2nd ed.). Strasbourg: Author.

Hauge-Moe, P. (1970). *TRIM—Realization of Sport for All.* Oslo: Information Department of the Norwegian Confederation of Sports.

Jackson, J.J. (1978). *Sport for all.* In B. Lowe, D.B. Kanin, & A. Strenk, *Sport and international relations* (pp. 486-504). Champaign, IL: Stipes.

Landry, F. (1979). Organizational patterns relative to the development of Sports-for-All: An international perspective. *Bulletin of Physical Education* (FIEP Bulletin), **49**(2), 15-25.

Levy, G. (1976). Participation could undermine public support. *Recreation Canada*, **1**(34), 41-47.

Palm, J. (1977). *Trimmszene international: Beobachtungen und Bermerkungen anläßlich der 5. Konferenz Trimm and Fitness International Paris 2. - 5 Mai 1977* [Trim Scene International. Notices and Remarks on the Occasion of the Fifth Conference Trim and Fitness International Paris May 2-5, 1972]. Frankfurt/M: DSB.

Palm, J. (1978). Freizeitsport als aktion—Trimm dich durch sport [Leisure sport as a campaign—Trim yourself by means of sport]. In J. Dieckert (Ed.), *Freizeitsport* (pp. 161-167). Opladen: Westdeutscher Verlag.

Rat für Kulturelle Zusammenarbeit (Ed.). (1972). *Sport für Alle. Erziehung und Kultur* [Sport for All. Education and Cultures]. Zeitschrift des Rates für kulturelle Zusammenarbeit und der Europäischen Kulturstiftung, **181**, 39-43.

CHAPTER 22

The Assessment and Improvement of the Physical Fitness of Members of the Hamburg Fire Service With Comparative Data From the Cheshire Fire Service

Clemens Czwalina
Kevin Sykes

According to the discussion on methodology on the first day of the symposium, the first step toward comparative studies is to start with international collaboration between researchers from different countries with the possible result of a comparative approach. The experience of the authors shows that informal personal contacts between individuals are a simple but effective way of establishing an international network of multilateral links between institutions (in this case Hamburg University and Chester College of Higher Education).

In contrast to many contributions to the symposium, this report deals with clearly defined physiological and anthropometric parameters on a micro level, so to speak, without the problems of macro studies such as the description of sport phenomena in China or Africa.

Firefighters need a good level of physical fitness. Aside from the obvious dangers to life and limb associated with the job, firefighting subjects the body to environmental and physical stressors that can adversely affect the various physiological systems. Firemen do not control the physical requirements of their work environment, but rather respond to the everchanging emergency conditions. Effective adaptation to these stressors requires optimum respiratory and cardiovascular health. Furthermore, lack of strength and obesity have been identified as important components limiting the performance of firemen (Dotson, 1977).

In the summer of 1978, preliminary discussions took place with senior officers of the Cheshire Fire Service and with the County Senior Medical Advisor in Occupational Health with the purpose of developing a survey of the current levels of physical fitness within the brigade. It was anticipated that the results of such a survey would lead to appropriate recommendations for the improvement and maintenance of the physical fitness of the personnel. A pilot study was set up and a test protocol was devised to assess the cardiorespiratory fitness and morphological characteristics of a large group of volunteers. In July and September 1979, 246 volunteers were assessed. This number represented over half of the full-time members of the brigade, covering a wide spread of ages, abilities, and ranks. In 1980, Clemens Czwalina visited Chester College and learned the details of the survey. They were reported to the home office and to the Chief Fire Officer of Hamburg and it was decided to invite Kevin Sykes and staff (M. Hawling, I. Jamieson, and A. Park) to conduct the same assessments on the firemen ($n = 106$) from two (out of 18) Hamburg fire stations. This was in April and September 1982. In addition to the testing done by the researchers from Cheshire, the Hamburg firemen had to perform the Cooper 12-min run/walk test and were asked to train according to a special running program during the period between the two assessments. Thus this report compares Cheshire and Hamburg fire services in regard to particular parameters and describes the enhancement of the Hamburg firemen's fitness after the completion of a daily running routine. The latter aspect is also an international one because the assessments were conducted on Germans in Germany by English scientists. These facts legitimate this report's being given at the symposium.[1]

Procedures

The cardiorespiratory fitness and morphological characteristics of 106 firemen from two stations in the Hamburg Fire Service were assessed using the CCHPL/JU79 test protocol. This protocol was developed in the Human Performance Laboratory of Chester College and has been used extensively for fitness assessments and for monitoring physiological adaptations to physical activity. Extensive studies on top-level athletes and sportsmen/women, occupational fitness studies, and results from fitness assessments with over 10,000 members of the general public make it possible for the results to be evaluated across a very wide data base.

The CCHPL/JU79 test protocol includes the following:

- Measurements of height, weight, and waist girth
- Measurements of systolic and diastolic blood pressures under nominally resting conditions, with informal observation throughout exercise and recovery
- Prediction of percentage body fat from subcutaneous fat measurements taken at biceps, triceps, subscapularis, and suprailiac (norms not reported here)
- Measurements of left and right hand grip strength (norms not reported here)
- Measurements of expiratory lung functions using Vitalograph determinations of Forced Vital Capacity (FVC), Forced Expiratory Volume in 1 second (FEV_1) and Forced Expiratory Ratio (FER%)—FEV_1/FVC
- Prediction of aerobic capacity (mls O_2/kg/min) from the work heart rate taken during the final minute of a 6–min bout of submaximal cycle ergometry.

- Fitness classification is then based on internationally recognized, age-related norms (norms not reported here).

The test protocol takes approximately 20 min to conduct, and as a standard practice, a 10 min consultancy is always added. The tests are highly mobile, robust, and socially acceptable and no changing or showering facilities are required. They are sufficiently intense to produce values of between 120 and 170 heart beats/min.

Results of the initial tests conducted in April 1982 ($n = 106$) are presented in Table 1. Additionally, data from a similar survey with 246 men from the Cheshire Fire Service also are shown for comparison. All of the men from Hamburg and Cheshire were full-time members of their local fire services.

In addition, the Hamburg group was then asked to perform a 12-min run, ideally every working day, at a pace that each man regarded as being fairly fast. Over the project period of 4 months, the frequency of runs varied widely: Some men completed up to 42, while others made only 6. The mean number was 18 runs. The running program was informally supervised by the Faculty of Sports Science from the University of Hamburg. Participation was essentially voluntary and training regularity varied widely between the two fire stations, among the three watch units within a fire station, and among the individuals within the watch unit.

A second series of tests (CCHPL/JU79 test protocol and COOPER test) were conducted in September 1982. Ninety-three firemen were tested, of which 66 completed both series of tests.

Results and Discussion of Results

The Comparison of Hamburg and Cheshire Fire Services

Table 1 presents the initial findings on 106 Hamburg firemen and enables comparisons to be made with similar tests conducted on 246 Cheshire firemen.

A clear, observable difference between the two groups was the age of the firemen tested; the mean age of the Hamburg men was 40 years while that of the Cheshire men was 32 years. This factor was in part responsible for the mean values of body weight, waist girth, percentage of body fat, expiratory lung function (FVC, FEV_1), and blood pressure being higher for the Hamburg group.

It is worth serious note that while all of these parameters were expected to show higher values as with advanced age, the observed increases were respectively slight—for example, a weight gain of only 0.5 kg per annum between the two groups. Moreover, expiratory lung function data reveal that both FVC and FEV_1 values are well above the norm for a general population in both Hamburg and Cheshire firemen (norms not reported here). In spite of the age difference, grip strength was slightly higher in the Hamburg firemen, although both groups were well above the norm

Table 1   Pretest Results of CCHPL/JU79 Test Protocol Conducted on Hamburg and Cheshire Firemen

Parameters	Hamburg (n = 106)		Cheshire (n = 246)	
	M	SD	M	SD
Age (yrs)	40.0	9.0	32.0	9.0
Height (cm)	177.0	5.5	177.0	5.2
Weight (kg)	82.0	9.0	78.0	8.0
Waist (cm)	90.0	7.0	88.0	7.0
% Body fat	16.5	3.0	14.0	3.0
Systolic blood pressure (mms)	132.0	10.0	122.0	4.0
Diastolic blood pressure (mms)	90.0	11.0	86.0	7.0
FVC (l)	5.35	0.8	5.8	0.8
FEV_1 (l)	4.2	0.7	4.7	0.7
FER%	78.0	7.0	80.0	7.0
Grip strength (kg)	55.0	6.4	51.0	6.5
Aerobic capacity (mls O_2/kg/min	39.0	10.0	37.0	8.0

Note.   Testing was done on Hamburg firemen in April, 1982; testing was done on Cheshire firemen in September 1979.

for the general population (norms not reported here). The predicted aerobic capacity was slightly in favor of the Hamburg group, again going against the 8-year age difference.

In terms of general fitness for all practical, operational purposes, it must be assumed that the physical work load of firefighting is virtually independent of age. Admirably, the Hamburg firemen have achieved this goal in the important areas of strength and aerobic fitness.

The Enhancement of Physical Fitness of Hamburg Firemen

Table 2 shows the changes of the Hamburg group in selected parameters after the running program.

Table 2   Posttest Results (in % of the Values of the Pretest of Selected Parameters for 66 Members of the Hamburg Fire Service

Parameters	% change
Weight	− 3.3
Waist	− 3.4
% body fat	− 10.6
Diastolic blood pressure	− 6.5
Aerobic capacity	+ 10.7

All of the observed changes were in the desired direction. Body weight and waist girth were reduced, and diastolic blood pressure decreased. However, the most notable improvements were the reduction in body fat and the increase in aerobic capacity. At the onset of the program, the cardiorespiratory fitness levels of the firemen were no different than those of a normal sedentary population. By the end of the project, the mean level had improved into the "Good" fitness category (norms not reported here). These changes correspond with a mean increase of 6.5% in the distance covered during the Cooper (1970) test, with 87.5% of the men achieving the "Good" or "Excellent" fitness category according to Cooper (norms not reported here). The results illustrate that, despite the variability and relatively informal nature of the exercise regimens, the beneficial changes are clearly and numerically demonstrable.

Concluding Remarks

There are some "weak" points in the investigation, such as the following:

• It was not possible to obtain a random sample.
• The number of members in the compared samples differed widely (246 to 106).
• There was a gap of nearly 3 years between the assessments (September 1979 to April 1982) of the two fire services.
• Supervision and performance of the running program were informal and on a voluntary basis; thus a wide range in numbers of runs was produced (42 − 6 = 36).

Therefore the authors only claim to show *tendencies* of comparison of Hamburg and Cheshire fire services and of fitness enhancement of the Hamburg group. Interpretation of the results has to be done carefully and diligently. Nevertheless, there seems to be a strong indication that even a modest 12-min running at a pace that the runner regards as being fairly fast is valuable in building and maintaining fitness. The fire services were advised to give serious consideration to regular running and other physical activities (e.g., circuit training) as an integral feature of keeping firefighters fit.

Note

1. Passages of text have been quoted from Sykes, K. (1983). *The assessment and enhancement of physical fitness of members of the Hamburg Fire Service, with comparative data from the Cheshire Fire Service* (1983, July). *Fire International, 3.*

References

Cooper, K. (1970). *The new aerobics*. New York: Bantam.

Dotson, C.O., Santa Maria, D.L., et al. (1977). *Development of a job-related physical performance exam for firefighters*. Washington, DC: U.S. Fire Administration.

CHAPTER 23

Development Patterns in the Chinese Sport Delivery System

Brian Pendleton

Since the mid 1970s, athletes from the People's Republic of China (PRC) have entered individual competitions, multinational events, and major international championships with predictable regularity. While much is now known regarding Chinese levels of proficiency and world rankings in most sports, to date little information has been available on the underlying support services that comprise the sport delivery system in the PRC. The concept 'sport delivery system' embraces such subsystems and networks as local, regional, and national organizational structures; talent identification and feeder systems; scientific and technical assistance groups; equipment and facility provisions; and training and competition opportunities—all of which nurture and sustain the high-performance athlete. Those data that exist in the literature have often been the products of travelers' tales: brief discussions with local authorities, hurried tours of recently opened facilities, visits to one or two schools, attendance at an international sporting event. While perhaps of general interest, these descriptive accounts have provided little data needed to understand, much less chart, China's progress as a sporting nation and, as such, have been of limited value to the study of sport from a comparative perspective.

Purpose, Methodology, and Limitations

The purpose of this study was to analyze the development patterns of selected components of the sport delivery system in China since the establishment of the People's Republic in 1949.

The data were gathered through review of Chinese language materials and personal interviews conducted in the PRC. With few exceptions, materials were willingly provided and discussions were candid and informative. The general time frame covered in the study was 1949–1979, with occasional reference to data and events in preceding and subsequent years. Romanization of Chinese characters to English has followed the *hanyu pinyin* system adopted for use in the PRC in 1979.

The major limitations in the project were (a) occasional gaps in published data, particularly during the years of the Cultural Revolution

(1966-1976); (b) variations over time in Chinese methods and procedures of data collection and reporting; and (c) unavailability of data on the essential base variable of monetary investment and financial support for sport.

Notwithstanding these limitations, a considerable amount of data was obtained; only a portion of the data is presented in this shorter version of the original paper. The results and discussion are presented in four sections: (a) national award and certification programs; (b) the human resource base; (c) spare-time sport schools; and (d) facility and competition provisions.

The findings have been analyzed and discussed in the context of China's recent social, economic, and political experience, taking into account stability of the social order, pending sporting competitions, and financial exigencies that might impact on the sport delivery system over time.

Results and Discussion

National Award and Certification Programs

Both participation and achievement in sport are promoted and recognized in the PRC through various normative systems; individuals are awarded titles, ranks, and grades (classes) for (a) mass fitness, (b) sport skill development, and (c) contributions to sport.

Mass fitness. Mass fitness standards were first promulgated in 1954 under the Labor-Defense System *(Laoweizhi)*. A further series of tests was implemented under the Youth Physical Culture Training Standards *(Qingshaonian Tiyu Duanlian Biaozhun)* program in 1964, only to be abandoned 2 years later during the Cultural Revolution. The most recent program, the National Physical Culture Training Standards *(Guojia Tiyu Duanlian Biaozhun)*, introduced in 1973 and subsequently revised and updated, sets performance criteria for males and females in four age categories: Children (10–12 years); Junior I (13–15 years); Junior II (16–17 years); and Youth (18+ years). Achievement trends for the most recent program are shown in Table 1.

Achievement totals in the Labor-Defense program grew steadily from 1954 to 1957; there was a dramatic increase in the number of people meeting the norms and standards in 1958 (from 1.5 to 23 million!). Similar high totals were maintained in 1959 and 1960 prior to drastic declines in both 1961 and 1962. A reversal in this trend occurred in the final year of the Labor-Defense program which carried over into the brief 2 years of the Youth program. During the period 1973–1976, the number of individuals reaching the national program fitness standards increased annually. However, from 1976 to 1978, declining totals were recorded in all but the Junior I category.

Attention to mass mobilization and involvement during the Great Leap Forward *(Da Yue Jin)* campaign perhaps accounts for the 1958 figures. The

Table 1 National Physical Culture Training Program Awards

Year	Youth class	Junior II	Junior I	Children	Total
1973	263,254	426,050	555,748	323,405	1,568,457
1974	188,410	490,134	539,924	583,426	1,801,894
1975	515,967	1,347,690	1,600,305	1,270,009	4,733,971
1976	781,094	1,546,109	1,454,804	1,439,622	5,221,629
1977	546,513	1,451,705	1,517,616	1,427,492	4,943,326
1978	366,095	1,040,302	1,699,071	1,124,215	4,229,683
1979	418,810	1,251,698	2,587,016	1,995,581	6,253,105
Total	3,080,143	7,553,688	9,954,484	8,163,750	28,752,065

Note. From *Tiyu Nianjian* (pp. 885-886), 1979, Beijing: Renmin Tiyu Chubanshe. Copyright 1979 by Renmin Tiyu Chubanshe. Reprinted by permission.

postLeap declines may be linked to the general socioeconomic downturn attributed to setbacks resulting from the withdrawal of Soviet technical assistance, several natural disasters (floods and droughts), and resistance to many of the communalization measures adopted at the time. The political and economic adjustments that occurred after the overthrow of the radical Gang-of-Four (*Si Ren Bang*) following the death of Communist Party Chairman Mao Zedong in late 1976 may account, in part, for the declines noted between 1976 and 1978. On the other hand, the increases evident in 1958-1959, 1964-1965, 1974-1975, and 1978-1979 are most likely a result of promotional campaigns launched prior to the holding of China's National Games (see "Facility and Competition Provisions" in this paper). It would appear, then, that economic and political stability have significantly influenced mass participation and fitness achievement in China since 1949.

Sport skill development. Sport skill development in China is encouraged through the Athlete Ranking System (*Yundongyuan Dengji Zhidu*), which sets performance standards in nearly 40 sports. The program introduced in 1956, was revised in 1958 and 1963 prior to being suspended in 1966 at the beginning of the Cultural Revolution. Unlike the mass fitness programs designed for the population at large which reappeared in the mid 1970s, the Athlete Ranking System was not revived until 1978, when athletes were again encouraged to undertake training to qualify for one of five rankings (classes): Youth, 3rd, 2nd, 1st, and Master of Sport. Figure 1 shows the number of athletes who earned the highest ranking of Master of Sport (*Jianjiang*) from 1956 to 1979.

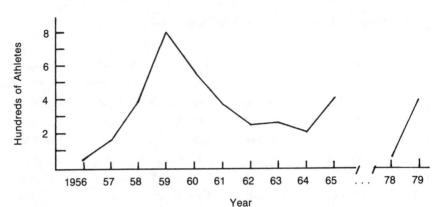

Figure 1.   Master of Sport ranked athletes: 1956-1979.

Note.   Compiled from data in *Tiyu Nianjian* (1979), pp. 902-903 and in selected issues of *Tiyu Bao. n = 3,801.*

   The probable impact of the Great Leap campaign noted earlier may likewise account for the dramatic increase in the number of individuals qualifying for state rankings from 1958 to 1960 (6 million in 1958 alone). The most popular sports among Master of Sport qualifiers ($n = 3,801$) from 1956 to 1979 were athletics/track and field (766), cycling (574), weight lifting (302), and gymnastics (292). Somewhat surprisingly, table tennis (113) tied with wrestling in 10th place. Caution is in order, however, when dealing comparatively with Master of Sport data, because performance criteria vary from sport to sport. In addition, the universality of the ranking system must be questioned because 1960 was the only year in which Master of Sport titles were awarded in handball, softball, and baseball.
   Similar ranking systems for officials and coaches were introduced in 1956 and 1958 respectively. Like the athlete ranking systems, these programs were suspended from the mid 1960s to the late 1970s. The current Officials Ranking System *(Caipanyuan Dengji Zhidu)* certifies individuals in four grades (classes): 3rd, 2nd, 1st, and National, while the Coaches Ranking System *(Jiaolianyuan Dengji Zhidu)* recognizes five grades (classes): Assistant, 3rd, 2nd, 1st, and National.
   Contributions to sport.   Honor medals and certificates have also been awarded in China in recognition of extraordinary achievement or contributions to sport. Since 1959, Physical Culture and Sport Honor Medals *(Tiyu Yundong Rongyu Jianzhang)* have been conferred on more than 300 athletes and coaches in such sports as athletics, diving, mountaineering, shooting, table tennis, and weight lifting.

The Human Resource Base

   China's human resource base of sport personnel includes coaches, officials, researchers, educators, functionaries, and administrative cadres.

These individuals serve either in (a) the centrally controlled state bureaucracy, which encompasses such ministries as Health, Education, the People's Liberation Army (PLA), and the Physical Culture and Sport Commission (*Tiyu Yundong Weiyuanhui*) or (b) one of the numerous "mass organizations," including peasant associations, trade unions, the Women's Federation, and the All-China Sports Federation (*Quanguo Tiyu Zonghui*).

Although data exist on sport personnel, they are less than comprehensive and, as such, should be considered as relative rather than as absolute measures of the human resource base in China. Both changes in classification categories and tabulating procedures over the period 1958 to 1979 have contributed to the incomplete nature of the data, particularly where comparative analyses are concerned. The previously noted periods of growth in the mid 1950s, 1960s, and 1970s and the subsequent periods of decline are, however, evident in the sport personnel sector as well. Furthermore, in response to the vagaries of climate, geography, economic well-being, and ethnic (national minority) peoples' needs and customs, PRC authorities have encouraged local autonomy and initiative through the mobilization of volunteer and part-time sport leadership at neighborhood centers, industrial enterprises, and agricultural work units. To date, data on volunteer and part-time leadership in sport has yet to be compiled on a nationwide basis.

Spare-Time Sport Schools

Modeled on similar institutions in the Soviet Union, China's first spare-time sport schools (*yeyu tixiao*) opened in 1955. Partial and incomplete data for the years 1956–1960 suggest that the spare-time school feeder system developed unevenly during this period. Although special instruction for promising young athletes was provided across the country, recruiting procedures, selection criteria, and training methods varied. Later restructuring of the system saw the creation of sport middle schools (*tiyu zhongxiao*) and key schools (*zhongdian*).

Since 1961, the data on spare-time sport schools have been among the most comprehensive available on any aspect of the sport delivery system in the PRC. Following the Great Leap Forward, there was notable growth in the number of spare-time schools and athletes enrolled—a pattern that was repeated, with minor variations, in the key schools during the same period. In the 1970s, both types of schools witnessed continuing growth, particularly in the number of specialized coaches assigned to the general spare-time schools, where the figure rose from 4,458 in 1974 to 7,721 in 1979. In the key schools, where the best facilities and coaches were to be found, the 1970s saw an increase in the number of specialized coaches and a reduction in both the number of key schools and the number of athletes enrolled—a situation that suggests that the "best" of China's better young athletes received even more attention and support as the system was further rationalized. Notwithstanding minor downturns in

1978 and 1979, the spare-time school network emerged relatively untouched by the economic and political adjustments demanded in most sectors of Chinese society in the immediate postCultural Revolution period. One possible explanation for this situation was the realization by government officials that the majority of the nation's world-class competitors were developed through the spare-time sport school network. Recognizing that athletes will continue to play a vital role in Chinese international diplomacy, the future of the PRC's nurseries for young champions appears bright.

Facility and Competition Provisions

Fundamental pillars in any sport delivery system are those material provisions which enable sporting excellence to emerge. Although data on financial investment on sport in China are limited, information is available on two key components: (a) construction of facilities and (2) opportunities for competition.

Construction of facilities. As the demand for facilities far exceeds supply, most regions of the country have undertaken major construction campaigns in recent years. In addition to swimming pools, cycle tracks, tennis courts, and lighted playing fields, scores of gymnasiums and stadiums have been built by local, provincial, regional, and national authorities. Figure 2 illustrates the development patterns for Categories A, B, and C gymnasiums and stadiums over four time periods.

As noted previously, many components of the PRC sport delivery system have been forced to make adjustments during times of economic and political uncertainty. This point is clearly demonstrated where major capital investment has been required, specifically for construction of sport facilities. Few gymnasiums or stadiums were built in the 3 years immediately following the Great Leap Forward, and similar restraint was evident during the early years of the Cultural Revolution. The one notable exception during the latter period was the completion of the 18,000-seat Capital Gymnasium (*Shoudu Tiyuguan*) in 1968 in Beijing (Peking). In the 1970s, the PRC again undertook major facility provision projects (Figure 2). Although Beijing, Chengdu, Nanjing, and Shanghai now have major sport complexes of international standard, provisions at the grass roots level are often left to local initiative and ingenuity. Where mass participation is the goal, facilities are often the poorest.

Opportunities for competition. Organized sport competition in the PRC is provided for through a pyramid structure of meets, contests, and tournaments held under local, regional, and national auspices and authority. China's major multisport festival, the National Games (*Quanyuanhui*), has served as a yardstick for sport planners in regard to contemporary training techniques, performance comparisons, talent identification, and regional sport development.

In the 1950s, the number of competitions held at the county level and above increased dramatically, particularly during the period of mass

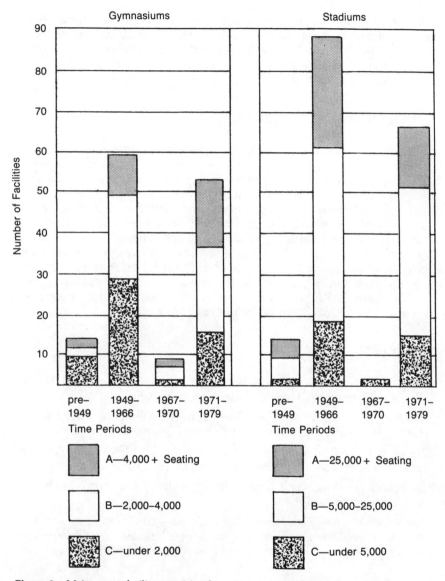

Figure 2. Major sport facility provision by category over selected time periods.

Note. Compiled from data in *Tiyu Nianjian* (1979), pp. 908-909.

mobilization and involvement associated with the Great Leap Forward. Although data on the period of the Cultural Revolution is incomplete, the relatively stable years of the early 1960s and 1970s saw similar growth patterns in the provision of organized sport competitions. With regard to the National Games, a trend toward decentralization is evident. Although the first four Games took place in the capital, the fifth was held in Shanghai in 1983, and the sixth is scheduled for the southern provincial capital of Guangzhou (Canton) in 1987. If the venue continues to change and if the quadrennial pattern remains, then both facility provision for and participant interest in competitive sport should increase throughout the country.

Observation and Comment

The findings of this study suggest that the development patterns of key components of the sport delivery system vary. Stability of the social order, from both an economic and political perspective, was found to be a significant factor in the PRC. In addition, as the country prepared for major national sporting competitions, interest and participation in sport and fitness activities increased. This finding may be of interest for future cross-cultural comparative studies. Although data on financial investment on sport in China are limited, a link seems to exist between economic stability and growth and the development of the sport delivery system. Further investigation in this area is warranted. As an area of study, sport in the People's Republic of China is recommended for researchers interested in sociocultural and comparative topics.

References

Zhongguo Baike Nianjian [Yearbook of the Chinese Encyclopedia]. (1980). Beijing: Zhongguo Dabaike Quanshu Chubanshe.

Zhongguo Dabaike Quanshu: Tiyu [The Chinese Enclopedia: Physical Culture].(1982). Beijing: Zhongguo Dabaike Quanshu Chubanshe.

Zhongguo Tiyu Nianjian [China Sports Yearbook]. (1949-1979). Various years/editions 1964-1982. Beijing: Renmin Tiyu Chubanshe.

Zhongguode Tiyu Yundong [China's physical culture and sport] (1980). Unpublished manuscript.

Zhongguode Yundongyuan Dengji Zhidu [China's athlete ranking system]. (n.d.). Unpublished manuscript–plus selected issues of *Tiyu Bao* [Sports News] newspaper and *Xin Tiyu* [New Sports] magazine.

PART IV

Teaching of Courses in Comparative Physical Education and Sport in Higher Education

CHAPTER 24

Internationalizing the Physical Education Curriculum

D. Margaret Toohey

In the United States, as well as in many other countries, curricula in physical education departments usually include courses in sport history, sociology, psychology, pedagogy, exercise science, and physical activity. Tagging along as the distant relative of this family may be one or two courses in comparative and international sport studies. The variety of courses is never sufficient. For comparative and international sport studies to be truly effective, steps should be taken to internationalize the entire physical education program. While they may appear to be somewhat grandiose and idealistic, ideas are offered here for such an internationalization of the physical education curriculum. Furthermore, integration of international physical education curricula within other departments in each institution is also considered. This paper is consequently divided into the following areas on the topic of internationalizing the sport curriculum:

- Infusion of Disciplines,
- Comparative Approaches,
- Issue-Oriented Approaches,
- Area and Civilization Studies,
- Intercultural Communication,
- International Development: Study and Practice,
- International Courses of Study: International Offerings Across Disciplines Within the Institution.

Finally, in a section called "Curriculum Planning in General," concrete consequences are indicated for internationalizing the physical education curriculum.

Internationalizing the Sport Curriculum

In approaching the internationalization of the physical education curriculum, a number of options, not necessarily mutually exclusive, need to be considered by each department in the context of its own makeup, tradition, existing and potential resources, and commitment. The major curricular options that might be considered for adoption, adaptation, or even gradual curricular change are listed later.

The Infusion of Disciplines

The available literature on curriculum content for international physical education appears to be intensely Western-oriented. For true universalization of the physical education discipline, the use of nonWestern materials is essential. For example, generalizations about the effect of media on the shaping of the sport curriculum in the societies of the United States and Western Europe may be lacking when applied within the cultures of Thailand, Kenya, or Peru. Often the most important factor in the development of such a study is the attitude and development of the particular instructor. Infusing the physical education discipline with non-Western materials calls for the instructors and textbook writers to make a conscious effort to treat that part of the discipline in which they are interested on as universal a basis as possible.

Comparative Approaches

One way the curriculum can be internationalized is by providing students the means to learn simultaneously about Western and nonWestern cultures and countries. In the sociocultural area of physical education the instructor can easily introduce sporting life-styles in India and Mexico for purposes of comparison with those in the United States. In this example not only has the instructional approach been internationalized, but the instructor has ensured that students will better understand family life in the american cultural context. Furthermore, abundant evidence supports the fact that a person only understands his or her own culture when at least one other culture has been experienced for purposes of evaluation and comparison.

The process of modernization and social change is one of the most challenging areas for purposes of research and teaching in the history of physical education. The tensions between the forces of tradition and those of modernization represent an enormously fruitful field of inquiry, both theoretically and practically, in relation to issues of national sport development.

The comparative analysis of the impact of sport science and technology in different societies, developed and otherwise, is another area of investigation critical for purposes of research and teaching. The transfer of sport science and technology across national boundaries is particularly appropriate to any Olympic Games discussions. Adaptation of this transfer to a variety of cultural environments evokes a wide range of ethical questions that impinge upon the increasingly complex net of global interrelationships. In the future, large numbers of physical educators will be increasingly involved in working with less-developed countries through government programs. The technical training of these physical educators should, therefore, include sensitization to the cultural factors that come into play when necessary skill learning is transferred across cultures.

Issue-Oriented Approaches

It is increasingly obvious that the major issues confronting the international sport world cannot be seriously studied through a traditional subdisciplinary approach (e.g., sport history, sport psychology, exercise physiology). Issues such as jurisdictional disputes, governance disputes, and ideological promotion of nations through sport are all multifaceted. The challenge here is to maximize the understanding of issues through the integration of subdisciplinary approaches. Social leadership and an abundance of persuasive skills are necessary tools here. Faculty must be persuaded that a degree of subdisciplinary integration is necessary if international issues surrounding sport are to be confronted. They must be called upon to extend themselves beyond the narrow focus of each respective subdiscipline.

As an illustration of topical curricular approaches, the participation of women in sport is offered. The theme of women's sport participation provides an umbrella for the study of international and domestic issues.

What does the sport psychologist have to say about women's aggression and its correlation with sport participation? Do sportswomen behave differently under stress than other women? Does this difference vary because of cultural conditioning? What impact does technological advancement have on the training of the sportswoman? What philosophical and ethical questions come into play when the subject of the impact of religion on women's sport participation is discussed?

Conflict situations lend themselves to interdisciplinary study within physical education. For example, the issues of the effects of peace and war on international sport are integrally tied to the conflicting ideologies of free enterprise with various brands of socialism and communism (e.g., the study of the pinnacle of international sport institutions—the Olympic Games—is necessarily tied to an understanding of the ideologies of the participating nations). A person does not understand technological or other advances or conflicts that are obviated in Olympic Games unless he or she understands the culture in which that advancement or conflict occurred.

Ways of creating necessary incentives for faculty to look at their discipline—sport—from a more global perspective must be devised. Here the department leadership must provide concrete incentives and other methods of faculty recognition in order to promote sound perspectives on international sport studies.

Area and Civilization Studies

A rationale easily can be made for an area studies concentration at the undergraduate level as one of the several viable options available to those people concerned with internationalizing the physical education curriculum; for example, an undergraduate physical education program in California could easily offer particular courses on Southeast Asian sport programs. Because of the number of foreign students from that area already ensconced in the institution and because of the number of Southeast Asian refugees who are living in the region, such an area study would be practical and self-serving. However, developing a successful area study is extremely difficult for many reasons. Certain conditions must be met before an area study is undertaken.

First, the department instructors must have the ability to offer knowledge in the area sports from a multidisciplinary perspective: sport history, politics, technology, philosophy, literature, and so forth. Second, the institution must offer the major language of the area as part of normal course offerings. In the case of Southeast Asian studies, many dialects exist within each culture. To understand the sport of a culture, a person must have an entry into that culture's language. Third, library sources must be readily available for students. These sources should extend beyond reading materials to audio-visual materials and archival programs. Fourth, the institution or the department must be willing to assume a large initial expenditure and future annual expenditures for resources and faculty.

Instead of area studies, curricular approaches to significant civilizations and cultures can be undertaken, for instance, a curriculum relating to China, Japan, Saudi Arabia, or Egypt. The object here is to view any of these civilizations through its history, culture, and social organization. Such approaches are successful when they combine broad chronological coverage with concentration on a selected number of topics. Those people who favor the comparative approach may want to compare the impact of Buddhism on Chinese and Japanese sport programs with the impact of the Christian religion on Italian and Spanish sport programs. The key here, as always, is competent and enthusiastic teaching. The issue of foreign languages in such approaches becomes less critical, but offering access to language study should be considered.

One of the drawbacks to area or civilization studies is that requiring students to enroll in all aspects of the program is difficult. For this reason a diffusion of the international approach with across-course offerings within a physical education department needs to be a sustained objective.

Intercultural Communication

Whereas *cross-cultural* implies the comparative, juxtapositional approach, *intercultural* is meant to cover the contact of two cultures—their collision, their interaction. Such situations create attention, adjustment, and learning experiences of value to students and researchers alike. The movement of students and faculty across cultures is a continuous experiment in intercultural communication.

The sport symbols and languages and the cultural values projected through sport participation can cause alienation and misunderstandings about the nature of the activity itself. The very act of eating, drinking, and playing sports with host family members often necessitates impromptu adaptation to a different socialization style. Certain communication skills can be taught in seminars and courses through direct contact with people from that other culture. Intercultural experiences that have been obtained prior to leaving the "home" culture have proven to be invaluable to both students and faculty. Certain principles of intercultural analysis and the deportment of good human relations can be learned.

Misperceptions and miscalculations can easily occur in sport participation situations. The tensions inherent in the collision of cultures, both on and off the sport field, are more easily understood when some form of intercultural education has been undertaken. A general curricular approach in intercultural communication could be accompanied by regional or comparative studies. Appropriate general education courses should be included in such a program of study. The greatest value of both intercultural and crosscultural studies continues to be helping students transcend their own cultural conditioning.

International Development: Study and Practice

Most developing countries are concerned with the development of human and material resources. Such development is incorporated in each country's sport programs. Coaching expertise, financing, technological developments, and sport organizational structures are areas in which more-developed countries can assist developing countries. The real challenge to the provider of the goods and services comes in the adjustment and creation of new techniques for the local societal and cultural conditions of the receptor nation. Such adjustment can be learned in academic training of an interdisciplinary nature. Such training and knowledge are acquired through the gathering of data on climate, terrain, and living conditions of the receptor culture. Here the student can be encouraged to seek out faculty in the institution from other departments who can provide the necessary understandings and skills training. Health science, agriculture, business, engineering, and economics departments usually have regional experts among their faculties who are willing to assist eager students and faculty in obtaining the necessary skills for use in sport programs to assist developing countries.

International Courses of Study: International Offerings Across Disciplines Within the Institution

All people interested in international and comparative aspects of physical education truly believe that such a study should be a requirement for graduate and undergraduate students alike. Unfortunately, such a belief has not been put into practice. It is therefore imperative that particular courses of study be developed for the student who shows interest in gaining knowledge and experience in international sport. Offerings can be developed in different ways. The first one has been already mentioned— the infusion of international learnings across the entire physical education curriculum. This is the ideal rather than the reality. It can be encouraged by judicial use of visiting faculty from other cultures. The second course of study usually comes under the sociocultural studies area within physical education. Whether it be sport history, sport sociology, sport psychology, or sport philosophy courses, it appears easier to incorporate an international and comparative dimension in those areas than in the exercise science of sport pedagogy areas. A certain degree of team teaching should be encouraged so that the use of faculty strengths can be maximized. Again, visiting international scholar programs also tend to heighten faculty interest in the international development of their instruction.

International study abroad programs should be well-publicized within the physical education department. Once students become aware that they are eligible for such an opportunity in their senior year, awareness of international aspects of all parts of the curriculum is increased. Once faculty become aware of student interest, an international dimension is likely to be added to instruction.

Encouragement from the administration of an institution does wonders in getting faculty involved in internationalizing the curriculum. California State University at Long Beach has just committed to building an international house for students and for visiting foreign dignitaries. The university president recently hosted a seminar on internationalizing the entire university curriculum. Speakers were brought in from all over the world. Faculty were given free registration and other inducements to attend the discussions.

The process of infusing courses with nonWestern materials and of promoting comparative international approaches and interdisciplinary studies in physical education thrives best in an atmosphere of visible, organized commitments in the curricula and intracurricular areas.

Curriculum Planning in General

In many institutions, international study from any disciplinary perspective is often considered to be elitist in character. It is therefore critical that international sport studies transcend schools at all levels and radiate to the community. Global attitudes and perspectives and the acquisition of knowledge can be shared through speakers' bureaus and other devices. To be most successful, the international dimension should touch all students.

General education or liberal arts are excellent target areas for including the international dimension. At California State University at Long Beach, two courses from physical education that have a pronounced international dimension are part of the general education or liberal arts course selection offered to all students. They are titled "Women's Sports" and "Sports Appreciation." It is in these offerings that faculty have an excellent opportunity to infuse their enthusiasm for international sport in the curriculum. Visiting professors from other countries are continually invited to share their knowledge in the subject area, and students are rewarded for seeking intercultural sport experiences.

Exchange programs of faculty, students, and administrators make it possible each year for hundreds of individuals to obtain new cultural perspectives, to strengthen their research and teaching expertise, and to obtain exposure to special academic programs and individual scholars. The international movement of faculty and students represents a concrete means of assisting in the internationalization of a physical education department above and beyond whatever other purposes these individuals might serve in the context of teaching research and public service.

Despite the vast literature in the field of international exchange, and regardless of the rationales offered for the training of foreign students, the receiving department needs to consider the following:

- How is the curriculum modified to meet the needs of foreign students?
- How can the department maximize the enrichment it receives from hosting foreign students?
- Is there a limit to the number of foreign students that can be accommodated? Why is there a limitation?
- What is the department's follow-up procedure once the foreign student has completed the course of study?

For department administrators who are interested in further internationalizing their respective curricula, the following questions are offered for discussion:

- Are adequate inducements offered to faculty to increase their participation in international programs?
- What kind of information services are offered to faculty and students on the international dimension?
- How can grants or other financial funding be obtained to assist faculty in international curricular development?
- How can the surrounding community be involved in international curricular offerings within physical education?
- Has a systematic inventory of existing international resources been taken to determine the mission and strategies of the international dimension of the physical education department?

This discussion has been intentionally general in nature and has covered many topics. It is hoped that it has provoked some thoughts and ideas on ways to promote the international and comparative physical education curriculum.

References

Anthony, D. (1966, Summer). Physical education as an aspect of comparative education. *Gymnasion, III*, pp. 3-6.

Association of American Colleges. (1980). *Toward education with a global perspective*. A report of the National Assembly on Foreign Language and International Studies. Washington, DC: Author.

Bao, T. (1981). Sports are flourishing in Taiwan. *China Sports*, **XIII**(5), 31-32.

Bennett, B.L. (1971, April). Critical incidents and courageous people in the integration of sports. *Journal of Health, Physical Education and Recreation*, **XLII**, 83-85.

Eisen, G. (1974, June). The Hungarian sport culture. *Quest*, **XXII**, 100-103.

Harari, M. (1972) *Global dimension in U.S. Education: The university*. New York: Education Commission on Pre-Collegiate Education of the American Political Science Association and Center for War/Peace Studies of the New York Friends Group.

Howell, M.L., & Mutimer, B.T. (1974, May). Toward comparative physical education and sport. *Canadian Journal of History of Sport and Physical Education*, **V**, 31-37.

Killanin, L. (1974, November-December). The Olympic movement brought up to date. *Olympic Review*, 572-573.

Miller, F.D. (1981, February). The blueprint for success in 1984. *The Olympian*, **VII**, 4-5, 30.

Peace on earth, happiness for all. (1981). *Sport in the USSR*, **5**, 2-5.

Shaw, S.M. (1976, September-October). Sport and politics: The case of South Africa. *Journal of the Canadian Association for Health, Physical Education, and Recreation*, **XLIII**, 30-38.

Williams, L.R.T. (1979). Undergraduate and graduate education in physical education in New Zealand over the next three years. *Quest*, **XXXI**(1), 71-76.

CHAPTER 25

Exchange Market for Ideas to Teach Courses in Comparative Physical Education

Bruce L. Bennett

During the first few minutes of this session, participants suggested topics for discussion. Eventually six questions were identified and selected for discussion by the moderator; equal time was allotted to each question. Following are the questions and ideas provided by members of the group.

What difference in content is appropriate between courses taught at the undergraduate and graduate levels?

Undergraduate courses should contain the following:

- More survey and multicountry-oriented material.
- More descriptive information.
- Aspects of physical education in foreign countries that might be new to the students.
- Emphasis on the cultural perspective, with comparisons of rituals, symbols, and movement forms that develop out of a culture's heritage.
- Descriptions and interpretations as defined by Bereday.
- Surveys for status determination.
- Activities that develop international awareness.
- Good examples of well-conducted and varied types of research, including studies and reports on some of these examples.
- The four stages of methodology by Bereday.
- Studies of one or two countries to illustrate the importance of knowing about geography, social systems, politics, economics, and climatic conditions because sport and physical education do not exist in a vacuum.
- The area approach.

Graduate courses should include the following:

- Comparative analyses, starting with sport in the students' own country.
- More in-depth analyses through research papers and so forth.
- More sophisticated approaches, including government, politics, and area studies.

- More comparative studies to analyze the similarities and differences among the countries.
- Activities that develop a research-minded attitude and a concern with the "why" and "how" rather than the "what".
- More methodology, greater depth, and fewer countries.
- Thorough studies of one country, comparing it with the students' own, or considering one topic from the perspective of several nations.
- The topical approach.

How many and what kind of countries should be covered in a course?

- Two or three countries should be covered at the most; otherwise sufficient background cannot be given for each country.
- At least one country from each continent should be included, more if possible.
- The students' own country should be studied first. It then should be compared initially with countries similar in government, size, population, climate, and so forth, followed by a comparison with the big powers such as the USA, USSR, and GDR.
- A country should be selected that is representative of an area.
- A minimum of four class periods should be devoted to each country; six or eight would be preferable.
- A superficial overview of numerous countries should be avoided.
- The students' own country should be studied well before one or two other countries are studied.

What are some problems and themes?
Themes and areas identified include the following:

- Social forces or influences (values and norms, economics) and professional concerns such as curriculum, use of leisure, and so forth.
- Aims and objectives of physical education; teacher training, history, and traditional attitudes toward physical education and sport; structures of sport organizations; public administration and self-government of sport organizations; economic and climatic situations; facilities; mass programs; international competitions; amateurism and professionalism; politics; influence of religion; and mass media.
- Inflation's effect on sport participation; democracies versus dictatorships.
- Sport for all; pursuit of excellence; education of coaches; role of physical education and sport in developing countries (examples drawn from China, Cuba, and Africa).
- Differences in ideological orientation; educational philosophies, the culture, and the role of sport and physical education within that culture; women and sport; physical education and competitive sport; significant individuals.
- Contemporary issues such as the Olympic Games for 1984; different kinds of school competitions; discrimination in sport and physical education.

What are requirements or qualifications for teachers?

- Have experience in traveling abroad.
- Be scholarly and insightful.
- Have a background of courses in comparative education, history, and sociology.
- Have an intimate knowledge, from a personal perspective, of at least one or two other countries.
- Have a broad background in the humanities or social sciences in appropriate theoretical and methodological perspectives.
- Have a genuine interest in broadening the perspective of parochially minded students.
- Have studied a foreign language.
- Have read the literature.
- Be open toward people from other countries and have little bias or prejudice.
- Correspond with people from other countries.
- Be an active member in the International Society for Comparative Physical Education and Sport; have a membership in other international associations such as the International Council for Health, Physical Education, and Recreation (ICHPER) and the Fédération Internationale d'Éducation Physique (FIEP).

How can teachers motivate students?

- Bring outsiders into the class.
- Encourage student exchange with other countries.
- Invite students and professors on campus from other countries to speak.
- Discuss controversial issues (with care!).
- Use slide presentations (not too long).
- Interview people who are native to the countries studied and find out about their physical education and sport experiences.
- Conduct experiential projects: eat the food, learn two sentences of the language, wear the dress, meet the people.
- Encourage students to research a country of their own ethnic origin.
- Draw attention to newspaper and journal articles or television coverage of international competitions or sport activities and integrate these into class.
- Put students in touch with individuals from another country for information.
- Bring in exchange students from other countries for information.
- Show movies.
- Visit another country (nearby, at first).
- Bring in speakers who can provide new ideas and different perspectives about your country.
- Read newspapers and magazines from another country.
- Have students attend special events on your campus such as travelogues, performances by visiting dance or gymnastics groups or exhibitions by visiting art groups, events sponsored by the International Students Association, and so forth.

How can individual study be conducted?

- Visit and stay in another country, preferably for 14-21 days (possibly during the holidays).
- Depending on student level, develop an annotated bibliography or make a comparison between two countries from the standpoint of some social force or professional concern.
- Have students report on developments in one country.
- Have students compare one aspect of a foreign system with an aspect in their own country.
- Visit ethnically based sport clubs.
- Require students to make a comprehensive review of the literature as it pertains to the various facets of the makeup of a particular country.
- Have students enroll in a study course abroad (advertised in various journals and flyers sent to individuals and universities).

At the conclusion of this discussion, Bennett read the following short paper dealing with the current world situation concerning the enormous expenditures for military spending, the awesome number of nuclear weapons, and the role of sport in contributing to world peace.

Today we live in an unparalleled age with the mutual threat of nuclear annihilation hanging over our heads—a fact recognized by other countries as well as ours. It would seem more imperative than ever to make all possible efforts to promote understanding and goodwill among the people of the world. This must come out of learning about other people and their cultures. But when this topic is mentioned to people, they invariably ask, "What about the Russians?" Well, what do we really know about people in the Soviet Union? People in the German Democratic Republic? People in Cuba? Have you ever met one? Have you ever talked to one? What do you actually know about their countries and their histories?

An exciting new development in the United States (nongovernmental) is the matching of nearly 1,000 cities and towns in the United States with 1,000 comparable communities in the Soviet Union. All kinds of information is exchanged between the countries' citizens. This is a movement of the people that reminds me of the time when President Eisenhower declared that "people in the long run are going to do more to promote peace than our government. . . . One of these days government had better get out of their way and let them have it."

But what is happening at the governmental and political level is very disturbing. It seems clear that politicians are doing a terrible job of promoting peace and international goodwill around the world. One notable exception was Canadian Prime Minister Pierre Trudeau's effort to encourage peaceful efforts in his recent tour of many national capitals. The nations of this planet, whose survival and wellbeing is vital to us all, spent $660 billion last year for military weapons, bombs, and other military procurement. This was an increase of $110 billion from the previous year. The global nuclear stockpile now totals 50,000 weapons, the equivalent of 1 million times the explosive force of the single bomb dropped on Hiroshima.[1] The bomb dropped on Hiroshima killed or injured 200,000 people. Thus the world has the capacity to kill or injure 200 BILLION people. In the world's approximate population of 5 billion, each person could be killed 40 times. Furthermore, each day weapons are produced to kill or injure another 1 million people.

This is a frightening situation which has no simple, easy, or quick solution, but an effort must be made to find one. At the 20th anniversary of the founding of the United Nations in 1965, Adlai Stevenson said "World order will come not through the purity of the human heart nor the purge of the human soul, but will be brought from a thousand common ventures that are at once possible and imperative." Melvin Maddocks, in an article in the *Christian Science Monitor* at the time of the USA's boycott of the 1980 Olympic Games, stressed the idea that we should have as many relationships with the Soviet Union as possible. He wrote, "Whatever became of the argument that any relationship between people of two countries was better than no relationship at all?"

What I wish to emphasize here is that art, music, dance, literature and sport afford "common ventures" to bring people together. CBS morning news recently had a wonderful report on the trip of Pearl Bailey to the Soviet Union. The genuine warmth of her personality and her musical talents evoked similar responses from the members of her audiences. People in the USA thrill to the beauty of the Bolshoi Ballet from the USSR, to the art exhibit from Leningrad, and to the music of Tchaikovsky.

And so it is with sport also. In spite of the many problems related to international sport competition, think of the enormous goodwill engendered in the 1983 World University Games by the treatment of the Peruvian volleyball team in Edmonton[2] or the outpouring of sympathy and sadness toward the Soviet diver who died from injuries suffered in a tragic accident.[3]

Yes, what I saw at the World University Games in Edmonton and what I watched of the Winter Olympic Games in Sarajevo on television have only reinforced my conviction that sports and games are another "common venture" toward world order and peace that are too vital to the people of this planet to be manipulated by our governments for narrow national political purposes.

This concludes my paper on the present world situation. The purpose of presenting it here was to find out if this group believes that such facts and materials are legitimate and relevant content for a course in comparative physical education and sport.

Notes

1. This statistic comes from the following publication: Sivard, R.L. (1983). *World military and social expenditures*. Washington, DC: World Priorities. It may be purchased for $4.00 from this address: World Priorities, Box 25140, Washington, DC.
2. The men's volleyball team from Peru arrived penniless in Edmonton after traveling by bus from Washington, DC. The citizens of Edmonton donated money to pay the team's

room and board during the games, and a Canadian airline flew the team back to Lima without charge.

3. Sergei Chalibashiwili was attempting the extremely difficult reverse 3-1/2 tuck from the 10-meter platform when he smashed the back of his head on the platform. He died five days later without regaining consciousness.

References

Hanna, E., Hicks, H., & Koppel, T. (1965). *The wit and wisdom of Adlai Stevenson* (p. 52). New York: Hawthorn.

Maddocks, M. (1980, January 14). Politics and the Olympics. *Christian Science Monitor*, p. 22.

Sivard, R.L. (1983). *World Military and social expenditures.* Washington, DC: World Priorities.

CHAPTER 26

Conceptions of Higher Studies of Physical Education in European Socialist Countries

Zygmunt Jaworski

This paper describes the history of higher studies of physical education in Poland and the contemporary academic study of physical education in European socialist countries.

Evolution of the Conception of Higher Studies of Physical Education in Poland from 1922-1984

In Poland, Poznań University started the first 3-year academic course of physical education in 1922. The aim of this course was to train physical education teachers for secondary schools. Course studies with similar purposes were organized in 1927 at Jagiellonian University in Cracow and in 1946 at Wroclaw University. In all of these universities, physical education departments existed within the faculties of medicine.

Other, more general (universal) course studies were established in Poland in 1929 at the Central Institute of Physical Education in Warsaw which in 1938 became the Academy of Physical Education.

In 1950, physical education departments in Poznań, Cracow, and Wroclaw moved out of the universities and were established as independent colleges of physical education. After this reorganization, general, unified curricula were introduced and functioned with some changes until 1970 in all of the physical education colleges and in the Academy of Physical Education in Warsaw. Because different branches of national economics existed there was an increased demand for physical education graduates with more specific qualifications. So in 1970 the general curriculum was abandoned. Four separate faculties were introduced in its place: teacher's training faculty, coaching faculty, recreation exercise faculty, and physical rehabilitation faculty. These faculties still exist in 1984, along with a modified version of the general faculty which was reestablished in 1981.

Between 1922 and 1984, the profiles of studies of physical education have undergone serious modifications (see Figure 1). The number of institutions that provide physical education on an academic level has doubled and new organizational units have gained the status of academies

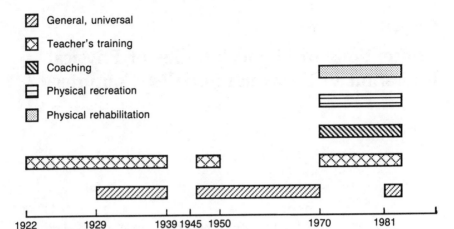

Figure 1. Timeline of studies of physical education in Poland.

of physical education. At present, six academies of physical education exist in Poland. They provide a 4-year academic course equal to university studies. Two of the academies organize additional departments outside the school location.

Since 1922, a serious change has taken place in the structure of the curriculum in Poland. First of all, let me explain the term *study subject block*. The term is understood in this case as a group of subjects, thematically related. A four-part aggregation of all study subjects was made, including professional training practice and training camps outside school. The respective subgroups of study subjects were given the following symbols and definitions:

A—theory, methodology, techniques of motor activities
B—natural sciences
C—humanities
D—other study subjects and elective class hours

It seems that this four-part aggregation expresses the current yet historically shaped curriculum structure in higher physical education well. The part of the curriculum occupied by the humanities and natural sciences has changed most among the curriculum subjects over time. The role of the humanities has increased significantly, while the part devoted to natural sciences has diminished. The part of the curriculum occupied by the main subject block, including theory, methodology, and motor activities techniques, has been very stable (see Figure 2).

The emphasis on natural sciences in curriculum concepts for higher physical education in the early period of its development is connected with the leading role of the natural sciences in shaping the theoretical basis for physical education. On the other hand, the increasing role of

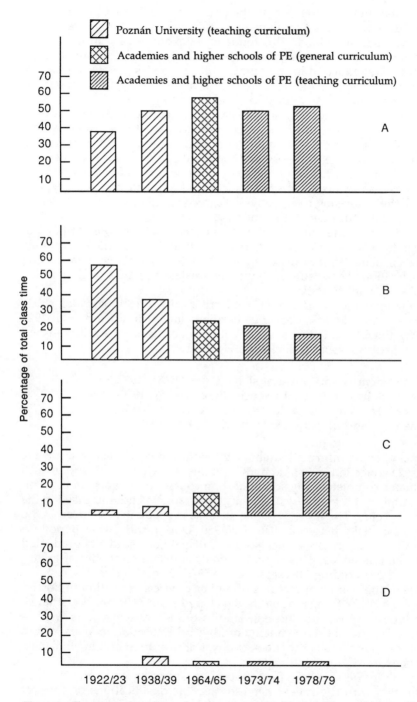

Figure 2. Changes in the relative class time assigned to blocks of the curriculum of higher physical education in Poland.

humanities in the curriculum in the later period of higher physical education development is a result of a general tendency to humanize university education in Poland. This tendency is expressed by an increase in such subjects as foreign languages, political science, philosophy, and sociology. The reduction in the number of class hours devoted to natural sciences has been made at the expense of such subjects as anatomy, chemistry, biochemistry, physics, and physiology.

In the period discussed, notable changes occurred within the subject block of theory, methodology, and techniques of motor activities, which, as a whole, occupied a stable part in the total class time. Within this block of subjects, the role of theory and methodology of motor activities significantly increased, mainly because the time for professional training practices was reduced. This latter fact may be considered as an expression of the decreasing role of physical exercise in the curriculum concepts for physical education in the country.

The data characterizing the number of class hours devoted to particular blocks of curriculum subjects may constitute the criteria for typology of the curricula. In this analysis, two blocks of subjects were taken into consideration. These subjects take the greatest numbers of class hours within the total class time.

Employing the earlier mentioned criteria in the typology of study courses to the classification of 25 curricula taught in Poland from 1922 to 1984, the following types of curriculum concepts may be distinguished (for symbols of subject blocks see Figure 2):

Natural sciences and physical skills (blocks B-A), 1922
Physical skills and natural sciences (blocks A-B), 1930-1964
Physical skills and humanities (blocks A-C), 1969-1978
Humanities and physical skills (blocks C-A), 1975

Finally, some information about the educational results of academic physical education in Poland may be of interest. Up to 1939, about 1,000 graduates completed physical education courses on the academic level. The number of higher physical education graduates has increased in the postwar years. The most dynamic increase in graduates occurred in the 1970s, especially between 1976 and 1980. During this 5-year period (in both the direct and in-service studies), over 13,000 students graduated from the academies. This number almost equals the number of graduates in the preceding 20 years (i.e., 1956-1975; see Figure 3).

One of the particular features of higher physical education in Poland is, among other things, a highly developed form of in-service studies. This type of physical education studies on an academic level was introduced in 1952 at the Academy of Physical Education in Warsaw and is still provided in all academies of physical education and in all departments except the general departments.

A peak in the number of extramural classes occurred in the 1970s in connection with the urgent need to raise the qualifications of physical

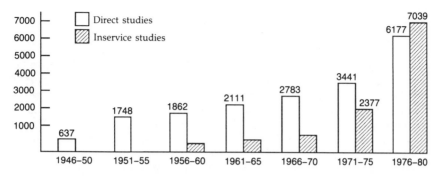

Figure 3. Numbers of graduates of physical education studies in consecutive 5 year periods.

education teachers. The dynamic development of extramural studies in the last decade is shown in the fact that from 1976 to 1980 the number of extramural studies graduates was greater than the number of intramural studies graduates (see Figure 3).

After 1980, the number of extramural studies graduates declined, but the studies still have a strong position within the academies of physical education in Poland.

Contemporary Conceptions of Studies of Physical Education on an Academic Level in European Socialist Countries

One of the most striking tendencies in the development of physical education on an academic level is the decline of the general, "universal" curriculum, which has been replaced by a course of study preparing the graduates for specialist professions such as becoming physical education teachers, coaches, recreation exercise specialists, or physical rehabilitation exercise specialists.

This process of dividing the general course of studies into various specialized faculties occurred most noticeably in the 1970s. The reason for this development can be ascribed to the dynamic development of knowledge about physical education, which indicates new scopes and possibilities of physical activity and its advantages. On the other hand, this fact has caused an increased demand for proficient personnel with specific qualifications.

In the late 1970s in European socialist countries, the faculties of higher physical education developed the following types of programs:

- General "universal"—Romania
- Teacher's training—Bulgaria, Czechoslovakia, German Democratic Republic, Hungary, Poland, Soviet Union, Yugoslavia
- Coaching—Bulgaria, Czechoslovakia, German Democratic Republic,

Hungary, Poland, Soviet Union, Yugoslavia
* Physical rehabilitation—Poland

These faculties constitute a unified course of university-level studies. The graduates are conferred a professional title of Master of Physical Education or an equivalent title. Only in Czechoslovakia and the German Democratic Republic were double-specialization faculties organized to provide the graduates with qualifications for school work in two fields, physical education and another school subject. These double-specialization studies lasted 5 years.

The organizational status of the institutions providing higher physical education is varied. Yet differentiating between two basic groups of these institutions is possible. Those two groups are the following:

* Independent units of the higher education system that exclusively provide physical education studies on the university level
* Units that function within universities or pedagogical colleges.

The first kind of educational institutions existed only in Poland in the late 1970s, whereas the second variant was found exclusively in Czechoslovakia. Both variants operated in the remaining European socialist countries.

In another aspect of the organizational status of schools providing higher physical education, it is necessary to ascertain which organ of state administration is responsible for direct supervision over its country's activities. On that score, the situation also differs. The majority of schools submit directly to the ministry supervising the entire structure of university education in a given country. The situation is different in Poland; all academies of physical education are directly under an organ of state administration dealing with physical culture affairs. In some countries two centers control the academies of physical education, each supervising different schools. In general, independent schools that provide physical education exclusively on an academic level are usually under direct supervision of an agency of the state administration dealing with physical culture. The remaining schools report directly to the ministry of schools of academic rank or to the ministry of education.

Often significant differences are observed in the numbers of class hours devoted to particular subjects or blocks. Considering the space limits of this study, only the pedagogical specialization of physical education on an academic level is presented according to the number of total class hours (with respect to the mentioned four-part aggregation of study subjects) in chosen schools of European socialist countries. The data are provided in Table 1.

Among other things, the data present two facts that are worthy of mention. First notable differences occur between the listed schools concerning the total time devoted to obligatory classes in the 4-year cycle of academic physical education.

Table 1   Percentage of Total Class Hours Allotted to Subject Blocks in Academic-Level Physical Education

Country, school, date of curriculum issue	Curriculum subjects blocks				Total no. of class hours
	A	B	C	D	
Bulgaria, Institute of Physical Education in Sofia, 1978	66.1	14.0	19.3	0.7	4507
Hungary, Hungarian College of Physical Education, 1977	60.3	10.4	27.6	1.6	2950
Poland, all academies of physical education—curriculum outline, 1978	55.6	14.4	26.2	3.8	3296
Soviet Union, all institutes of physical education—curriculum outline, 1972	52.5	18.2	24.4	4.8	4074

Secondly, in spite of the differences in the total number of class hours, in all schools the time allotted for each subject block in the overall total for obligatory classes is analogous. In each school listed in Table 1, most class time was devoted to the scope of theory, methodology, and motional activities techniques (block A), in second place were humanities (block C), and in third place were subjects of natural sciences (block B).

In the analysis of the evolution of curriculum changes in physical education on the academic level in Poland, classification of the types of study courses was done considering the two subject blocks that require the most class hours. In analyzing the data in Table 1, it can be seen that, according to this criterion, in all countries studied the "humanities and physical skill" type of study course is dominant.

CHAPTER 27

Curricular Models in Physical Education: Professional Preparation or General Education— Sponsored or Contest Mobility

Joy Standeven

This paper seeks to raise the question of common definitions. Is there a shared body of knowledge and method of practice that is defined as physical education irrespective of a person's location in the world? Or are subject definitions bound to social contexts and therefore culturally specific? Can comparative physical education be satisfactorily defined unless the meaning of physical education has been clarified? Should educational models seek to come together; is this part of what comparative physical education should be about? Should physical educators rise above their contexts and work together despite cultural differences? Can there be universal definitions?

If we were to examine only the British model of physical education, what measure of agreement would we find as to what constitutes the subject? In 1972 Crunden stated that "considerable confusion exists as to what actually constitutes physical education" (Crunden, 1972, p. 6).

In an article entitled "Physical Education—An Obituary" Mawdsley claimed that "physical education is dead. Death occurred in the late 1970s following a long and painful illness due to constant efforts to hold the various body parts together in a unified whole" (Mawdsley, 1978, p. 5). Nevertheless, a year earlier, the Department of Education and Science (DES) published a document that identified the physical area of experience as one of eight areas of experience that all children should be introduced to during the compulsory years of schooling (DES, 1977).

With increasing pressures toward accountability (not only in terms of resources but also in implying curricula relevance for pupils and parents as well), what rationale do we offer for our subject? And how do we undertake professional preparation for a subject that some believe has become a mile wide and an inch deep? Is the fitness account a defensible rationale for an educational activity? And in any case, what do we mean when we describe an activity as educational?

Education implicitly demands positive values or "good" ends, which are generally described in terms of changing a person for the better, that is, learning occurs in activities that are considered worthwhile. Professor

Peters, an eminent philosopher of education in Britain, describes activities as "educationally worthwhile" if they:

- Have a wide-ranging cognitive content which is such that it can change a person's view of the world;
- Are rich in skills and are open-ended enough to afford endless opportunity for elaboration;
- Have standards of correctness or style built into them in such a way that anyone who is seriously committed to them comes to care about their inherent standards (Westthorpe, 1974, p. 4; see Peters, 1966).

If our account of physical education can meet such narrow criteria of educationally worthwhile activities, then we should be in a position to argue a case for our subject in terms of any account of education. Peters himself rejects physical education, which he sees only as games, as a worthwhile activity educationally on the grounds that its skills are limited; because it bears little relation to the seriousness of life, it is unlikely to change a person's view of the world. But Peters's conception of physical education is just as much a truncated view of the subject as that held by incoming students in Britain who are preparing to enter the profession, who normally view the skills aspects of their courses as physical education, and who see the theoretical aspects as lending no more than an academic respectability to an otherwise atheoretical study. Such a view raises one of the biggest, as yet unresolved, problems in physical education—that of the relationship between theory and practice. It also raises the question of whether there is a unitary concept that binds the many different activities together.

Physical education may be seen as the study of movement—a term that embraces all physical activities but is not to be confused with the diverse interpretations (some of them very shallow) of a particular approach to physical education commonly known as *movement education*. Participation in movement can expose a person to a body of knowledge that has cognitive content, that enables concepts to be learned and understanding to be gained, and that has the potential to change a person's view of the world. Such understanding may be acquired through many kinds of experience, and to the extent that practical participation affords illumination of theoretical principles, it becomes an important way of understanding.

The relationship between theory and active participation varies according to the intention and context in question. But undeniably, both are ways of learning something that has demonstrable cognitive content concerned with the effective positioning, shape, and action of the body in space, the significance of body tension coupled with the timing of actions, the flow of energy, the use of rhythm, the recognition and understanding of spatial patterns, and the ability to respond to other people's movements to understand their significance and to initiate and control the movement of one's own body. Such knowledge constitutes a theory of physical education and gives a *raison d'etre* to the practical activity. It is clear that in learning something intrinsic to the activity itself we are focusing on education *of* the physical as our primary account. Movement knowledge, dependent on active participation and observation, will be extended and illuminated by a study of human anatomy, physiology, kinesiology, and biomechanics, motor competence and skill acquisition, psychology of performance, aesthetics, communication, creativity, the arts and culture, and perspectives that permit access to ways of explaining and interpreting movement. Such a body of knowledge meets the criteria proposed for judging worthwhileness in that it clearly has, implicit within it, wide-ranging cognitive content and a capacity to change a person's view of the world.

Peters's second criteria of being rich in skills and open-ended enough to afford the opportunity for endless elaboration necessitates a critical examination of the activities to be selected from the wide range of forms of human movement. Three criteria may be proposed for selecting activities. First, they should be intrinsically worthwhile to meet educational criteria. Second, in order to allow for the development of conceptual understandings, it should be possible to derive common principles that would permit some degree of transfer to be effected, thus enabling the possibility of illuminating wider frames of reference. Third, activities should be selected for their cultural relevance and meaning as forms of activity specific to certain people in particular contexts. Acceptance of such criteria permits placing hierarchical value on the many different activities that could be embraced within the notion of human movement.

Physical activities such as gymnastics, games, dance, swimming, and track and field have recognized standards for judging good performances. Efficient and effective movement can be distinguished from inefficient and ineffective movement, improvement can be learned and discerned, and performers, including children, can be taught to value correct performance in both their own movements and in those of others; thus such activities meet Peters's third criterion of educational worthwhileness.

Turning in more detail to the curricular model that was devised and is in the process of development within my own department, Table 1 illustrates the components of the 4-year specialist physical education program and the periods of practice teaching in schools. Because all course content is selected on the criterion of professional relevance, subject and teaching studies are fully integrated. This is particularly the case in the practical aspects of physical education. The curriculum is designed so that in the first 2 years students take a common set of courses that cover a wide range of practical activities and introduce students to the various disciplines that form the study of physical education. Years 3 and 4 are more specialized, and students progressively limit their focus of study according to their needs and interests. Analysis of the course shows both total class contact hours and relative proportions.

The rationale for the curricular model that we devised is based on the need to present a carefully planned and selected sequence of related experiences that involves coming to terms with the medium of movement. That, after all, is the distinctiveness of physical education, and it is that which holds together the range of disparate activities. Our rationale stems from our definition of a physically educated person as one who is

Table 1   Class Hours and Percentage of Total Hours for Components of the 4-Year Physical Education Program

Courses	Years 1	2	3	4	Total hours	% of total
Subject studies						
Physical education theory	116	98	136	68	418	19
Physical education practical	248	199	136		583	26
Physical education teaching and professional studies			68	34	102	5
Second subject	81	87	96	6	270	12
Educational and professional						
Education theory	80	82	102	51	315	14
Professional studies[a]	34	26	36	34	130	6
Dissertation/enquiry method			37	5	42	2
Total excluding school-based experience					1860	84

	Practice teaching	
School-based experience	18 weeks	13
Polytechnic-based preparation and follow-up	4 weeks	3

Note. The total curriculum is 137 weeks.

[a]Included under professional studies are teaching skills (40 hours), language across the curriculum (26 hours), computers and the applications (30 hours), and teacher as professional (34 hours).

knowledgeable about a range of physical activities and has a familiarity and facility with that knowledge that results in a high level of confidence and articulateness in movement. He or she has the ability to handle complex movement tasks and ideas competently, to initiate and control movement efficiently, and to communicate effectively. Such an individual will have developed his or her powers of judgment and discrimination in terms of appropriate standards of correctness and style of different movement forms. In other words, the individual will not simply "know about" movement; his or her knowledge will be part of himself or herself in the way he or she moves.

Many of the wide range of practical activities subsumed within physical education give rise to similar types of experience and can therefore be grouped together in terms of the knowledge and the understandings to which they give access. The areas of experience that we differentiate are the same as those identified by the DES:

- Activities where movement has expressive and symbolic content (e.g., creative dance, synchronized swimming)
- Activities where movement is functional but which also depend on qualitative performance and efficiency (e.g., gymnastics, ski-jumping)
- Activities where competition versus others is an essential element involving the use of psychomotor skills (e.g., games)
- Activities where there is a contest but where the challenge is in remaining in control of oneself in the natural environment (e.g., windsurfing and other outdoor activities)
- Activities where body-training leads to increased physical performance; this may also be used in competition with others (e.g., track and field, speed swimming) (see DES, 1979)

The basis of our physical education curriculum is this range of experiences, rather than the range of specific activities. While activity-specific concepts are learned only by being exposed to selected activities, more general concepts transcend the boundaries of differentiated activities. These include, for example, body action, space, dynamics, and relationships. While activity-specific concepts are covered in activity-specific classes, the emphasis is on categories rather than on specific content, on understanding principles and concepts and developing ways of thinking and learning. Thus specific activities are taught, but a Movement Concepts course also is offered in which students are encouraged to reflect on their practical experiences, to conceptualize them, and to make something of them in wholistic terms. Phase 1 of the course is structured around the need for the student to experience all major categories of activity, and the categories' associated principles and basic concepts. Supporting theoretical studies that are drawn from a range of disciplines focus on the capacities and biological limitations of the developing, individual learner, the teaching-learning process and situation, and the social and artistic influences of the culture. These latter elements provide an interpretive framework to assist in the understanding and evaluation of movement behavior in its different forms. In Phase 2 of the course, students select two areas of experience and take two theoretical options carefully designed to illuminate their practical activities. A strand of teaching and professional studies, followed throughout this latter phase of their course, is designed to enable students to keep in contact with the full range of physical education content, and retain contact with children and the teaching situation.

To examine the place of comparative physical education within the context of the total course, it is necessary to look in more detail at the core course, Aesthetic and Cultural Forms (ACF), in which it is rooted. This course runs parallel with Motor Behavior and Learning; the two together form the multidisciplinary theoretical support in the first 2 years of the course. While few people question the relevance of science to the physical educator, many question the relevance of "culture" for the same student. Yet both science and culture give the prospective teacher cognitive models that will help him or her acquire a fuller understanding of physical education. The ACF course draws on a range of approaches within social studies and philosophy in an attempt to introduce ways of thinking about the meaning of physical activity and to explore ways of understanding physical education in wider contexts. The course begins with a double stress—one on how culture is experienced and the other on how physical education has had distinctive meanings in particular times and places. This leads into a consideration of particularly significant figures in spheres of physical education and sport and proceeds with a focus on the origins and development of modern team sport. The course continues with an examination of the cultural experience of dance and then divides into two strands offering students specific ways of thinking—the first is concerned with theoretical or analytical models to understand the aesthetic experience of sport and dance, and the second introduces dominant ways that sociologists and cultural critics have explored social and cultural life. The final part of the common core course examines case studies of particular kinds of cultural movements. The comparative-historical cases focus on the Bauhaus movement alongside the development of athletic nationalism, which is compared with social realism and the development of sport in the Soviet Union. Such a course introduces students to interpretive and analytic modes of thinking, gives them knowledge of the cultural base and development of physical education, and helps them to be aware of the relationship between the individual and culture. Thus all students are exposed to comparative studies through an in-depth study of culture.

A 68-class-contact-hour option in historical and comparative studies is offered in Phase 2 of the course. Here the focus is on the explanation of cultural differences and the appraisal of the significance and values attached to physical activity in a variety of sociopolitical contexts. Commencing from selected descriptive studies of a representative range of societies, individuals pursue an in-depth case study that possibly includes a term of exchange abroad. Attention is drawn to different methodological approaches and underlying assumptions of the empirical material studied, and students are expected to demonstrate an increasing capacity for analysis, synthesis, and evaluation. The course concludes by focusing on themes such as the Olympic Games or physical education and sport for women and girls that are examined cross-culturally. Importance is placed on the appraisal of competing theories and methodologies used to explain cultural differences. Seminar discussion is the major teaching mode used in the course and is strongly supported by a range of excellent video materials accompanied by comprehensive worksheets. Lectures and tutorials are also used.

To engage briefly in comparative study within the context of this paper, we can examine the structure and balance of two further curricular models from other institutions. This comparison arose in connection with obser-

Table 2   Percentage of Total Course Hours Devoted to Various Course Areas

Course areas	Chelsea School of Human Movt.	Schools Dalhousie University	McGill University
Physical education studies	50	56	50
Elective(s)/Second subject	12	20	13
Education studies	20	10	19
School-based experience	16	14	18
Dissertation	2		

vations made by students engaged in an exchange program. The data were provided by students and checked against specifications given in course catalogues, from which Table 2 is constructed.

Defining particular inputs as belonging within certain categories is likely to involve a degree of arbitrariness; many substantial differences may be masked in Table 2 but similarities are obvious in the overall balance of courses.

A 4-year program at Chelsea and Dalhousie is being compared with a 3-year program at McGill. Such a tabulation gives little indication of underlying philosophy. A more detailed analysis supported by documentation and experience would be necessary to reveal the finer differences. Exchange students are particularly aware of the attempt to achieve overall coherence and integration within the Chelsea School and of the school's professional emphases. Chelsea students who study abroad note the differently stressed curricula: more emphasis is placed on the scientific illumination of physical education and less is placed on its cultural significance; course components are more self-contained, permitting students a wider range of individual selection and course construction; the lecture mode of teaching is used more frequently; and reporting and analysis of resources is stressed more than evaluation and manipulation of them to achieve reasoned, self-constructed arguments.

Turner, in a paper presented in 1960, suggested a framework for relating differences between North American and English systems of education to the prevailing norms of upward mobility in each country. His proposal of organizing norms of sponsored mobility and contest mobility provides a way of relating differences in curricular rationale and planning, a way of understanding differences, and a way of raising the question of whether definitions of physical education can transcend space. Turner proposes that these ideal-types can be readily applied between countries other than the United States and England (Turner, 1960, p. 121).

Sponsored mobility is the controlled and early selection of restricted recruits who hold appropriate qualities for elite status and who are destined to pass through a process of sponsored induction. *Contest mobility*, on the other hand, is more open, offering elite status to those people who can take it by their own efforts. One system values achievement; the other values ambition. Control is exercised through ideology and restrictive access in a society based on sponsored mobility, but in a contest-based society, the principal control seems to lie in the insecurity of elite position. Thus the contest system avoids any absolute points of selection and delays recognition of the realities of mobility as long as possible. Sponsored mobility, as we see its application in England, values the content of education as an end in itself; schooling is valued for its cultivation of elite culture. In the United States, Turner suggests that the contents of education are not highly valued in their own right but are valued only as a means to an end—the means of getting ahead. Thus in England, education did not need a practical value to justify it because it was defined by its intrinsic value, while in the United States, practical value emphasizes skills to compete for material gain.

It is necessary to point to changes occurring in England that suggest that sponsored mobility is changing. Removal of the 11+ examination and the selective tripartite system of secondary schooling has delayed the point of selection to the national examinations at "O" and "A" levels. Contest at this point is increasingly intense because of the reduced number of student places available and the freedom for the colleges to set more academically rigorous criteria for entry. College curricula may also be changing, state involvement may be becoming more and more significant, and emphasis may be placed on the vocational relevance of courses. Thus a major current concern is to develop a more rigorous concept of professionalism. The extent to which state intervention may change interpretations of professionalism is critical; Johnson argues the concern of professionalism with power and control (Johnson, 1972). In systems where contest mobility is increasingly becoming the organizing norm, new definitions of professionalism are required. Yet these may not be universal because we retain a capacity for arranging technical forces in our own way—in terms of the social relations within our own cultures. Attempts, then, to universalize definitions and values of physical education may be frustrated. It may be most appropriate to use comparative studies, journals, and meetings as forums for sharpening our own rationales, yet we must always endeavor to overcome ethnocentrism and promote international understanding.

References

Much of the work in this paper owes a debt to unpublished papers by Mrs. G.M. Burke and the Chelsea School of Human Movement.

Crunden, C. (1972, January). The uncomfortable relation of physical education and human movement. *British Journal of Physical Education*, 3(1), pp. 6-7.

Department of Education and Science (DES). (1977). *Curriculum 11-16*. London: Her Majesty's Stationery Office.

Department of Education and Science (DES). (1979). *Curriculum 11-16 Supplementary working papers of physical education.* London: Her Majesty's Stationery Office.

Johnson, T. (1972). *Professions and power.* London: Macmillan.

Mawdsley, H. (1978, Spring). Physical education—An obituary. *Bulletin of Physical Education,* **XIV**, pp. 5-8.

Peters, R.S. (1966). *Ethics and education.* London: Allen & Unwin.

Turner, R.H. (1960). Modes of social ascent through education: Sponsored and contest mobility. In A.H. Halsey, J. Floud, & C.A. Anderson (Eds.) (1961), *Education, economy and society* (pp. 121–139). New York: The Free Press.

Westthorpe, G. (1974). P.E. as a worthwhile activity. *British Journal of Physical Education,* **5**(1), 4, 9.

CHAPTER 28

From Physical Education and Sport to Physical Culture: The Case of Hungary

Aniko Varpalotai

It has been said that the East European countries possess one distinct advantage—terminology. *Physical culture* has helped socialist countries avoid the constant terminological disputes facing other physical educators and has "helped them avoid the 'either-or' reasoning which has separated sport from physical education in some countries. In physical culture, championship sport and sport-for-all are seen as twin pillars of the same movement, as equal parts of the same sports spectrum" (Anthony, 1978, p. 9).

Eastern European nations, perhaps more than other countries, have realized and harnessed the power and appeal of sport to promote ideology—in this case the cause and creation of socialism. In Hungary, this has been a particularly attractive public forum because of the centuries of tradition related to Hungarian sport (Veto, 1965). But the instrumental promotion of sport to promote socialism has its inherent contradictions. Over the centuries, much of Hungarian sport had been the exclusive domain of royalty, lords, and the bourgeois classes. Consequently, historical traditions must be addressed in a new way in socialist Hungary.

Cultural studies theory seems to be an appropriate vehicle for understanding the subtle nuances that underpin the emergence of a true physical culture in Hungary. The purpose of this study was to address the relationship between the theory and practice of physical culture in a socialist society. A review of literature confirmed the difficulty that people are still having in accepting sport and other forms of physical activity as genuine cultural forms. The tendency to relegate sport to a realm separate from life or to view it as a mirror of society persists. The culturalist tradition negates both the reflective and the separate-from-life arguments. By introducing the process of mediation, the significance of human agency, and historical interplay, cultural studies shed a new light on the everyday experience of human existence.

The Study

A participant-observation study was carried out over a 2-month period at the Hungarian College of Physical Education in Budapest on the basis of a number of general premises:

- Education is considered an extremely significant element of socialist society.
- Physical education is an integral part of physical culture.
- In choosing the level of physical education teacher training, the assumption was that human agency is ultimately responsible for the transmission of theory into practice and of culture into the realm of the everyday experience. Thus the most immediate mediation of state policy occurs at this significant stage.
- Within this context, the Hungarian College of Physical Education was chosen because of its centrality within the Hungarian system of physical education and sport.

Through extensive discussions, interviews, questionnaires, and observations of the administration, faculty, and students at the college, I sought to understand how official policies were mediated through the experience of those who would implement the policies. The study makes a case for cultural studies because it illustrates the complexities of translating the ideals of physical culture into actual day-to-day practice.

Discussion

It is imperative to remember the following:

> Saying that men 'just do' certain things, on the micro-level, ignores the fact that they are doing so in an historically specific situation, and ignores the evolution of the culture and the institutions of which this behavior is an organic part. It also ignores the personal history of the individuals concerned. (*Whitson* quoted in *Pearson*, 1980, p. 29)

Cultural studies have created a new awareness of the complexities of human and social relations. A close interplay between culture and ideology must be recognized. Neither can be understood as a separate, isolated entity. An awareness of this becomes especially important in comparative studies. While the importance of ideology has been overemphasized in the past, the influence of culture has been underestimated.

Williams's concepts of the dominant, residual, and emergent "ruling ideas" (Williams, 1977) are highly appropriate in discussing the case of the Hungarian College of Physical Education. The *residual* idea refers to traditions of the past that continue to have an undeniable and immeasurable influence on the present and the future. The *emergent* idea refers to the new values, practices, and relationships that are continually being created and that are a very conscious part of socialist development. The *dominant* idea can be understood best as the status quo of the present. In true dialectic fashion, these "ruling ideas" reinforce the ideas of the "ruling class" and succeed in establishing themselves as legitimate (Marx & Engels, 1968, p. 61). Because the dominant ideology becomes so deeply imbedded in all social relations, change is a slow, often tension-ridden, and always complex process.

For example, despite the existence of an official public policy that states the importance of physical culture, it has been found that the average Hungarian does not take advantage of the opportunities to participate in it (Foldesi & Foldesi, 1981). The state has, and continues to, overcome many of the structural restraints that face other societies in this regard (i.e., high participant costs, long work day/work week, lack of facilities, low priority of school physical education). And yet the average Hungarian continues to resist the incorporation of physical culture into his or her lifestyle.

Some plausible reasons for this discrepancy are to be found in the discussions with those directly responsible for the everyday dissemination of physical culture activities—the faculty and students of the Hungarian College of Physical Education.

Findings

The primary purpose in this analysis was to investigate the relationship between the individual perceptions of the Hungarian physical culture professional and the state aims and objectives of the profession. Interviews were conducted with approximately 50% of the faculty ($n=37$), representative of all departments and disciplines in the College. Written questionnaires were also completed by a sample of 1st- and 4th-year students ($n=54$ and $n=74$, out of approximately 100 students per year).

The interviewees included several generations of physical educators, ranging from those who had experienced both pre- and post-war developments (many having taught, coached, and administered professionally at all levels of age and expertise) to students and young athletes who were only just beginning their teacher training. Given the frequently distinct polarization of faculty members, they were arbitrarily categorized as "theoretical," "practical," or "theoretical and practical," depending on their major teaching responsibilities and orientations.

One of the fundamental underpinnings of the thesis is the necessity of fusing structure and culture to get a more complete and realistic picture of social reality. If we were simply to take the academic recruitment procedures, the bureaucratic organization of the College, and the official policies as stated in the physical culture literature, then the tensions that exist among faculty and students would not surface. Conversely, simply noting these tensions, such as student dissatisfaction with having to achieve high skill standards, would not help us to understand why performance is stressed at the College, nor would it help to distinguish the structural factors that contribute to this tension. The application of Raymond

Williams's concepts of the dominant, residual, and emergent allows us to not only understand the historical developments of the College's organization but also to understand the growing dissatisfaction with a program geared to skill improvement.

The greatest tension I found concerned high-performance sport and "sport-for-all," which is an important underlying factor in the continuing development of Hungarian physical culture. The dominant ideology, which equates the two as equal physical culture partners (see Anthony's quote earlier), does not seem to correspond to the everyday experience. The Foldesi's (1981) discovered that for the average Hungarian citizen, physical culture was synonymous with high-performance sport. Similarly, the structural conditions of the College of Physical Education also suggest that excellence is given first priority. This is evident from a number of factors. There is the residual notion that the Golden Age of Hungarian sport that occurred in the 1950s can be recaptured in the 1980s.

Although this may not be a deliberate or consciously arrived-at assumption, indications are that it is true. The student entrance examination emphasizes an ability to perform; given the competition to earn a place at the College, the vast majority of students must be highly skilled athletes. The faculty, with the exception of some who teach specialized academic subjects, are themselves graduates of the institution. Consequently, they also have developed in a structure that emphasizes skill. Indeed, given the earlier preoccupation with success at the international level, many are still more skilled than the students they currently instruct. Finally, the monetary incentives that are awarded for coaching (as opposed to teaching) also suggest, rather powerfully, that sport is what is important.

It is not surprising, therefore, that almost half of the faculty saw sport as dominating the College curriculum, and that the major source of tension was between those who wished to return to the residual (excellence equals physical culture) stance and those who supported the emergent notion (usually cited by the theoretically based faculty) that physical culture is a much broader concept.

The students tended to side with the latter group, noting that no direct correlation existed between international athletic prowess and success as a physical culture professional. A second major concern involved the lack of sensitivity of students toward the socialist project. The faculty noted that many of their charges lacked sufficient consciousness to carry the project forward. Not only was there a lack of general socialist awareness, but also there were specific examples of the tension between the dominant and the emergent supporters. Thus, for instance, there were many students who would deemphasize the practical component of the program. There were those who saw little need to develop high personal standards of performance to teach physical education. Finally, there was the small group of students who, despite the materialist philosophy of sport, desired a program that was apolitical—no Russian language, no political economy, no Marxism-Leninism.

What do these tensions imply? Simply, that the future development of Hungarian physical culture is a complex and tentative issue. As the students graduate and move into positions of influence, their particular philosophical stance will influence and be influenced by the structure. We can be certain that those who expressed an interest in contributing to the development of international performers are going to approach their daily activities in a fundamentally different way than those students who would deemphasize skill, practical course work, and so forth.

While the College illustrates some "evergreen" issues common to physical education everywhere, some significant differences exist. There is a conscious effort to relate physical culture to the new dominant ideology; the new structures, curriculum, and theories are all coordinated to facilitate this development. Though the structures are highly developed and the theories are sophisticated, there remains the problem of individual mediation. Structure alone does not account for all of the problems, nor does it contain all of the solutions.

My thesis was not intended to be a definitive statement on the development of Hungarian physical culture. It is rather an exploration of an ideal policy in the process of being realized in practice. Utilizing the theories of cultural studies, we may achieve a little more insight into both the ideal of physical culture and the process of its mediation through institutional and human agency.

References

Anthony, D. (1978). Introduction. In J. Riordan (Ed.), *Sport under communism*. Montreal: McGill-Queen's University.

Foldesi, T., & Foldesi, T. (1981). Expectations related to physical culture in Hungary. *International Review of Sport Sociology, 3*, 45-60.

Marx, K. & Engels, F. (1968). *The German ideology*. Moscow: Progress.

Pearson, K. (1980). Cultural interpretation in sport: The outside world and pictures inside heads. *International Review of Sport Sociology, 15*, 19-40.

Veto, J. (Ed.). (1965). *Sports in Hungary*. Budapest: Corvina.

Williams, R. (1977). *Marxism and literature*. London: Oxford University.

Closing Remarks

Message from the President

John C. Pooley

It has been a privilege to be directly associated with the Fourth International Seminar on Comparative Physical Education and Sport, capably directed by Herbert Haag at Malente, Federal Republic of Germany. The smoothness of the Seminar was matched by the quality of the papers and the warmth and enthusiasm of the participants. It really was a splendid week.

The Seminar provided an excellent balance among formally delivered scholarly papers, suitable question and answer periods, and discussions on a variety of issues. The breadth of topics was encouraging. An important decision made at the Seminar was to set in motion an international empirical study about competition in schools, the fruits of which are expected at the Fifth Seminar in Vancouver in 1986.

The only disappointment was the narrow range of national representation. Recognizing the problems facing members and potential members with respect to the finances required to attend any international gathering, it was nevertheless sad that other countries, especially in Europe, were not better represented, especially because the site of the Seminar was relatively centrally placed with respect to that continent. Consequently, the question of broader representation at future seminars is an issue for consideration. However, the Society continues to expand and continues to draw a growing number of concerned and dedicated researchers and teachers from different parts of the world. With the enthusiasm and spirit generated at Malente, the Society can look forward to continuing progress and expansion.

John C. Pooley
President

Summary and Conclusions

João Piccoli

Aniko Varpalotai

We would like to begin by expressing our thanks to the executives and members of the International Society for Comparative Physical Education and Sport for the honor of being chosen as the recipients of the C. Lynn Vendien Student Scholarship. It has been a great privilege for us to have taken part in the seminar and to rub shoulders with those whom we have until now only known through books and journals.

We would like to express a few personal thank-yous to our respective academic advisors and mentors with whom we have been most closely associated during our studies and who are, in large part, responsible for us being here today. Namely, we owe our gratitude to Professors Bruce Bennett, Hart Cantelon, and John Pooley for inspiring and encouraging us in our comparative research and academic work to date.

As recipients of the Vendien Scholarships, we have been asked to give a summary of the week's events and proceedings; without further ado we will launch into the "meat" of our collective reason for gathering in Kiel/Malente.

At this, the Fourth International Symposium of our Society, we have tried to develop four major themes: (a) comparative research methodology, (b) comparative research relating to physical activity within the schools, (c) comparative physical activity research outside of the schools, and (d) courses in comparative physical education and sport in our institutes of higher education.

Dr. Grupe's opening paper addressed a common theme—the scientific uncertainty of a new subdiscipline. He recommended the using of an interdisciplinary approach without losing sight of our own disciplinary roots. An international exchange of mutually useful information needs to be applied in a truly comparative manner.

Welcoming "outsiders" to our discussions was very refreshing, particularly our guests from the areas of sociology and comparative education. Professor Postlethwaite related the evolution of comparative education and suggested that the most fundamental problem for researchers is the question of scope. He offered a challenge to us to begin team research, even as we continue to develop our methodology, and determine the direction that our society should take.

Drs. Willimczik and Zeigler instructed us to wear "bifocals" in our work, once again stressing the need for a variety of research methods. We were also made aware of the problems of language and terminology in our field. We must be careful to compare like to like and be prepared to ask many different questions to ensure that we are receiving the information that we are seeking to compare.

One of the wonderful advantages we have in being able to attend international conferences around the world, especially in a field such as ours, is the multidimensional insights we gain into others' practices and cultures. Our German hosts assured us that we would get the most out of our brief visit to their country. Through visiting German institutions of sport and education, observing typical German sports demonstrations, and listening to the theory behind their organization and development, as explained by Drs. Rehbein and Hanke, we are able to observe yet another case study and perhaps gain useful comparative insights. Despite our interest, however, we have learned through both Dr. Pooley's and Dr. Broom's presentations that there is a great dearth of comparative research reported or apparently even conducted in a truly academic manner, and thus the potential utility of our insights are lost.

Although our work is fundamentally problem-oriented and reform-oriented, research must be more than that—it must be daring. As Dr. Saunders quoted in his paper (paraphrased here), "Comparison involves choosing and provoking, not necessarily proving. . . .Questioning, not always answering."

Sociocultural research, especially in a comparative way, as we all know from our own experiences, is a complex, sometimes frustrating, and never straightforward matter. This is one of the reasons that research methodology, the decisions related to the scope of our organization, and subjects for team research are such problems.

As Dr. Krüger pointed out, everyone has done some form of comparative study in sport since the beginning of the modern Olympics in 1896. Many developed countries have increasingly used the Olympic "barometer" to measure their nation's standings and have developed their sport's—not their physical education, leisure, or recreational policies— accordingly. This sort of comparative study is not what we are after—on that, at least, I think we have some consensus. We seem to be in general agreement that, for the lack of a better term, physical culture, coined by our colleagues from the socialist countries, is a better descriptor of our interests.

We welcome our new members from Poland, the first from the Socialist countries. This, too, is an indication of the growth in scope and potential of our broad and diverse area of study. We need this exchange of ideas: only if we face differences as challenges rather than as threats will we continue to grow and progress.

Those of us in the academic disciplines of physical education and sport have perhaps had more difficulty than other disciplines in achieving academic credibility; but no field, regardless of age or status, should be willing to relax its standards and its level of inquiry. Despite the fact that our world is increasingly becoming a "global village" and that problems of travel, communication, and so forth quickly are becoming nonissues, the complexities of the world, never before within our grasp, are now waiting to be tackled.

We have the means today, even in the less-developed nations, to improve the quality of life for people of all walks of life. We acknowledge that physical education and sport are vital elements of human society. As *the* international society for comparative research in this area, we must lead the way toward bridging the gaps, learning from and teaching one another in the most responsible, professional, and critical way. This process sometimes includes harsh criticism and deep introspection, but the spirit of this week spent in Kiel/Malente should have proven that we are among friends and colleagues with mutual interests at heart. If it means calling on the expertise of older, perhaps more experienced professional organizations, so be it. We are, after all, a problem-oriented group, and we should welcome the opportunities for exchange with related disciplines.

Finally, I think we speak on the behalf of all of the delegates here when we say that this week in Kiel/Malente has been most enjoyable, thought-provoking, and worthwhile. We wish to thank Professor Haag and all of his hard-working assistants for a superb seminar. And thank you all, once again, for honoring us with the C. Lynn Vendien Student Scholarships. We hope we will live up to your expectations as soon-to-be active and contributing members of the International Society for Comparative Physical Education and Sport.

See you in Vancouver in 1986!

João Piccoli
Aniko Varpalotai
May 1984